THE

COUNTRIES AND TRIBES

OF THE

PERSIAN GULF.

COLONEL S. B. MILES.

[*Frontispiece.*

THE COUNTRIES AND TRIBES OF THE PERSIAN GULF.

BY

COLONEL S. B. MILES

VOL. 1.

ISBN: 978-93-5128-883-1(HB)

First Published in 1919
Indian Reprint in 2017

Published by

Kalpaz Publications
C-30, Satyawati Nagar,
Delhi – 110052
E-mail: kalpaz@hotmail.com
Website: kalpazpublications.com
Ph.: +91-9212142040

Cataloging in Publication Data—DK
Courtesy: D.K. Agencies (P) Ltd. <docinfo@dkagencies.com>

Miles, S. B. (Samuel Barrett), 1838-1914, **author.**
The countries and tribes of the Persian Gulf / by Colonel S.B. Miles.
volumes cm
Reprint. Originally published: London : Harrison and Sons, 1919.
Includes index.
ISBN 9789351288831

1. Oman—History. 2. Persian Gulf States—History. 3. Tribes—Oman—History. 4. Tribes—Persian Gulf States—History. I. Title.

DS247.O6M55 2017 DDC 953.53 23

CONTENTS.

VOL. I.

VOL. II.

LIST OF PLATES.

PREFACE.

The present volumes, dealing with the ancient and modern tribes and peoples of the countries around the Persian Gulf, were compiled by the late Colonel Samuel Barrett Miles, of the Indian Army and Political Service, Consul-General of Muscat and Baghdad, etc. He had looked forward to revising his notes, many of which were jotted down on odd bits of paper as he rode through the desert on his camel, but was prevented from doing this by failing eyesight. His blindness was aggravated by serious internal troubles, and in spite of the heroic attempts which he made, he found it impossible to set down in writing even a hundredth part of the vast store of Oriental learning which he had accumulated during his prolonged residence in India, Persia, Arabia, and Mesopotamia.

The reader will note that the system of transcription of proper names used in these volumes is that which was generally employed by Orientalists and British Indian officials some forty or fifty years ago. Had Colonel Miles lived he would undoubtedly have abandoned this system and adopted that now commonly in use in India, England, and on the Continent; and it is very probable that he would have modified certain portions of his narrative and supplied full references to his authorities, both ancient and modern. After much thought his widow decided to publish the manuscript of his work as she found it. With it she has included the rough notes which he made on his travels in Mesopotamia, and added a good, full Index.

She is indebted to Dr. Wallis Budge, Keeper of Egyptian and Assyrian Antiquities in the British Museum, for much friendly help in seeing the book through the Press.

F. A. W.

BIOGRAPHICAL NOTE.

Samuel Barrett Miles was the son of Major-Gen. Miles, of North Villa, Regents Park, and Cheshunt, and was born on October 2nd, 1838. He was educated at Harrow and entered the Indian Army in 1857. He was appointed Resident at Aden in 1867; Political Agent and Consul at Muscat in 1874; Consul-General of Baghdad in 1879; Agent and Consul-General of Zanzibar in 1881, etc. He was the author of several papers in the publications of the "Royal Geographical Society." In 1877 he married Ellen Marie, eldest daughter of Sir Brooke Kay, Bart., who survives him. His only son, Major H. W. Miles, R.M.L.I., was killed on H.M.S. *Vanguard*, July 19th, 1917. Colonel Miles died August 28th, 1914, and was buried at Hinton Charterhouse, Somerset.

CHAPTER I.

HISTORY OF EARLY COLONIZATION.

THE history of the ancient colonization of Oman in Eastern Arabia is naturally connected very closely with that of the rest of the peninsula, but the subject is so veiled in obscurity, from the absence of materials, that our knowledge of it is shadowy and fragmentary in the extreme. The only available authentic sources of information and guidance, in addition to the book of Genesis, are the monuments and documents of Mesopotamia and Egypt, which afford a few scattered rays of light.

The question, however, regarding the origin of the pristine inhabitants of the land is by no means an uninteresting one, in view of the part taken by them in promoting the cause of civilization by connecting the East and the West in commercial relations, the most prominent and active of which was probably taken by the people of Oman.

The earliest race known to have spread over and occupied the peninsula are the Cushites, of whom we read in the Bible, but of whom the origin is uncertain, though it is generally believed to be Egyptian. The epoch and duration of their occupation can only be conjectured, but of the important consequences resulting therefrom we can entertain but little doubt. For to these bold, adventurous Cushites, possibly, are due, not only the beginnings of inland trade by caravan, but also the navigation of the Arabian Sea and the infantile efforts of maritime commerce. The reasons for supposing that these seafaring efforts were more particularly the work of the Cushites of Oman will appear later on. Though the Hamitic Cushites spread over Southern and Eastern Arabia and founded most of the settlements on the coast, they were perhaps not the only race who dwelt in that region at that remote period. There were, for instance, the Phœnicians, who, according to Herodotus, came to Palestine from the Persian Gulf and appear to have sojourned in Oman during their former migrations.

The port of Soor, near Ras al-Had, has a name identical with that of Tyre or Soor in the Mediterranean, and was, beyond doubt, the prototype of it. The town of Soor, part of which is called Eijah, is situate on a rocky eminence at the mouth of a serpentine creek, and has always possessed one of the most useful, safe, and commodious harbours for native craft on the Oman coast.

The Cushite inhabitants of Arabia, though enriched by commercial enterprises, gradually dwindled in course of ages, and were overwhelmed eventually by a great wave of Semitic invasion from Northern Arabia, by which they were partly expelled and partly absorbed. These early Semitic tribes, as we learn from Caussin de Percival's great work, are known to the Arab historians as the "Baida" and "Ariba," and are considered as extinct races.

The tribes that now dispersed and took possession of Arabia were composed of two main stocks, derived from the fourth and fifth generations from Shem. One of these stocks was Kahtan, who, identified with Joktan, son of Eber, colonized the Yemen, or the southern half of the peninsula, while the other, Adnan, who descended from Ishmael, occupied the northern part, where his posterity are mostly found at the present day. Under the one or other of these great progenitors, Kahtan and Adnan, the whole Arabian race is comprised.

In the tenth chapter of Genesis we are informed that Joktan had thirteen sons, "and that their dwelling was from Mesha as thou goest towards Sephar, a mount of the East." The identity of Joktan with the Kahtan of Arab tradition and of Sephar with Dhofar has been sufficiently recognized, and it is known that it is this stock of thirteen branches or tribes whose posterity has continued to occupy uninterruptedly and almost exclusively the southern half of the peninsula for 4,000 years.

Regarding the distribution of these tribes much has been written, but so far only a few of them have been traced with certitude. The identification of three of them, Hazarmaveth, Uzal, and Sheba, are perhaps indisputable. Yerah and Hadoram may be Yarab and Jorham; Havilah is probably Khaulan, a well-known district in the Yemen; while Hommel has connected Diklah with Hiddekel or Dijla, the River Tigris.

The name Obal or Wibal, as that of an ancient tribe, appears to survive in Oman, where a town so called exists in a valley now known as the Wady Beni Ruwaihah. The descendants of Kahtan, however, are differently named by the Arab genealogists, who also vary in some degree from each other. It may suffice here to give the list compiled by Kremer—numbering sixteen—Yarub, Khatar, Anmar, Mutenier, Madi, Lawi, Maiz, Gasib, Meina, Gorhum, Multenies, Katami, Zalim, Gusem, Aufar, and Nafir. We now have to fall back on the traditional accounts of the Arab historians, as we search for more light in other quarters in vain. In genealogy the Arabs have ever taken great pride and much pains, and have preserved with tolerable accuracy their pedigrees from very ancient times; indeed, it is not a little wonderful how far they have surpassed all other nations in this matter. Considering the many difficulties of the subject, it is not surprising that these genealogies abound with gross inconsistencies and contradictions, yet on the whole they may be accepted as fairly correct and trustworthy, though it was not until after the death of Mohammed that the ancient traditions were elaborated and reduced to writing by the Arabs.

The earliest inhabitants known to the genealogists are denominated by them as the Al-Ariba, who are also called the extinct tribes. Of these tribes, several are enumerated, and we are furnished with fabulous accounts of their exploits and adventures, as well as of their extirpation. The most famous of all were the Ad and

Thamood, who are said to have been of gigantic stature; others were Tasm and Jadis, who were sisters of the two brothers Thamood and Sohar; Jasain, Waber, Hadboora, Abel, and Emin, nearly all of whom are known to have been represented in Oman.

The sections of the Tasm and Jadis, who migrated to Oman, appear to have settled in Al-Jow and Towwam, giving to those districts the names of the places they had occupied in their old home, Yemama. According to Wüstenfeld, Sohar is the name of the sons of Said bin Zaid. Hamza, after Bekra, thinks it identical with Ghuma Said al-Hodsin. The Sohar tribe occupied the Batineh, and gave their name to the present town on the coast. The Jasain were Amalekites and dwelt, it is said, also in Oman, where their descendants, under other names, still exist. The Thamood were probably the last of the Ariba, as they survived till the time of Christ, and are alluded to by Diodorus, Strabo, and other classical writers.

Besides the extinct tribes which existed in Oman in ancient times, there were, of course, many famous ones that helped to people the country, and whose descendants, mostly of mingled blood, were subsequently divided into branches under other names, and it may be as well to mention a few of these once renowned tribes whose history is hidden in the mists of tradition.

The Azd, who form such a large proportion of the population of Oman at the present day, are of rather obscure origin. Some derive them from the patriarch Kahtan, others from Al-Gauth bin Nabt bin Malik. There were three divisions of them: (1) the Azd Shenoo; (2) the Azd Sarat; and (3) the Azd of Oman. They were further divided into nine principal families—Ghassan, Aus, Al-Khusraj, Ibn Khodjer, Barek, Dows, Ateek, Ghafeh, and Beni Julanda. From each of these descended many tribes now known under other names. The Mazen, after whom East Arabia obtained the name of Mazoon for some centuries, were a great seafaring race and were descended from Mazen bin Azd. Sprenger thinks the Maceta of Nearchus, who sighted Cape Mussendom on his voyage, obtained its name from this tribe. "The Kamoos" says "the Mazen are of South Arabia and are Azdites and long afterwards joined the

Ghassanites." The Mazen had, it is said, four divisions. They appear to have occupied the Shemal or Cape Mussendom, and were succeeded there by the Shihiyyeen, a small tribe.

The Kamar or "Moon" tribe was a large and important one in Southern Arabia in remote times, and gave its name to the Kamar Bay, and also, it is supposed, to the Comoro Island on the east coast of Africa; the tribe is now represented in Oman by the Beni Ryam, who occupy Jebel Akhdar, and also by the Beni Hadeed and probably other tribes. The Beni Kodhaa were a great tribe stretching along the southern coast from the Yemen to the Gulf of Oman, and many branches sprang from it; also some genealogists derive it from Malik bin Hamza, but it is probably of higher antiquity. The tomb of Khodhaa, the personification of the tribe, is said to have formerly existed in Shihr. Ptolemy calls the tribe Kattabene. Its descendants are still in Oman; it had a branch called Khaulan or Chavila, which formed a colony and dynasty in Oman, but at what time is not known.

The names of many other powerful and distinguished tribes have come down to us by tradition from antiquity, and some of them have left their mark in the name of the valley, town or district where they resided; for in Oman, as in Arabia generally, they called the land after their own name.

Among these may be included the Akk, a well-known tribe of doubtful origin and dwellers in the Yemen. The Azdites took refuge with them after leaving Mareb. The Wady Akk, in which they resided in remote times, is situated about fifty miles from Muscat; and the gorge in the Wady Akk is very steep and narrow.

The Bahila, an ancient tribe of dubious derivation, which founded the town of that name in Oman Proper.

The Dibba, or Lizard Tribe: a Modhar tribe of Nejd, which probably founded the town in Cape Mussendom, where a decisive battle was fought in the year 11 A.H. [632 A.D.].

The Jaalan, or Water Beetle tribe, derive from the Abdul Kais or "Slaves of Kais," who was one of the divinities of the ancient Arabs; the Jaalan occupied the district of that name in the Sharkiya.

Caussin de Perceval, in his essay, informs us that Yarab, descendant of Kahtan, after having destroyed the power of the Azdites, established the exclusive domination of the Kahtanites over all Southern Arabia and founded the kingdom of the Yemen, consolidating his rule by appointing his brother Jorham, to the government of the Hejaz, and his other brothers, Hadhramaut and Oman, to rule over the provinces designated by their names. This noteworthy event is reckoned by him to have occurred in the year 754 B.C., which would make it contemporaneous with the founding of Rome, and if this chronological calculation be accepted, it would mean that the Oman tribe first migrated to East Arabia in this year. The date, however, of 794 B.C., ascribed to the birth of Yarab by de Perceval, who calls him the brother of Hadhramaut, is not easily reconciled with the period usually allotted to Hadhramaut, the third son of Yoktan, or about 2,000 years before the Christian era. Moreover, if we accept Oman as the brother of Hadhramaut, the omission of his name from the list of Yoktan's sons in the tenth chapter of Genesis is certainly singular. But whatever the period may have been, it is probable that the migratory movement of the Omanis was on a large scale, as on their arrival at their destination they were enabled to take possession of the central and most productive parts of the country, known to this day as the province of Oman Proper, a name which was subsequently extended to the whole land, in the same way that the province of Fars has given its name to the whole kingdom of Persia.

The successor of Yarab in the Yemen was Yashjob, a feeble prince, who allowed many of the provinces, including Oman, to become independent. On the death of Yashjob the succession fell to his son, Abdul Shams, to whom many remarkable actions are attributed. He invaded Egypt, completed the construction of the great dam at Mareb, the metropolis of the Sabeans, and reduced to obedience the dependencies that had revolted from his father. We may conjecture that Eastern Arabia, like the others, returned to his sway, but of this we have no certain record.

Abdul Shams left many sons, the most famous of whom were

Kahlan and Himyar. Kahlan, according to some, succeeded his father and was followed by his brother Himyar, whose real name was Azanjaj, but was called Himyar on account of his wearing a red dress. His power over the whole of South Arabia was complete, extending from the Yemen to Muscat. He was the founder of the two dynasties of the Himyarites, which held paramount sway in the Yemen until the time of Mohammed. Himyar, during his reign, appears to have made his son, Malik, Governor of Oman, but on the death of Himyar the kingdom fell in disorder, and, like other governors, Malik made himself independent. Then two of his brothers, one of whom was named Wathil or Waïl, resolved to try and wrest the country from him. They were unsuccessful in their efforts, and Malik not only retained his authority in Oman but left the succession to his son, whose name has not come down to us. Malik's son, however, appears to have been attacked and defeated not long afterwards by Wathil's son Sacsac, who then ruled over Oman. During the reign of Yasar bin Sacsac disorders broke out against him and he was constantly at war with the children of Malik. In the minority of Yasar's posthumous son Norman, the regency was held by Dhul Raish. This account, it must be observed, conflicts with other historians, who state that Wathil was himself sovereign of Oman for many years. The subjugation, however, of Oman to the first Himyar Dynasty could not have been of very long duration, as, like the rest of the Yemen, it seems to have fallen in the middle of the sixth century B.C. to the armies of the great Cyrus, who was then engaged in extending the limits of the Persian Empire.

How long and to what degree Persian domination extended is uncertain, as traditional history of Oman at this period is extremely vague and hazy, but it is probable that Cyrus was content with merely nominal submission and the payment of tribute, and the country continued under the hegemony of its native Arab rulers.

In the history of Isidore of Charex is mentioned a king named Dhu Joaisos, who lived at Shihr and ruled over the Omanis. This king is identified by Blau with Dhu Joaisham bin Akran bin Ali Malik, who is spoken of by Hamza Ispahani. Blau further states that Dhu Joaisham reigned in the time of Dara bin Dara bin Bahman and for seventy years after. He made war on Tasm and Jadis, and his successor lived to the time of Hadhr bin Kinana. Dhu Joaisham was of royal Himyaritic family, and his presence in Oman was due to the fact that one of its progenitors was Kahlan bin Arib bin Zoheer bin Ajam bin Hamoza, who was the first to subdue Oman. Kahlan was King of Oman and his adviser was Mazen bin Azd, who was Lord of Oman. His proclamation began—

> "From Mazen a document in which is a message to all who inhabit Ajam, Arabia and Shihr."

This fragment is of value, and indicates how much remains to be unravelled of Oman traditional history. It may be as well here to notice the legend given by Persian historians, which relates that Kai Kaoos, King of Persia, having subdued Oman, made peace with the Arab ruler, Dhul Sogar, on condition that the latter gave him in marriage his daughter, Sibarba, who was of rare beauty. The story of Dhul Sogar, who is variously styled Dhul Saris and Dhul Zind, is narrated by Merkhond in the "Rouzat al-Safa," and the subsequent adventures of Sibarba and Prince Siawash, son of Kai Kaoos, are poetically described in the "Shah Namah" of Firdusi.

It was in the time of Alexander the Great that the land of Oman was first seen by Europeans. His admiral, Nearchus, when passing up the Persian Gulf, sighted Cape Maceta or Cape Mussendom, and heard from the pilot of a great Omani emporium. This port, it is almost certain, was Sohar, which was still an emporium in the time of Mohammed. Alexander, on hearing his report, determined on sending an expedition to circumnavigate the Arabian peninsula, but his early death at Babylon put an end to this and other schemes, and for nearly a hundred years no fresh light was thrown on the land.

The first king of the Second Dynasty of the Himyarites was Harith, a descendant of Himyar through Wathil bin Gauth: Harith was a conqueror and is supposed to have invaded India, and ruled over all the provinces of Southern Arabia. He took the title of

"Tobba," which applies to all his successors, but more strictly only to those kings who possessed besides the Yemen, Hadhramaut, Shihr, and Oman. He received the sobriquet of "Al Raish," on account of the rich spoil he brought from foreign countries.

De Percival, in his work above mentioned, accepts the computation of Thaalibi as to Harith's having lived about 700 years before Mohammed or about a hundred years before Christ. For some time Oman appears to have been under his subjection, but it subsequently passed under the dominion of the Parthians. It was probably in the days of Mithridates that East Arabia fell under Parthian dominion. This king, who founded the empire, ruled from 174 B.C. to 136 B.C., and extended his conquests over an immense area, including Susiana, Persia, and Babylon; and as Oman was at that time a dependency of Persia, it necessarily followed the fate of that country and remained so until the advent of the Azdites.

We have now come to a period when we might have expected a flood of light on the general condition of Arabia, from the literary and commercial activity of the Greeks, who, after its conquest by Alexander, took possession of Egypt, and at once began to undertake trading operations with the East. Unfortunately, though we certainly have some valuable works such as the "Periplus" and "Ptolemy's Geography," the more important labours of the Greeks on Arabia have perished. The first Greek writer to mention the Arabs was Eschylus, but the first to produce a description of Arabia was the astronomer Eratosthenes, who composed a cosmography when he was Curator of the Library of Alexandria, where he died in 196 B.C. As Eratosthenes had abundant opportunities of collecting information, his work would doubtless have contributed much to our knowledge of the Yemen, but he appears to have known nothing of Eastern Arabia, as of the four great tribes mentioned by him, only one, viz., the Beni Kodhaa, extended as far as Muscat.

From Agarthacides, who at one time resided in Egypt, and who about the year 120 B.C. wrote a work in five volumes on the Red Sea and Southern Arabia, we might have gathered a still more complete and trustworthy account of the Arabs and their country.

but his labours, with the exception of a few fragments, have, like those of Eratosthenes, been lost. We learn, however, from Agarthacides, of the existence of Arabian colonists in the ports of India.

As Egyptian trade increased, so the knowledge of Arabia extended, and Pliny's account of the Oman coast is fairly accurate, but he knows little of the interior and he gives no historical information whatever. The Periplus of the Erythrean Sea, which was written about the year 80 A.D., is very accurate as far east as Cape Fartak, but the author knows little or nothing of Oman, and does not mention any port between Muscat and the Persian Gulf. His notions about the position of Oman are very vague and confused, and the only political information we glean from him is that Oman was then subject to the Parthians.

Even Claudius Ptolemy's extensive work, valuable as it is, gives little assistance in compiling the early history of Oman. He furnishes the names of many towns, villages, and tribes in Eastern Arabia, but most of them, if they ever existed, have long since disappeared. He gives the name of Cape Mussendom not incorrectly as "Asabon Promontorium," a name which has survived in Khasab, a hamlet in a small valley, probably the residence in former times of a tribe so called. One of the Oman townships, however, mentioned by him, *i.e.*, Rabana Regia, was doubtless the residence of the tribe Rabban bin Holwan bin Imran, a branch of the Kodhaa, which, migrating from Nejd, and wandering through Yemama—where it left a portion of the folk—settled in Oman near the Azd, though the exact locality is not now ascertainable, as the name Rabban has passed out of memory.

With regard to the early history of Eastern Arabia, Ptolemy is distinctly disappointing, as he provides no data on which to form any idea of the political conditions at that period. Little as we know, however, of the manner in which in ancient times Oman was peopled, of the migrations of the tribes, of its wars, invasions, or of its dynastic successions, we are sufficiently acquainted with its history to see that any glory and renown it could boast of was gained not on the land but by sea, and that it was the Cushites of Oman, who, inhabiting a poor and sterile country, largely dependent on external resources, and being the pioneers of navigation in the Indian Ocean, took the initiative in transporting the valuable wares and products of the East through the Persian Gulf to the Western World, thus promoting the cause of civilization in Western Asia; and it may be suitable here to subjoin an outline of the maritime commerce in which they were engaged.

Situated as it is midway between Mesopotamia, on the one hand, and Western India on the other, Oman occupied an unrivalled and most commanding position for inaugurating maritime commerce with those countries, and it seems reasonable to conjecture that the bold, enterprising Cushites, who possessed the land, soon learned to take advantage of their opportunities to become a great seafaring race, and that having stretched across to the shores of India, they became from the beginning masters of the whole Oriental commerce. In their control of this commerce, which it seems difficult to controvert, the only possible competition they could have had to encounter would have been that of the Cushites of Western India, but as there is little or no testimony of the existence of the latter, we need hardly discuss it. But although we may ascribe to the early Omanis the merit of having been the first to supply in their own vessels the spices and other productions of the East to Mesopotamia, they were, of course, powerless to reach the equally important markets of Egypt and the Mediterranean.

Had Oman been as admirably situated as regards commerce by land as she was by sea, had she, for instance, been able to attract foreign merchants to her ports and to despatch caravans directly across Arabia, she might have grasped the monopoly of trade throughout the whole route, and have become a most powerful and wealthy kingdom. But the great sand desert to the westward isolated her from the rest of Arabia, and proved an insuperable barrier to land traffic from her ports by caravan, and compelled her to disembark the wares at Gherra, further up the coast, and entrust them to merchants of other countries for transport.

We see, therefore, that, taking advantage of their position the inhabitants of Oman were the great mediaries and carriers of Indian goods to the West, successfully monopolising it and excluding all others from the Indian Sea, navigating their vessels between India and the Euphrates and enjoying a most lucrative trade. This commerce was, of course, unknown before the civilization of Babylon and Egypt had begun, as the articles imported to them were those of luxury, acceptable to a refined people.

As Babylon, on the banks of the Euphrates, advanced in civilization, and began to appreciate more and more the products of India and Africa, she became the chief emporium of goods between the East and the West, and the greatest consumer of luxuries; while the traffic of the Omanis developed and increased in proportion, their vessels landing merchandise at Erridu, Mugheir (the Biblical Ur of the Chaldees), and other places. Gherra, which is probably identical with the Dedan of Genesis and Ezekiel, seems to have been situated where Lahsa now stands and had a port on the coast opposite Bahrain (or Al-Bahrain), but it may have had this appellation when the Gherra tribes arrived there and gave it their own name. It was, no doubt, originally selected as the most suitable anchorage and depôt to the northward of Oman, where Oriental goods could be landed for transport to Palestine and Egypt. For this purpose it was frequented by Phœnicians and other merchants, who loaded their caravans with the articles brought by the Omani ships. In this way, maritime commerce poured prosperity and wealth into the lap of the great cities of Mesopotamia and Syria, Palmyra—which was founded by Solomon—Opis, Baalbec, Damascus, Nineveh, Tyre, and many others, which all owed their greatness to Oriental commerce.

During the palmy days of the traffic, Syria was intersected by a network of roads, along which were built "serais," or rest houses, for the caravans to camp in at night. At this time Egypt confined herself to agriculture and did not care for trade, indeed, sailors and foreigners were dreaded and distrusted, and the demand for Eastern wares must consequently have been small.

Ezekiel, who died about 570 B.C., gives a valuable account of the trade of Tyre, but it is inaccurate as regards Arabia, as his knowledge of that country was very vague. He mentions no place between Dedan and Kane, except Raamah, the site of which is unknown. He alludes to gold as an article of trade, but it must have been brought from Africa or India, as little was found in Southern Arabia, though Ibn Haik al-Hamdany in the "Iklil" gives a list of sixty mines in the Yemen, including ten gold and eleven silver.

Next to the Tyrian and Carthaginian navies in the Mediterranean, the Omanis, at this time, probably possessed the most numerous and powerful fleet in the world, trading between India and the Persian Gulf. At this time, also, or perhaps still earlier, the Arab trade was doubtless the means of introducing into India the civilization of Nineveh, Babylon, and Susa. It was from those kingdoms that the Hindoos learnt their astronomy, philosophy, astrology, and mathematics, and indeed all that they ever possessed in the way of civilized and intellectual advancement, for it is beyond doubt that the civilization of India was not indigenous, and that the Hindoos originated nothing, but received everything from Mesopotamia and Persia. One of the relics of this ancient trade is the word "man" or "maund," which is of Accadian or Babylonian origin, and was made use of in Persia, Arabia, and India by the Arab traders. It is in common use to this day, and has remained a unit of weight and measure for some 5,000 years.

About this period of seven centuries before our era, the Muscat Arabs, according to Professor de la Couperie, taking advantage of the experience they gained, determined to essay their strength in a still more distant and difficult navigation to China. In thus extending their sphere of operations they increased commercial relations and spread much useful knowledge while enriching themselves by trade. But this early intercourse with China is not sufficiently well founded to be accepted without confirmation.

It was not until the time of Nebuchadnezzar that the Persian Gulf trade began steadily to decline and its rival channel by the

Red Sea was rapidly gaining the ascendancy. That great monarch, however, did his utmost to encourage and revive the old course of trade; he dammed up the Tigris, made two canals near Babylon, and built Teredon (afterwards known as Obolla) as a trade emporium and as a frontier defence against the Arabs. Having thus done what he could in his own dominions, he crossed the Syrian Desert to attack and ruin Tyre, whose merchants had then turned their attention, almost exclusively, to the Red Sea route. But his efforts to stem the ebbing tide of Mesopotamian commerce were in vain. Not long after his death, which occurred in 561 B.C., Nineveh and Babylon were captured and ruined by the Medes and Persians, and two of the greatest markets in the world for Indian goods disappeared for ever; the Persian Gulf route never wholly recovered, and never entirely ceased, but rose and fell alternately for centuries with that of the caravan route by Aden and along the western coast of Arabia to Egypt, and partly by water up the Red Sea.

Let us now consider, as a matter of no small interest, the commodities brought from India to the Eastern Archipelago and from Africa to Arabia by the Omanis, as the great carriers and intermediaries of commerce in ancient times, many of which are enumerated by the Bible, Herodotus, the Periplus, etc. The more important articles were, first, olibanum or frankincense, which Sprenger thinks was the foundation of the trade, and which was brought chiefly from the neighbourhood of Cape Guardafui, and also in a far less quantity from Dhofar; slaves, spices, ivory, gold, precious stones, silks, and embroideries. Other items were ebony, sandal-wood, lignum, aloes, teak, cassia, metals, and cotton fabrics of many kinds. Besides the above articles from India and Africa, others came from the ports of Arabia itself, such as gum, balsam, myrrh, pearls, etc. In the importation of negro slaves from East Africa, the Muscat Arabs had a monopoly, in all probability, from remote times, and poured them into Mesopotamia in immense numbers. In this trade, which must have required a large number of boats of all sizes, they were facilitated to an astonishing degree by the south-west monsoon, which enabled their vessels to run a distance of over 2,000 miles from Zanzibar, in a few days.[1] The Arabs, in fact, knew of the north-west and south-west monsoons thousands of years before the modest Grecian Hippalus took the credit of their discovery to himself.

The mart of Maceta (mentioned by Arrian in his account of the voyage of Nearchus), Hereen says, was probably Soor, and he adds that an emporium like this, at the entrance of the Gulf, strengthens our idea of an ancient Indian trade with the Oman coast. He then decides the great question as to whether the Arabs or Indians were the carriers of trade in the Persian Gulf, in favour of the Southern Arabs. He considers, further, that this trade was extensive and existed long previous to the foundation of the Persian Empire, and that the Arabs, who were very early a navigating people, brought the Indian commodities to Babylon.

The anarchy that prevailed in Persia and Mesopotamia after the Battle of Arbela, or more correctly, perhaps, after the death of Alexander, in 323 B.C., to the rise of Mithridates, must have tended still further to depress trade in those regions by diminishing the demand for luxuries and foreign products, and at the same time to make that by the Aden route more brisk and active, especially, too, as Egypt had at the time fallen under the sway of a foreign dynasty, more enterprising, intelligent and vigorous, than the decrepit one it had superseded. The wealth and magnificence resulting from this traffic in Mareb and other cities of the Yemen, which were under the influence of Greek art, are described in glowing terms by Agarthacides and other writers of a later period. Oman, however, though she must have acquired great opulence from her monopoly of maritime commerce in the palmy days of Babylonia, seems never to have felt the influence either of Persian or Grecian art, and certainly no traces of architectural splendour can now be found throughout the land. From the time of Christ to the rise of Islam, the legendary history of Oman continues to be very fragmentary and disconnected, and indeed, with the exception of a few noteworthy events, there is but little to chronicle, as even the names of most of the rulers are lost.

The ordinary works on Arab history may be ransacked in vain for information on Eastern Arabia at this period, and the only native chronicle on which we have to rely gives us but little help. This Arabic work, which bears the name of "Kashf al-Ghummeh," or "Dispeller of Grief," was composed at Zikki about the year 1728 A.D., and was discovered at Muscat by Colonel Sir E. C. Ross, whose translation of it was printed at Calcutta in the *Journal of the Bengal Asiatic Society*, in 1874, under the title of "Annals of Oman." It may be observed here that an almost verbatim transcription of the "Kashf al-Ghummeh" forms the greater part of the supposititious work issued by the Hakluyt Society, under the name of *Imams and Seyyids of Oman*, but curiously enough the author, Salil bin Rizak, omits the first chapter of the "Kashf al-Ghummeh," which treats of the Azdite immigration into Oman in the second century after Christ. In this chapter, the author of the "Kashf al-Ghummeh," Sirhan bin Said, begins by quoting the famous genealogist, Al Kelbi, who states that the first of the Azd that came to Oman was Malik bin Fahm bin Ghanim bin Dows bin Adnan bin Abdulla al-Azd, and the cause of the migration was that his nephews, the sons of his brother, Amr bin Fahm, were wont when taking their flocks to pasture to pass by the house of a neighbour, who had a dog that used to bark and scatter the flocks, and which was killed by one of the nephews with a spear. The owner of the dog, being under Malik's protection, complained to him, and Malik in anger said he would no longer remain in a country where a person under his control suffered such treatment. Another story is that a herdsman was set on by a dog belonging to a bondsman of Dows, and slew it with his spear, on which the owner of the dog slew the herdsman.

It is certainly true that tribal feuds have often arisen from trivial affronts, but in this case it is probable that the word for a dog has led to a confusion in the tradition, and that it was a war between the Beni Kelb bin Wabara, who were a branch of the Kodhaa, and the Azd of Sorat, and that this feud was in some way connected with the migratory movement of the latter to Oman.

The most singular part, however, of Sirhan's account is the

entire omission of any allusion to the bursting of the dam of Mareb, which according to all other writers was the main cause of the dispersion of so many tribes.

The "Kashf al-Ghummeh" gives some details of the tribes accompanying Malik on their march through Hadhramaut, and of their expulsion of the Parthians, which are valuable and interesting, and are not recorded by any other writer. Before proceeding with the narrative of this migration, however, it would be as well to give some account of the calamitous event which is usually regarded as the real cause of the upheaval, cleavage, and departure of the Azdite group of tribes. The original construction of the great sudd or dam of Mareb, the rupture of which has been the theme of so many Arabian historians, is ascribed to Lokman, who lived about 1700 years B.C., and it is said to have been rebuilt by Abdul Shams Saba about eleven centuries later. The city of Mareb was situated to the north-east of Sanaa on an eminence not far from a small valley formed by two converging ranges of hills, one of which was called Jebel Ablak, the other Mareb. At the lower end of this valley a wall, about 1,000 feet long and 120 feet high, was thrown across the bed of the torrent to restrain the waters of the six or seven ravines, which flowed into it. The wall was built of solid masonry, the huge squared blocks of stone being bound together with metal clamps, and so wide that houses were erected on the top of it, and thus was created a lake over two miles in length.

The dam was supplied with several sluices at various heights, to supply water when required to a large tank below, from which the water was drawn to irrigate the cultivation around. Part of the dam is still standing and some of the sluices are in excellent condition, according to the French traveller, Arnaud, who describes the bed of the torrent and the banks on each side being strewn with blocks of stone.

Mareb, which is called Mariaba by Eratosthenes, Strabo, Artemidorus and Pliny, was in ancient times of circular form and about four miles in circumference. The extensive remains and architectural débris covering the area on which it stood are evidence of splendour and magnificence of the great city in its prosperity, when, inhabited by the rich merchants engaged in the lucrative trade between India and Egypt, Mareb rose to be the largest, finest, and wealthiest town in Arabia.

Before the dam gave way, obvious signs had not been wanting that it was in a dangerous condition, owing chiefly to the neglect of repair, and its destruction had been foretold by Dhareefa, the wife of Amr (" The Tearer "), who attributed its impending fall to its being gnawed by rats with iron teeth. The Tobba Akran bin Abdul Malik, however, paid no attention to the warning and no steps were taken to strengthen the dam. He had succeeded to the throne when he was very young, and the power had been usurped by two of the Azd, Amran and Amr (" The Tearer ") who dwelt at Mareb, and much political dissension and trouble was occasioned thereby.

While the Yemen was in this distracted state, the intertribal complications and wars were interrupted by the occurrence of the event that had been predicted, and the dam gave way to the pressure of the water in the lake, inundating the villages and cultivation in the most populous district of the country, destroying many lives and carrying away property of all kinds. It is not difficult to imagine the terrible havoc and devastation that must have swept over the country, when the restraining wall broke, but as no contemporary Greek or Arab writer has described the catastrophe, we are in possession only of the traditional tales told by later writers.

The reigning Tobba of the Himyarites at this time was Al-Akran, whose real name was Zaid, who ruled from 120 to 140 A.D. The date of the rupture, therefore, may be put down approximately at 130 A.D. It is not much to be wondered at that, as a consequence of the animosities of the people and the disastrous deluge, a great dispersion of the tribes took place, but the accounts given by their historians are as discordant as they are meagre.

After the collapse of the dam, which was never rebuilt, the city of Mareb began to decline, the trade languished, the Greek and other foreign merchants forsook its markets, and the population melted away until about a century later the Sassanians, having revived the Persian Gulf route, drew the Indian trade from Egypt to Ctesiphon, and Mareb gradually fell to the condition of a small Arab village. Of the dispersion of the tribes inhabiting the fertile valleys and plains near Mareb, we only know that those of the Adnani race marched northward to Nejd, and Hejaz, the Azdites and their kin, who formed the most important group, moved partly to the Hejaz and partly eastward.

Amr bin Ameer Mazeikeya (" or Tearer ") with his followers wandered first to the territory of the Akk tribe, the leader of which, Shenluke bin Jubab, received him hospitably. On the death of Amr Mazeikeya, his son Talib led his people on to Mecca, from whence they proceeded to Bahrain. The greater portion of the Azdites, however, from the districts of Surat and Oman in the Yemen, took the road to Oman, not at once, but by two or three successive waves or detachments, and it would seem at intervals of many years.

Some writers give the command of the first body of emigrants to Nasr, son of Al-Azd, but most authorities, including the local historian, agree that Malik bin Fahm was the pioneer on this occasion and led the Azdites on their toilsome journey to their future abode.

On leaving Mareb, Malik bin Fahm and the Azd made their way across Hadhramaut direct to the sea coast until they reached Raysoot, at that time a thriving town and trading port about 500 miles from Mareb, where they remained for some time to rest, and where they were joined by many of the Mahra, Beni Kodhaa, and other tribes, who had resolved to separate from their own folk and settle in Oman.

By the time they had reached Raysoot the wanderers were doubtless worn out with fatigue and privation, after journeying for many months through a barren and sparsely inhabited country with their families, flocks, and other impedimenta, and as the road that lay before them to Oman passed through a still more wild and desert land than that through which they had already traversed, it was deemed expedient by Malik bin Fahm to send the weaker portion of his tribe by sea to Oman, in order to avoid the dangers of a land march of 400 miles, and we are informed in the "Annals" that the families and baggage eventually reached Kilhat, a castle and seaport on the Oman coast, where they were temporarily placed under a strong guard.

Having learned at Raysoot that the Parthians were in possession of Oman, Malik selected 6,000 warriors, horse and foot, to precede the Azd emigrants, and sent forward a body of horse as an advance guard, under the command of his youngest son, Honat, or as some say, Ferahid, to reconnoitre. On reaching Oman, Malik is said to have proceeded first to Kilhat, to arrange about the families, and then returned to the Jowf, or the valley between Adam and Bahila, to look after his people and found a colony there. He then began to negotiate with the Parthian satrap, and sent an envoy requesting permission to settle in the country. When the messengers arrived at Sohar, which was then the capital, the satrap held a council and finally decided to reject the Azdite claim to colonize, and returned an answer accordingly. Malik is said to have then sent a second envoy, deprecating the satrap's refusal to comply with his request, and insisting on his demand. The satrap, however, not only remained firm, but began to prepare a force to expel the intruders.

The Parthian armies, consisting of 30,000 or 40,000 men, with a few elephants, advanced up the Wady Semail and halted at Saloot, between Zikki and Nezwa. Malik, as stated in the "Annals," had only 6,000 men, but after four days' fighting the Parthians were completely routed and their commander killed. As a result of this battle, a truce was made between the combatants, by which the Parthians agreed to evacuate the country after a year, leaving the Arabs in possession. The truce was made use of by the satrap to report the affair to his monarch, Vologaces II., and to ask for reinforcements; while Malik, on the other hand, spent the time in distributing his people among the valleys in the vicinity of Jowf.

On receiving news of what had occurred in Oman, the Parthian king appointed a new marzaban, and despatched him with reinforcements to Sohar, with orders to expel the Azd intruders. Malik, however, did not wait to be attacked, but on hearing of the arrival of the new satrap, at once assumed the offensive and moved down against the Parthians, and in the battle that ensued was again victorious, compelling the enemy to abandon everything and quit the country. Honat and his brother Maan are said to have killed one of the largest elephants used in the fight with their own hands.

Malik bin Fahm, having now made himself master of all Oman, continued to rule it for many years, well and justly, until at the age of 120 he was shot with an arrow by his third and favourite son Solima, who thereupon fled to Kirman in Persia.

After making due allowance for the native chronicler's exaggeration and partiality, the narrative of the Azdite invasion in the "Kashf al-Ghummeh," the author of which, Sirhan bin Said, states explicitly that it is based on ancient lays and legends current among the Arabs, may be taken as fairly authentic and trustworthy. With respect to Malik bin Fahm, some historians state that he led many of the Azdites to Bahrain and thence to Hera on the Euphrates, where he founded a principality, being succeeded by two of his sons, and that he was slain there by his son Solima, who fled to Oman for refuge. Much information relating to Malik and his family is contained in the interesting notes to Ross's "Annals of Oman."

About sixty or seventy years after the first invasion of the Azdites, a second immigration into Oman appears to have taken place, by which the predominance of the Yemenites was still further strengthened, and the tribes composing this second are probably indicated in the following passage, which is here transcribed direct from the "Annals of Oman":—

> "Then came to Oman many tribes of the Al-Azd. The first of the Al-Azd to join Malik was Imran bin Amru bin Ameer Mael Sema with his sons Al-Hajr and Al-Aswad. From the two latter many tribes in Oman derive. Afterwards Rabiah bin al-Harith bin Abdullah bin Ameer al-Ghitrif went forth with his brothers, also Muladis bin Amru bin Adi bin Harithah came

and entered Hudad, also Arman bin Amru bin al-Azd, then came Al-Yahmad bin Homma, also the sons of Ghamn bin Ghalib bin Othman ; and Ziyad or Al-Nadab the junior. Then Mawalah, the sons of Shams, and Al-Nadab the senior went forth, also Al-Dheyyak, and some of the Benu Yashkar and of the Benu Amid, and men of Khawaleh. All these tribes went forth, each tribe with its banners. As they journeyed on, they consumed the substance of all by whom they passed, until they reached Oman. They extended themselves throughout Oman, and settled in its rich and spacious lands. The Al-Aẓd named it Oman, because their dwellings had been in a watered valley (Yemen) which was probably called Amman, and to which they likened their new home. The Persians called Oman by the name of Mazun.

" The tribes of the Al-Azd ceased not to migrate to Oman, until they became numerous therein, and their power and fame increased. At length they overran the country and extended as far as Al-Bahrain and Hajar (Al-Hassa). Then came to Oman, Samah bin Loweij bin Ghalib and settled at Towwam which is Al-Jow, in the vicinity of the Al-Azd. There were also in that place some of the Benu Said, and Benu Abd al-Keis. Some of the Benu Tamim also settled in Oman ; the Al-Khazaah bin Hazem settlers, too, arrived from the Benu al-Nabat, whose abodes were at Obri and Al-Seleyf, and Tenam, and Al-Sirr. Some of the Benu al-Harith bin Kaab came and settled at Dank. About one hundred persons of the Khadhaah also settled at Dank. Some of the family of Benu Ruaheh ben Katiah bin Abs came to Oman, amongst them Abu al-Hishm."

During the minority of Sapor II., who ruled in Persia from 310 to 330 A.D., the Arabs raided Persian territory, and Sapor, a few years later, landed an army at Kateef and overran Al-Hajar and the adjacent region, where he almost exterminated the Arab tribes.

The terror inspired throughout Central Arabia by the ruthless ravages of Sapor's troops caused a great dispersion of the Adnani tribes, many of which came to Oman, and smaller influxes continually followed to such an extent as almost to threaten Yemenite supremacy. Some of these tribes are enumerated in Badger's *Introduction*, such as the Safir, Sahban, Batl, Arabah, Said, Rashid, Akhzam, Wahib, Main, Benu, Samit, Hadiyeh, and Ashraf.

In the beginning of the fifth century further contingents of Adnani tribes, numbering 30,000, poured down into Oman, but many of them pushed on to Hadhramaut and settled there. Among the Nejdean tribes that entered Oman, about two centuries later, were the Abs, whose descendants, the Benu Ruwaihah, now hold the valley called after their name.

The forty years' war between the Abs and Dhobyan, resulting from the race between the horse Dahis and the mare Ghobra, which took place in 563 A.D., is one of the most famous in Arab history. The chivalrous Kais bin Zoheir, the Shaikh of the Abs, then retired to Oman with part of his tribe, turned Christian, and became a monk.

At this epoch the number of Christians in Southern and Eastern Arabia was very considerable. Subsequent to the well-known mission of Frumentius, the most vigorous effort at converting the Yemenite Arabs, as Wright informs us, was made about the latter part of the fourth century, when Theophilus Indus, a native of Dabul, near Karrachee in Sind, and a man of superior capacity, who had been carried to Rome as a hostage, was sent on an embassy with valuable gifts to the King of the Himyarites, by Constantius II.

Theophilus succeeded in converting the Tobba and many of his people, and was empowered to erect three churches in the Yemen empire—one at Zhafier near Sanaa, one at Aden, and one in the Persian Gulf, most probably at Sohar in Oman, which was visited by Theophilus in his travels, and where, as we have seen, Kais bin Zoheir 200 years later lived in seclusion until his death.

The conquest of the Yemen by the Christian Abyssinians and the destruction of the Himyarite Empire in 525 A.D., with the concurrent increase of Roman influence, must have greatly augmented the progress of Christianity, and this religion would soon have become the dominant one in Arabia had it not been for the unexpected rise of a new one, *i.e.*, Islam.

From the invasion of the Azd, under Malik bin Fahm, to the advent of the Sassanians our knowledge of dynastic succession as well as of political events is almost a blank.

Malik bin Fahm may have left the power to one of his sons, of whom he had many; and we read in the "Annals of Oman" of one Malik bin Zoheir, whose authority was nearly equivalent to that of Malik bin Fahm himself, but the only dynasty we know of is that of the Julanda Princes, regarding whose family Abufeda says that every one who came to the throne took the name of Julanda. The Julanda are said to have belonged to the Maawali tribe, which still exists in one of the valleys of Jebel Akhdar. Another tradition, however, asserts that they derived from the Amalekite Beni Kerker, and this view appears to have been adopted by Sale.

The Julanda were ruling in Oman at the time of Mohammed and are mentioned in the Koran, but how and at what period the family rose and assumed the reins of government we are entirely ignorant. The success of the Abyssinian expedition in 525 A.D. had led to the founding of a new and powerful dynasty at Sanaa, the capital of the Yemen. This welcome succour to the cause of Christianity was naturally hailed with joy by the Emperor of Constantinople, who despatched an ambassador to Axum to negotiate a treaty of alliance with the Negoos and to bring about his friendly attachment to the Roman Empire, but the court at Madain or Ctesiphon, as may well be supposed, viewed the matter very differently, and the news of the Abyssinian conquest was received by the Kesra in a resentful spirit.

The gain to Roman prestige and the stimulus to the world-wide commerce of Constantinople were too evident to be denied or overlooked. That sagacious ruler, Anoushirwan, saw plainly how necessary it was for Persian interests to check Roman progress in that quarter and to crush the new dynasty in the Yemen before it became too active a religious centre, or powerful enough to give Rome effective aid, and he watched for an opportunity to lay his hand on the African usurper. For many years the Roman and other campaigns distracted his attention, but the wished-for moment came at last with the treaty with Justinian of 562 A.D., which arranged for fifty years' peace, and which was fraught with eventful results for Southern and Eastern Arabia. In the first place the relaxation from war gave Anoushirwan the leisure and opportunity he had so long desired, to project an expedition against the Abyssinian power in the Yemen, and he lost no time in directing his energies towards the furtherance of this enterprise. The undertaking, however, was one which was calculated to tax his resources to the utmost.

Aden, the final destination of the force, was distant over 2,000 miles by sea from Obolla, the point of its departure, and notwithstanding the extent of the commerce that existed at that period, it must have required no little time to collect transports and lay in the requisite stores for so remote a voyage. Yet however ardent may have been Kesroo's desire to attack Roman influence in the Yemen, it is doubtful whether the design would ever have been put into execution had it not been for the appearance at his court at Ctesiphon of the Himyarite King, Dhul Yezen Abul Murra, who had been driven to seek refuge there by the tyranny of the Abyssinian King, Mezrook bin Abraha.

According to some, Dhul Yezen went first to solicit the aid of the Roman Emperor, and having appealed to him in vain, proceeded to Hera, and thence to Ctesiphon, where he died soon after his arrival. Most of the writers mention only his son Saif, who in his interview with the Kesra represented the wealth of the Yemen in such glowing terms that the expedition was determined on.

The valuable advice and information, political and geographical, afforded by Saif bin Dhul Yezen, enabled the Kesra to form a wide and comprehensive plan for attacking not only Yemen but the whole of the Arab coast. The command of this expedition was entrusted to a high official who is called by Al-Tabari Wahraz, but according to Hamza al-Ispahani his name was Kharzad bin Narsis—Wahraz or Vaphrizes being a family title. He was of royal blood, and belonged to the line of Ardeshir, and his conduct of the expedition shows him to have been an able general.

The strength of the army, which embarked at Obolla, probably in the year 570 A.D., on this famous voyage has been very variously estimated by the Arab and Persian chroniclers, one of whom gives 3,600, while Ibn Koteaba mentions 7,500 as the number of men. Al-Tabari tells us that the expedition comprised eight ships carrying one hundred men in each, and that two of them foundered on the way with all hands, leaving a force of only six hundred to land at Aden, and we may safely assume that these low figures are due to Persian vanity.

Probably Tabari knew nothing of the conquest of Oman, and imagined that the discrepancy between the number of troops shipped in the Shat al-Arab and the number actually landed at Aden was due to the loss of one-fourth of the expedition at sea. It may be fairly assumed that the effective strength of the Persians was 16,000 men, of whom about 12,000 were engaged in the attack on the Abyssinians in the Yemen.

Sailing from Obolla, Wahraz first led his fleet to the Bahrain Islands, which were at that time a dependency of Oman. These islands were easily seized and occupied, and Vaphrizes then steered for Sohar, the capital of Oman, where he disembarked his troops and proceeded to overrun the country and reduce the Arab tribes to submission. The only account of this conquest that has come down to us is contained in the "Kashf al-Ghummeh," whose author gives a meagre notice of the event. This record, scanty as it is, bears the stamp of truth and may be accepted without reserve. The passage in this work is as follows:—

> "The Persians did not return to Oman after their expulsion by Malik until his reign terminated, and his children reigned in his place, and the kingdom of Oman came into the possession of Al-Julanda bin al-Mustatir al-Maawali, and Persia fell into the hands of the Benu Sasan. There was peace between them and Al-Julanda in Oman, and the Persians kept a force of 4,000

warriors in Oman and a deputy with the kings of the Al-Azd. The Persians abode on the sea coast, and the Al-Azd ruled in the interior plains and hills and districts of Oman, the direction of affairs being entirely with them. The Persian monarchs used to send persons who had incurred their displeasure, or whom they feared, to their army in Oman. So it continued until God caused Al-Islam to be manifested."

The author relates further on that the Persians resided at Jamsetjerd near Sohar, a place built by the Persians as their headquarters; this locality is now known as Jebel Gharabeh, also as Felej al-Sook, the ruins of which are still visible.

The force of 4,000 men left in the country to overawe the population and retain it in subjection is sufficient evidence that the conquest of Oman was fully contemplated and provided for by the Kesra, and further, that it was not achieved without a long struggle and a vigorous resistance on the part of the Arabs.

A marzaban or governor, whose name was Dad Firooz Hashmushfan, and who was known as Al-Mukaabir, was appointed over the two provinces of Oman and Bahrain, and established his residence at Jamsetyerd, where he built and founded a town. But he was probably subordinate to Mundhir bin Naaman of the Beni Lahm, to whom, according to Al-Tabari, the Kesra had entrusted the provinces of Oman, Bahrain, Yemama, and part of Hejaz.

With regard to the relative position of this viceroy and the Julanda Prince, we are informed that the latter was allowed to retain Nezwa as his capital, and to continue to exercise jurisdiction over the Arab tribes, on condition of his acknowledgment of the vassality to Persia and agreeing to pay tribute. The marzaban, on his part, appears to have limited his troops to the long maritime plain called Al-Batineh and to have refrained from immediate interference with the interior.

After leaving Sohar, the Persian fleet continued its course along the Arab coast, and annexing Dhofar and Hadhramaut on the way, anchored at length in the port of Aden. Here the troops were disembarked, and after a long contest, in which the native adherents of Saif bin Dhul Yezen co-operated with the Persians, the latter secured a complete triumph. The brilliant success of this venturesome enterprise, which added to the Persian Empire some 1,500 miles of new coast line, and four Arabian provinces— Bahrain, Oman, Hadhramaut and The Yemen—caused great exultation in the Sassanian capital, and during the remainder of the reign of Anoushirwan—who died in 579 A.D.—these conquests were firmly held. But the grasp of his successor was more feeble, and the first wave of Islam, 66 years later, swept the Persians from Oman and the other states.

The subjugation of Eastern and Southern Arabia is remarkable as being the last notable episode in the history of the peninsula before the introduction of Al-Islam, and it is unfortunate we have so little information regarding it at this interesting period. The remembrance of the Persian invasion still lives clear and distinct in Arab tradition, and traces of the occupation are to be found in many places.

CHAPTER II.

THE PERSIAN GULF UNDER ISLAM.

ALMOST simultaneously with the appearance of the Sassanians in Southern Arabia there was born at Mecca one of the most extraordinary men the world ever produced—a man who was destined to revolutionize Western Asia, to lay the foundations of a magnificent Empire and to be the prophet of one of the most important religious systems that have influenced mankind.

Much discrepancy exists as to the exact date of Mohammed's birth, but European writers are now generally agreed to place it between A.D. 569 and 572. Moslem writers are fond of asserting that he was born in the "year of the Elephant," the year in which Abraha, after erecting a splendid Christian cathedral at Sanaa, marched to the destruction of the Kaaba, at Mecca, but was defeated and routed by the Meccans through the miraculous assistance of birds sent by heaven to destroy the Abyssinian host. This event must have preceded the Sassanian invasion of the Yemen by some years, as it was Abraha's grandson, who was in power there when Vaphrizes arrived, but it is natural the Moslems should wish to ascribe his birth to the eventful year in which danger to their sacred city and shrine had been so providentially averted.

It was not for some years after Mohammed's announcement of his prophetic mission that the convulsive throbs of the new movement, partly political, partly religious, that soon shook the peninsula from end to end, extended to Oman. The news of Mohammed's first victories did not perhaps reach very far, but as his power and fame grew, the remotest corners of Arabia must have been gradually affected by the military events and religious revolution transpiring in the Hejaz. In tracing the manner in which the earliest waves of Islam rolled into the south and east of Arabia, we meet with a few notices in Arab authors that must be quoted. According to Al-Nawawi, one Abu Bashair bin Aseed or Otba, who had embraced the new faith, having taken refuge for some reason in Oman, collected round himself there a few fellow Moslems and endeavoured to spread their doctrines, but success did not attend him, and his party was soon reduced to sixty or seventy. The tradition given by Omani chroniclers is to the effect that a man named Mazin bin Ghadhubah set out for Medina from Oman and was the first of his countrymen to visit and swear allegiance to the prophet. These indications, which need not be rejected, are sufficient to show that Mohammed's letter to the Shaikhs of Oman, demanding their submission, and a copy of which (doubtless spurious) is given by Al-Sohari in his "Ansab al-Arab," was not the first signal of the coming great change in the moral condition.

That Mohammed did write to the chiefs of Oman, as he wrote to all other chiefs and princes far and near, is certain, and the letter is said to have been brought to Oman by Amr bin al-As, who, passing through Al-Beraimi, brought the missive to the Persian Governor in the Batineh, from whence he probably proceeded to Nezwa, where the two Azdite chiefs in Oman resided. These chiefs are variously styled Jeifar or Habkar and Abd or Ayadh, and were the sons or grandsons of Julanda bin al-Mustenir.

The reply of the Persian Viceroy, whose name was Moskan, was a direct and scornful refusal, but the Azdite chiefs, with the usual wariness and circumspection of their race, took time to deliberate on their decision.

Hitherto the Omanis had been watching the course of events taking place in the Hejaz and the progress of the strange crusade against idolatry led by the son of Abdullah with interest and wonder. The passage above quoted from Al-Nawawi shows clearly that they had no desire for a new religion. They would take it if necessary, but had no intention of spontaneously making submission to the new reformer. Conscious of the strength of their isolated and remote position, with a desert frontier placed as a barrier against the rest of the peninsula, they deemed themselves secure from molestation, and calculated they could afford to wait and see whether the new prophet would be able to hold his ground.

It was in the ninth year of the Hijrah [630 A.D.], "the year of Deputations," that Amr bin al-As, a man of subtle intellect, who had been converted to Islam the year before, had been sent to Oman, and it was probably the same year, or the year after, that a general council of the Shaikhs of Oman, both Nizar and Yemen, was convened at Nezwa, at which it was resolved to submit and pay the tax demanded by Mohammed, whose divine mission could no longer be gainsaid.

Several considerations weighed with the shaikhs in coming to this conclusion and served to support the arguments brought forward by Amr. Doubtless the tidings of the general deputation of envoys to Mohammed, after the capture of Mecca, and the decisive defeat and humiliation of the Howazui and Thakeef tribes, at the Battle of Honain, had already reached Oman and had had its effect; but more than this, the hope of getting rid of the Persian yoke, and the political advantages to be gained from an alliance with the new and powerful Arab Government at Medina, must have chiefly swayed the council of Nezwa in its decision, for, in truth, it must have begun to dawn on all the inhabitants of Arabia that a master mind had arisen in the land and that a central power had been formed, to which all could look for guidance and support. Religious conviction, manifestly, had little or nothing to do with the matter. There was no display of bigotry. The Council was guided in its deliberations by a simple question of policy. The adoption of the new faith and friendship with the new ruler at Medina was clearly in their sight of far greater importance to Oman than the retention of idolatry, and, therefore, they were adopted. The decision come to by the authorities at Nezwa was at once put into execution.

Some of the leading shaikhs were selected and despatched to Al-Medina to tender allegiance and to accept the new faith on behalf of the people of Oman. At the same time Abd and Jeifar sent out messengers to Muheyreh and Dhofar in the south and to Dibba in the north, admonishing the people in those parts to accept Islam and abandon idolatry. The people offered no overt resistance and the change effected in the religion, though purely nominal and on the surface, was bloodless and peaceful.

We hear of no religious persecutions or tumults in Oman. No martyrs suffered in the cause of heathenism. The people simply ceased to adore idols openly and to frequent the temples to worship the graven images. In truth the people did not understand what they were doing. They could not yet know the details of Mohammed's system, nor could they realize or foresee the immensity of the change which the new religion would make in their moral and social condition. The Koran proscribes the whole of the religious observances of paganism; the idols and temples, the stones, trees and shrines are to be ruthlessly swept away, and the Moslems are taught in it to look back with shame, regret, and contempt on their former idolatry. The phallic stones and carved idols were ordered to be rigidly suppressed and destroyed, the tutelary deities of every tribe and family to be obliterated from the memory.

Probably the people long maintained the existing order ot things and offered an inert resistance to the encroachments, while nominally accepting the change; but their feelings and interests were not much affected, and it was only as time went on that the insidious invasion of Islam swept away the old system. It was by degrees that the people acquired pride and enthusiasm about Islam and its founder and stamped out paganism as an accursed thing.

The grand central idea of Islam was Monotheism, as a protest against the Trinity of the Christians and the idols and nature worship of the heathen. It is this fundamental truth that has formed the strength, vitality, and moral elevation of the religion. In reforming the Arabs, the object contemplated by Mohammed was to introduce among them new habits which would give them manners more compatible with the wellbeing of society than their old heathenism —moral influence, not violent interference, was his method. He wisely left their future progress to time, example, and tuition in his new dispensation.

Many, however, of the superstitions and usages of paganism became insensibly and permanently engrafted on to the Prophet's new faith, as had already happened in the case of Christianity; and certain tribes, the wilder and more ignorant Bedouin tribes in particular, retained their worship of the stars and other points of the Sabean religion for centuries. A few tribes in Oman, such as the Awamir and the Al-Waheebeh, are said at the present day to have but a veneer of Islam over their old paganism, and to carry on certain reprehensible practices.

The payment of zakat or tithes was simply carried on by Mohammed as an ancient and very convenient institution. It was the only national tax ever paid by the Arabs from time immemorial. In truth it is not easy to say exactly how many of Mohammed's ideas were real innovations, as we know so little of the details of the inner life and of the ceremonies observed at the birth, the bridal and the burial of a pagan Arab.

When the Omani shaikhs, deputed to take the reply to Mohammed, started on their journey, Amr bin al-As did not accompany them but stayed behind to watch the new faith and to instruct the people.

Incensed at the rejection by the Persians of his demand for submission, and anxious to remove the followers of a rival creed, Amr encouraged the people of Oman to attack them. The expulsion of the Persians from the soil of Oman had long been an object of ambition to the Julanda chiefs as well as to the inhabitants, but their strength had not been equal to the task: The Persians represented an autogenous race, the Aryans, between whom and the Semites a racial antipathy had existed from remote times. To this day the distinction between them is unmistakable and unalterable—the hatred of one towards the other is intense, avowed, and undisguised.

Nothing could have been more in accordance with the wishes of Abd and Jeifar than to draw the sword on the Persians, therefore the opportunity was eagerly grasped. With the moral support of the agent of the new government at Al-Medina, the tribes rose and prepared for the struggle. An ultimatum to the Persians to embrace Islam and to renounce the claim to suzerainty over the country was disdainfully refused and a contest ensued in which the Sassanian Governor Mazkan was killed and his troops worsted. The remnant retired to their strongholds, where they were besieged by the Arabs, until at length they capitulated on condition of being permitted to retire to Persia, and the land was then purged from the invader.

The deputation of shaikhs sent to Al-Medina from Oman appears to have been well received by Mohammed who, either from motives of policy or because it was thus stipulated for by the shaikhs, consented to forego the zakat and agreed that the money, annually collected for the purpose, should be distributed to the poor and needy in Oman, instead of being remitted to Al-Medina. The shaikhs, we may be sure, made use of their opportunity to ascertain the true state of political affairs in Western Arabia, and must have been impressed with the strong personality of Mohammed and the enthusiastic veneration of his adherents before they turned their steps homeward to report the result of their mission to the Julanda Princes at Nezwa.

Although the representatives of the great majority of the tribes in Oman, assembled in Council at Nezwa, had decided to submit to the new prophet and to adopt his faith, this was by no means universally the case, and some tribes had held severely aloof from the new movement. Even among the Azdite tribes, which might have been expected to follow the lead of their own chiefs, some still clung tightly to the skirts of their idols, and a bold and ambitious leader was not wanting to them in their opposition to the Julanda Princes. This was Dhul Taj Lakeet bin Malik, an Azdite shaikh, but of what tribe is not stated, who defied Amr bin al-As and strongly opposed the acceptances of the new doctrines by his compatriots.

In less than two years after the return of the deputation,

the great reformer and monotheist, Mohammed, fell sick and died in the eleventh year of the Hijrah. At this time all the Arab provinces and tribes had submitted to him, but the tide of victory had not yet begun to flow beyond Arabia.

The death of the Prophet was a shock to the believers in divine inspiration, which nearly caused the collapse of the new faith. At all the more remote parts of Arabia rebellion broke out instantly, as well as in the provinces nearer to Al-Medina. Oman proved no exception, but rose in revolt like the rest, and the delegate, Amr bin al-As, lost no time in returning to the Hejaz to report what had occurred.

The Julanda Princes remained staunch and with many of the tribes steadfastly adhered to Islam. But the bulk of the population were disaffected. Dhul Taj Lakeet at once assumed the lead in the insurrection and, taking advantage of Mohammed's death to proclaim himself the True Prophet, summoned the people to rally round him and swear allegiance.

His success was immediate and pronounced. Like the rest of Arabia the inhabitants of Oman had accepted Islam, not from conviction but from policy, and not doubting that the death of Mohammed would cause the downfall of the structure he had raised, the Omanis now turned eagerly to the new leader and prepared to follow him as the champion of their national and religious independence.

Abu Bekr's reign began under a stormy sky. His election had caused much heart burning and dissatisfaction, and he had not adopted the title of Khalif many days when messengers bearing tidings of insurrection and apostasy began to arrive at Al-Medina from all directions. .

Abu Bekr was a man of strong character without much strength of intellect, and at first dismayed and paralyzed at the new and mighty edifice raised by Mohammed being so suddenly and so roughly shaken, he was unable to do more than concentrate his forces upon the more important revolted districts near Al-Medina; but when these were subdued and the threatening clouds began to rise and drift away, he prepared vigorously for the reduction and chastisement of the more distant rebellious provinces.

Meanwhile the Omani tribes which remained faithful to Islam gathered round the Julanda Princes, Abd and Jeifar, at Nezwa and calmly awaited the arrival of succour from the Khalif.

As all southern and eastern Arabia had revolted, it was necessary that the Khalif's plan of campaign for the reconquest of these widely scattered regions should be a comprehensive one. Three generals were accordingly selected for the purpose and were instructed to act at first independently on the service entrusted to each and then to converge on Oman, where they were to unite their forces. Their names were Ikrima bin Abu Jahl, who had been censured by Abu Bekr for his defeat by Moseilama and had been sent to Oman to retrieve his tarnished reputation; Arfaja bin Harthema al-Barida, and Hodhaifa bin Mohsan.

The plan of campaign was successfully carried out by these generals, who after a long and weary desert march from Bahrain and Yemama reached Towwam (or Al-Riyam, as Tabari has it), from whence they sent orders to the Julanda Chiefs, Abd and Jeifar, to meet them at Sohar, under the walls of which fortress the combined Moslem army was soon assembled.

The warriors of Oman were thus divided into two hostile camps; one of them, and the more numerous, being headed by Dhul Taj Lakeet bin Malik, who presuming that the disintegration of the new government at Al-Medina had taken place simultaneously with the death of Mohammed had raised his own standard as a prophet, and seduced many tribes to abandon the profession of Islam. In the other camp were the Omani Moslems under their rulers, Abd and Jeifar, who with more discernment had appreciated the force of the arguments used by Amr bin al-As as to the stability and vitality of the new dispensation and had believed that the Khalif Abu Bekr would not forsake them but would send them aid to confront the enemies of the Faith. It was but another instance in the world's history of the rancour and bloodthirstiness created by religious intolerance when the new Moslems of Oman did not hesitate to join with Ikrima in a crusade against their countrymen, with whom a short time before they had been associated in idolatrous and heathen worship.

Being much inferior in numbers to the Omani force collected by their opponent, Dhul Taj Lakeet, the Moslem generals did not deem it prudent to commence the attack until they had tried the effect of intrigue, and they accordingly employed Amr Mozeikiyeh to seduce the Azdite tribes from their allegiance to the impostor and induce them to return to the fold of Islam. In this they succeeded beyond their expectation; a large portion of Dhul Taj's force fell away from him and helped to swell the ranks of the Moslems, thus placing the two armies more on an equality. Doubtless the arrival of Ikrima and Hodhaifa with a primitive expedition from the distant capital, Al-Medina, had been a sufficient proof to them that the new government had not collapsed but was prepared to support its authority with vigour, and led the more timid or more thinking of those who had lapsed from the Faith to consider their position and to seize the opportunity offered them to rejoin the ranks of the Faithful.

The Moslems, now reinforced by these seceders, no longer hesitated to march upon the rebellious tribes who had taken up their position at Dibba, a town situated in a small bay a few miles to the north of Sohar. A great and decisive battle was fought here between Islam and paganism, which raged the whole day with great fury and slaughter, and the issue of which was for a long time doubtful. The undaunted followers of Dhul Taj, befriended by their strong position, not merely sustained but repelled the attacks of their adversaries, and so wearied and intimidated the Moslems by their onsets that they would probably have come off victorious had it not been for timely and unexpected succours arriving on the scene and giving support to Ikrima's exhausted troops near the close of the day. This opportune reinforcement consisted of some of the Beni Abdul Kais and Beni Najia tribes forming part of the Khalif's army, which had apparently been delayed on the march across the Dahna and Sabkheh from Bahrain, and its sudden appearance so dismayed the Omanis and encouraged the Moslems that the tide of triumph was soon changed into a defeat, and Dhul Taj's army was utterly routed. The victory was dearly purchased, but it was followed by an unrelenting pursuit and carnage, and the loss of the vanquished is stated to have been 10,000 men. Dibba, an opulent mart and seaport, was sacked and burnt and an immense spoil became the prize of the victors. The town has never emerged from its ashes to this day, and the site of the battle is now regarded by the people with a kind of reverence as the place where Providence interposed to smite the idolators and put them to shame before Islam.

Henceforth there was no word to be said in Oman against the truth of the Mohammedan Faith; paganism was killed by the sword and the establishment of Islam in the land dates from the "Day of Dibba." The Julanda chiefs and the tribes who had remained faithful to the cause with them were rewarded with a share in the booty, and participated in the triumph of the Moslems, while such of the erring tribes as had escaped massacre hastened to make contrite submission to the Khalif's generals. What became of the false prophet, Dhul Taj Lakeet, is not related; but he was probably hunted to death by the zealous and haughty Hodhaifa, who remained, in accordance with Abu Bekr's previously given instructions, to restore order and obedience, to consolidate the new regime, and to engraft the new faith firmly in Oman.

Hodhaifa having been installed in the government, the other two generals prepared to carry out the duties apportioned to each by the Khalif when he entrusted the three officers with the task of quelling the insurrection in eastern Arabia, which had been so successfully accomplished.

Arfaja, charged to convey to the Khalif at Al-Medina the fifth share of the booty, which was the sovereign's right, and to conduct thither the fifth part of the captives, started at once on his journey. Among the captives, it may be here noted, was Abu Sofriya, then a youth, who became the father of the celebrated Muhalleb, "the Conqueror of the Kharejites."

The written instructions held by Ikrima were to the effect that, after assisting his two colleagues in pacifying Oman, he was to take the supreme command of the army and to proceed with it along the coast to Hadhramaut which, like Oman, had thrown off the yoke of Al-Medina, on the Prophet's death, and had relapsed into heathenism. After reducing that province he was to push on to the Yemen and put himself under the orders of Mohajir.

These orders Ikrima now prepared to carry out, and having mustered his Hejazi troops, he broke camp and started on his arduous expedition to the Mahra country and Hadhramaut, accompanied by two auxiliary bodies furnished by the Abdul Kais and Najia tribes, as well as by a small reinforcement from the tribe of Saad ibn Zaid Monat ibn Temeem.

Ikrima found the people of Mahra divided into two factions, one led by Sikhreet and the other by Musabbih; this disunion facilitated the triumph of the Moslems.

Sikhreet was won over by Ikrima and Musabbih was routed and slain. The Mahras and Hadhramautis then assembled and solemnly accepted Islam and vowed obedience.

On the departure of Ikrima with his army Hodhaifa was left to rule the country, now outwardly tranquil, but in what a perplexed and strange condition of domestic turmoil and transition! But, of course, Abd and Jeifar could not have contemplated and understood the momentous consequences of their action when they and their people resolved to accept the teaching of the Apostle of God; nor could they have foreseen the changes that would result not only to themselves but to the world.

Three years before the Arabs were in a rude state of ignorance and barbarism, split up into numerous principalities and shaikhdoms, now they were a great and united nation with a higher and purer faith to bind them together and a chief—the Khalif—to guide them and lead them to conquest.

The new religion was not merely a collection of theological dogmas they were called on to believe, but a code of religious laws containing the obligation to abandon their old faith, their social and domestic customs, and to adopt others that would affect not only themselves but their relations with each other and their attitude towards strangers.

There was change in everything; but the main points insisted on were the acceptance of Mohammed's Code of Laws, the five daily prayers, and the payment of the zakat.

Instead of a degraded idolatry, a great reformer had conferred on them—next to Christianity—incomparably the most exalted and noble religion the world has seen. It is indeed difficult to realize and appreciate the extent of the benefits that Mohammed bestowed on the people, the marvellous amelioration he effected in their condition.

Mohammed, to at least the same extent as any other lawgiver, is entitled to the applause, veneration and gratitude of the world. It is the business of a lawgiver to demarcate the boundaries of men's actions, to lay down just ordinances for the protection of the oppressed and helpless, to screen offenders from partial punishments, etc., and this is just what Mohammed did. His code was crude and imperfect, short-sighted and inadequate perhaps, but it represented the spirit of the age and nation, and was intended for the Arab race. The difficulty is that his laws are not elastic enough; they are so mixed up with religion that they are unchangeable. But they took the place of chaos, and worked an unexampled change in the condition and in promoting the social welfare of the Arab.

To understand this better it is necessary to take here a glance at the moral condition of the people in pagan times. It is unfortunately impossible to delineate the Arab accurately in his idolatrous and barbarous state, as the iconoclastic zeal of the Moslem has swept away nearly all traces of the time of ignorance, but a few notices and facts concerning them have been gleaned by scholars from the field of Arabic literature.

By the people of Oman as well as by the Himyarites, Sabeism or Stellar worship, the most obvious and primitive of all idolatries, was generally practised and was the prevailing religion; but

Christians, Jews, and Zoroastrians were numerous, and a few sectaries of Brahmanism, or Hindoos, were to be found in the seaports. The divinities were extremely numerous; those which were worshipped by certain tribes being (as in ancient Egypt) animals, plants, rocks, stars, etc. But each tribe and almost every family had a divinity which it looked to for protection. Under the figure of many of their idols they adored angels, whom they imagined to be of the female sex. These divinities were, however, only looked upon as intercessors, though powerful ones, before the supreme God. Some believed in the resurrection of the soul after death, but for the most part they expected nothing but annihilation.

Among the many barbarous and cruel usages abolished by Mohammed were the inhumation of living girls; the unrestricted power of marriage and divorce allowed to men; the slavery of woman; the marriage between stepsons and stepmothers, a ceremony that was called "Nikah al-Makt," or "the Hateful Marriage," by the early Moslems; trial by ordeal; indulgence in drink and gambling, in both of which vices they took both pride and delight. Circumcision and the slavery of captives were retained, but the last institution was fettered by wholesome laws and never became the frightful engine of cruelty and wickedness that subsequently disgraced certain more civilized and Christian countries.

In the Sabean religion of the times of ignorance there had been no priesthood, and one of the most important and significant decisions made by Mohammed was to continue the old system and to avoid the example set by Moses, Christ, and Zoroaster in creating a priestly hierarchy and to leave the rulers and the people free to appoint their own kadhis and imams, by selecting from among the learned such as were qualified by their piety, character and attainments. That Mohammed was led to this decision by what he had learned and observed of the state of affairs in other religions, and among the Christians especially, cannot be doubted. The degradation of the Christian clergy in Syria and other parts, the immorality, ignorance, and depravity of the shaven monks were so flagrant and notorious, that he wisely determined to save his own church from similar evil and pollution, and he took care to prevent, as far as he could, any possibility of such an institution being organized; his wisdom in not establishing a hierarchy was inspired by the true instinct of genius.

Christianity had a start of six centuries and would in all probability have supplanted every other religion in Western Asia had it not been encumbered and weighed down by the character and example of some of its churchmen. But when Islam appeared, the superiority of a free religion, untrammelled by a clerical hierarchy, was so apparent and incontestable, that Christianity in those regions sank into a lower condition, and in the thirteen centuries that have elapsed has never been able to recover its position. Mohammed unquestionably introduced the rudiments of a new life, intellectual, social, and political. His reforms impressed the Arab mind as Christianity had never been able to do, and next to Christ, he must be regarded as the greatest reformer the world has ever seen. For the rest the energetic and effective vitality of the new faith was as much, or more, in the sentiments and emotions it inspired as in the doctrines and precepts of the Koran, and the predominance of these motives clearly distinguish the character of the age—the early events of Islamitic history are always present to the minds of the faithful and have, not a little, affected the general character and attitude of the Moslems.

The radical change in ideas and customs effected by the introduction of Islam into Oman must, of course, have taken a considerable time to permeate the people, and the reform could not have been thoroughly effected until the old generation had passed away and a new race had sprung up, which had not known the old order of things; but the new Faith and law were as palpably and immeasurably an improvement, so admirably calculated to increase the general happiness and welfare, that the merits of Islam could not remain unrecognized and unwelcomed.

The new Ameer, Hodhaifa, ruled Oman for three years, apparently with judicious moderation, and no complaints are recorded by the Omani historians against the character of his administration. His efforts, supported by the iconoclastic zeal of his Hejazi adherents and followers, and calmly acquiesced in by the people, were mainly directed towards the obliteration of all traces of the "Days of Ignorance," in tutoring the people in the laws and precepts of the new Faith, in smoothing the path of this great religious revolution, and in guiding the mind of the population to a full recognition of the fact that a new era of light, of moral elevation, and of general prosperity, as a component part of the new commonwealth, had dawned for them.

By this time the fabric raised by Mohammed, which had fallen asunder when the master hand was withdrawn, had been reared again throughout Arabia. The revolt had been everywhere suppressed and the central government at Medina having reunited all the provinces of the peninsula into one harmonious, religious, and political system, with ample revenues, was about to wield the mighty engine of martial enthusiasm, to propagate the creed by the sword, and to overwhelm the neighbouring nations like a flood of lava, until it had ultimately established the most widespreading empire the world up to that time had ever seen. The rotten civilization of Sassanian Persia, the repulsive religion of Zoroaster, the debased form of Christianity and the immoral monkeries of Syria were to disappear in a great degree, and a comparatively sturdier and healthier regime was to hold sway from the Atlantic to Samarcand.

Doubtless the people of Oman generally did not give up all their old and cherished customs and superstitions without reluctance and without a struggle, and doubtless also some bitterness of feeling and some persecution, perhaps, occurred before the transition was effected. The revolt of Lakeet had shown how deeply the old pagan institutions had taken root in the Arab mind, and how the people clung to their ancient and cruel usages and superstitions.

More than a generation must have elapsed before the worst prejudices had passed away and the beneficial changes and aspirations of Islam were imbibed and assimilated. The Arab writers, however, tell us nothing about the gradual process of these changes, and we must picture to ourselves, as best we can, the way in which the old errors were eliminated and the new ideas filled their place. Our knowledge of the moral state of the Omanis after Islam must be taken from what we know of the inhabitants of Damascus and Baghdad, of which capitals the Omani towns offered a very subdued reflection.

Of the two Julanda Princes who had been in power when Mohammed arose, Abd and Jeifar, the latter appears to have resided quietly at Nezwa during Al-Hodhaifa's reign, but Abd proceeded to Medina with the caravan of spoil and captives that accompanied Arfaja. On arrival there, he temporarily took service with the Khalif Abu Bekr, in whose expedition against the Jifneh he is said to have taken part.

The year 13 A.H. [634 A.D.] witnessed the death of the austere and single-minded Abu Bekr, who, after only two years of deep anxiety and incessant toil in promulgating his master's work and in holding together the discordant elements of the rapidly growing empire, had sunk into the grave at the age of 63 years. He was followed by Omar bin al-Khattab, who was a prince of stern and unbending character and more fitted for the position than his predecessor. For some reason, not mentioned, this Khalif soon withdrew Hodhaifa from his command in Oman and prudently accorded permission for the local chiefs Abd and Jeifar al-Julanda to resume their hereditary position as rulers, placing them, however, in subordination to the Ameer of Bahrain, Hajar, and Oman, a famous warrior named Othman bin Abi al-Asi al-Sakeefi.

This Ameership over three minor provinces was afterwards subordinated to the government of Irak Arabi, and the arrangement continued undisturbed for about six centuries.

The concession made by the Prophet, on the submission of Oman in the year 9 A.H. [630 A.D.], to the effect that the zakat collected by the Julanda Chief should be given to the poor of the province, seems to have been withdrawn after the revolt of Lakeet in 12 A.H. [633 A.D.], and the Ameer then received instructions to forward the collections to the Khalif.

The new Ameer, Othman bin Abi al-Asi, did not tarry long at Bahrain, but having appointed his brother Hakam to act for him, he proceeded direct to Oman, where he found much to occupy his attention, and began to busy himself in the preparation of his great naval expedition, which in the following year, 16 A.H. [637 A.D.] sailed from the ports of Sohar and Muscat to pirate and ravage the rich and prosperous dominions of the idolatrous Hindoos. Of the strength of this armament we have no details, but we know that it reached as far as Tanna and, fortunately for Othman, was completely successful, having met with but faint resistance, and enriched the Arabs with a splendid booty. This enterprise was quite in Arab taste, but it had been undertaken without the knowledge of the Khalif Omar, who, on hearing of it, censured the Ameer, Othman bin Abi al-Asi, and wrote to him the following singular reproach: "If your expedition had been defeated, be assured that I would have taken from your own tribe as many men as had been killed and put them all to death."

Omar, it is well known, had a strong antipathy to maritime enterprise and adventure, and we may safely conjecture that he did not fail also to reprimand Othman's brother, Al-Hakam, who had been left to carry on the administration at Menamah and who about this time had despatched a similar piratical fleet from Bahrain against Broach.

Throughout the Khalifate of Omar, the government of Oman continued to be administered by the Julanda Chiefs, Abd and Jeifar, who ruled conjointly; the conditions of their thus retaining the sovereignty in practical independence being submission to the Khalif and the acceptance of the obligatory remission of the annual tax through the Ameer.

The facility and success with which the Ameer Othman had organized his expedition and accomplished his descent on the Tanna coast are sufficient evidence not only of the pacification of Oman but also of the infusion of a new spirit of martial enthusiasm and fierce ardour which were leading the people to emulate the deed of the home tribes and to imitate them in the career of conquest and plunder.

The Arabians indeed, who had hitherto been content with their own peninsula and buried themselves in their own affairs, had now cast their eyes abroad and were gazing with cupidity at the rich and populous countries in their vicinity. Becoming conscious of their own strength, they now saw in their neighbour's lands a fertile source of wealth which they only required to stretch out their hands to take possession of. Oman, from its seagirt position, fenced in by the salt sea on one side and by a sea of sand on the other, was perhaps by no means the least advanced province of Arabia at the time of the Prophet's mission, but the impetus to progress derived from the beneficent change introduced by Islam must have been enormous. It had its sea commerce with India and the Persian Gulf, but the interior tribes, isolated as they were from other provinces by the practical difficulties of the land journey—for a desert march meant considerable hardship, though the Omani is as much at home on his camel as in his swift and handy bateel—could have but little inter-communication with Hadhramaut or Nejd and were but little troubled with the permeation of new ideas. With Islam, however, Oman awoke like the rest of the peninsula from its trance; a new spirit of religious fervour, of literature, of warlike enterprise was quickly engendered; the population began to increase, industrial occupations were eagerly learnt and followed; many of the youths took service in the imperial wars; every family sent some member to push his fortunes as a merchant, sailor, or adventurer; internal feuds and quarrels passed into at least temporary oblivion; wealth began to pour into the country; luxury and progress made their appearance; domestic happiness and social fraternity were augmented; property became more secure in the country; flourishing towns and villages grew up everywhere; cultivated land increased, and in an astonishingly short time the order and regularity, conveniences and benefits of civilized life permeated the inhabitants of a country which a short time before was sunk in the rank and stagnant mire of paganism.

Such was, we may suppose, the hopeful condition of Oman when, about the thirtieth year of the Hijrah, the venerated King

Jeifar al-Julanda died at Nezwa. Having no sons living he was succeeded by his nephew, Abbad bin Abd, in the reign of the Khalif Othman.

Under the good impulse and influence of Islam, Abbad continued to rule his state with peace and prosperity until the assassination of the Khalif Ali bin Abi Talib, when the religious dissensions and political wars that had arisen in Islam almost caused for the second time the disintegration of the empire, and produced a general revolt against Moawiya.

Oman, like the other provinces of Arabia, refused submission to the first Ommiade Khalif and remained for some time independent.

It is interesting to note that the half century occupied by these events—620 to 670 of our era—was marked in England by the final struggles of the Celtic Britons to recover their country from the Angles and Saxons who had invaded it, and the firm establishment of the latter in England as at present.

With the accession of the Khalif Ali may be said to have begun those dire political troubles that shook the Mohammedan empire, and especially those burning schisms in the Faith that soon divided it into sects, and even imperilled the stability of the state itself. The waves of discord surged throughout the Moslem world to the remote provinces, and the grandsons of the "Apostle of God" were yet living when the Kharejites introduced into Oman the peculiar doctrines that, with some modification, exist there to the present day.

In the first century of Islam the more acute and discerning minds among those who were engaged in the study of theology and law began to perceive the crudity of the sacred book and to entertain vague doubts as to its meaning.

As the examination and criticism of the Koran proceeded, the numerous dogmatic difficulties, inconsistencies, and contradictions became more manifest, and some of the more profound of these doctors began openly to discuss its dogmas and publicly to avow their dissent.

On the important doctrines of predestination and free will, for instance, the teaching of the Koran is by no means consistent.

For while it affirms the absolute predestination of human action it does not fail to promise eternal reward and punishment, by which it infers the moral responsibility of man for what he does. This was a rock on which the ship of the Faith was sure to strike. The Jabarites accepted the doctrine of Fatalism and taught that man had no power of control over his own actions and that good and evil deeds were alike predestined by God.

The sect of the Motazilites or Kadarites, which was founded by Waseel bin Atha (born 80 A.H.) [699 A.D.], on the other hand, looked upon this view as impious, rejected the idea of Fate and taught that man was the complete master of his own actions.

Among the Jabarites may be reckoned the followers of Abdullah bin Ibadh, the founder of the prevailing sect in Oman.

So long as the disputants confined themselves to wordy controversies and polemical argument, the Church alone was affected, but there were other sects which were more dangerous and whose attitude threatened the existence of the empire.

As early as the third decade after the Flight, doctrinal divisions had arisen out of the contest between the Khalif Ali and Moawiya bin Abi Sofyan, the Governor of Damascus.

Ali, having by compulsion assented to the rightfulness of his claim to the Khalifate being submitted to arbitration, was deserted by 12,000 of his followers, who had held back in the campaign and had thereby prevented him from crushing his adversary as he might have done. These deserters he was now forced to attack in his own defence.

At the Battle of Nahawan, which took place in 37 A.H. [657 A.D.], the rebels were completely defeated and put to the sword. A few only escaped and fled: some to southern Persia, some to Mesopotamia, and some to Oman, in which country their doctrines were eagerly accepted and rapidly disseminated over the land.

The story of what had occurred, as related by these Kharejites, as they were termed, naturally excited great resentment against both Ali and Moawiya and, on the murder of the former and the accession of the latter to power, the Omanis at once refused their allegiance, withheld payment of zakat and continued to assert their entire freedom and independence during the reign of Moawiya and his successors, until Abdul Malik bin Marwan reduced the province to obedience.

We must look back to the lifetime of Mohammed for the earliest indication of the Kharejite schism, as the Prophet himself sowed the seeds of dissension by his partiality for the Koreish and by his unequal and imprudent distribution of the spoil after victory over the Howazon at Honain in the year 8 A.H. [629 A.D.], whereby much discontent and indignation had been caused among the Ansar who had been allotted no share at all.

With true Arab intrepidity the Shaikh Dhul Khowaisira openly accused Mohammed in the Wady Joghranah and pointed out to him the mischief of allowing oligarchical ideas to predominate over the principles of religious equality and brotherhood.

The Kharejites not only denied the claim of the Koreish tribe to the Khalifate but also objected to hereditary succession in the Khalifate and Imamate, holding that any Moslem, who was in all respects suitable, might be elected. The bold and uncompromising attack they maintained upon the hereditary right of succession and their insistence on the privilege of election by the people were unquestionably the real causes of the bitter persecution and final destruction of this sect by the Khalifs; the other views and heresies held by them would otherwise have been allowed to pass.

Abdul Malik's expedition against Oman was doubtless undertaken as part of the campaign against the Kharejites, which was so successful in the north under Mohallib.

The Kharejite schism was indeed a most formidable one and constituted a real danger to the Khalifate.

After Mohallib's campaign they again revolted under later Khalifs, and their rebellious movements continued to increase until shortly before the change of dynasty in 132 A.H. [749 A.D.] they reached the highest point of their power—in Mesopotamia under the Sofrite Dhahak ibn Kais al-Sheibani, and in South Arabia under the Ibadhy Abu Hamza Mokhtor bin Auf.

In Oman, after the introduction of Kharejite doctrines, it was a constant struggle between the elective and the hereditary system. The Kadhis tried to force their view by causing an Imam to be elected whenever they could, while the reigning Imam was usually anxious to leave the succession to his son.

The people were generally indifferent and allowed matters to take their course. Had the Imam been a purely secular king the practical wisdom of the hereditary system in averting disputed succession would soon perhaps have become the established custom, but as the Imam combined both spiritual and temporal powers, like the Popes of Rome, the Kadhis could put forward strong arguments in favour of the elective system.

The Imam Abbad bin Abd left his kingdom in tranquillity and independence to his two sons, Suliman and Saeed, who ruled conjointly and appear not to have been interfered with by Moawiya's successors, the Khalifs Yezard and Merwan, probably because these sovereigns found their hands too full at home to pay attention to so small a state.

It was not until Abdul Malik had consolidated his power, after the death of Abdullah bin Zoheir and until the famous Hejaj bin Yusof had been appointed for his services at Mecca, Governor of Irak in 75 A.H. [694 A.D.], that the conquest of Sind, Oman, and Mekran were resolved on.

Al-Hejaj bin Yusof at first contented himself with envoys, charged to demand submission and payment of zakat to the Khalifate. The Omanis, however, encouraged by the rapid extension and success of the Kharejites in other parts of the empire, rejected these demands with disdain, and Al-Hejaj thereupon determined to reduce the rebellious Julandaites by force, and having equipped an army placed it under the command of Kasim bin Shiwah al-Maziny.

It was deemed more convenient to despatch this expedition by sea, and it sailed for the Oman coast probably about the year 77 A.H. [696 A.D.].

Passing by Sohar and Muscat, where his disembarkation might have been resisted, Kasim appears to have anchored his fleet in the little cove of Jisseh, thus taking his enemy in the rear and by surprise.

Jisseh is cut off from the interior by an amphitheatre of rugged hills, and Kasim must have landed his troops about a mile to the east on the sandy beach of Yiti, where the Wady Maih disembogues, up which he marched as far as the Wady Hatat, a broad and stony valley remarkable for its curious monolithic pillars. In the meantime the Imam Suliman, being assured of the support of all the tribes, Azdite and Nizar, which had embraced Kharejite doctrines, in his determination to defy the imperial troops and maintain the independence of Oman, had prepared his force and only awaited the news of Kasim's arrival to concentrate the tribes at the point of contact.

The appearance of Kasim's fleet was speedily communicated to the Imam, and then the national levy pouring down the Semail valley, the great natural highway of Oman, and through the various passes converging on the Wady Hatat, met together on that plain, which is extremely favourable for defence, to confront the invader.

Though the respective strength is not given us it is probable that, numerically, the Omani array greatly preponderated, and that, strong in their numbers and confident in their thorough knowledge of the locality, they felt assured of victory. The battle was toughly contested, and the imperial army fought bravely, but the Omanis were able to attack from several quarters and their onset was irresistible.

Kasim al-Maziny was slain on the field, the carnage of the imperials was terrible, and very few escaped in safety to the boats.

Oman was saved for the time, but the triumph was shortlived. The first shaft of danger had been shielded off, but it had been thrown by one who had despised his adversary and who was not likely to repeat the mistake. The Khalif Abdul Malik, whose power had been so easily repulsed, was exasperated, and after some hesitation gave orders for an overwhelming force to be sent to wipe out the disgrace of the disaster and to chastise the heretical and refractory Omanis.

In the new expedition, of which Kasim's brother Mujaah bin Shiwah was appointed to the command, Al-Hejaj bin Yusof, who was now thoroughly in earnest and vindictive, took a great interest and exercised his undoubted military talents in personally organizing and superintending the preparations of it, even going as far, it is said, as to restrain the chiefs of the Al-Azd, at Busra, from taking part in it or aiding the Omanis in any way.

The strength of this army of revenge is stated to have been no less than 40,000 Nizar troops, cavalry and infantry, and though this number is probably an exaggeration, there can be no doubt that the force greatly exceeded the previous one. It was divided into two corps, one of which marched by land to Oman through Al-Ahsa and the Nefood, while the other was to be transported by sea down the Persian Gulf.

Owing to want of co-operation, through misunderstanding or jealousy between the two leaders, the Khalif's troops again suffered defeat, although the Omani success did not tend to augment the security of the country.

The Imam Suliman, who had under him only 3,000 horse and 3,500 camel men, appears to have received intelligence first of the approach of the land force across the desert and marching through Al-Beraimi attacked his enemy near Abu Thubi. The Imam's troops rushed on the invaders with an impetuosity which nothing could withstand, and though the imperials were this time in superior force, they gave way, then broke, and fled back into the Dahna desert.

While these events were occurring in the west, Mujaah, with the main body of his army in the fleet, sailed down the Persian Gulf and landed on the Batineh coast, probably near Mesnaah, and moved on to Burka, where he joined battle with Saeed bin Abbad al-Julanda, whose small force was easily routed.

Saeed fled to the Jebel Akhdar, whither he was pursued by a part of the Nizar army and besieged there. Suliman having cleared his frontier of invaders to the north-west, and being apprised of Mujaah's arrival, now turned back to the Batineh, and on reaching

Muscat found the Khalif's fleet, numbering 300 ships, riding at anchor in the harbour. Many of these vessels were surprised and boarded by Suliman's men, who captured and burnt fifty of them, but the rest managed to get under weigh and stood out to sea. Pursuing his career of success, Suliman now hastened up the Semail Valley, hoping to effect a junction with his brother, Saeed, and crush his enemy in the hills, but Mujaah's force was strong and well posted, and the battle that ensued was indecisive.

Mujaah, however, felt his position so insecure and hazardous that he resolved on retreat, and, quitting his position, retired along the Batineh to Julfar.

Al-Hejaj, on hearing of the repulse of his land force near Abu Thubi by Suliman bin Abbad, was greatly disappointed, but refusing to be beaten, lost no time in sending reinforcements, and a body of 5,000 horse, under Abdul Rahman bin Suliman, were already on the march overland to Oman at the time when the two armies encountered each other at Semail.

The arrival of Abdul Rahman on the scene with this splendid force changed the whole aspect of affairs and enabled Mujaah at once to resume the offensive. The Omanis had become exhausted by the contest and were intimidated by these repeated and formidable armaments and reinforcements being sent against them. They saw that the Khalif and Al-Hejaj were implacable and that the whole power of the empire was arrayed against them. The Julanda Princes, Suliman and Saeed bin Abbad, felt that they could expect no mercy or consideration at the hands of Al-Hejaj, and that their lives would pay the forfeit of their unsuccessful struggle for independence. Gathering their families, their property and adherents, therefore, they embarked for East Africa, where they ended their days, and thus brought to a termination the rule of the Julanda Dynasty in Oman.

The conquest of Oman by Mujaah and Abdul Rahman was then completed by the submission of the people, who suffered very vigorous and oppressive treatment for the brave and determined resistance they had shown. Al-Hejaj was greatly elated on hearing of the subjection of Oman by his troops, after so many reverses, and he despatched Al-Kheyrai bin Sirah Al-Mujashai, with the title of Ameer, to govern the province on behalf of the Khalif and to collect the mukatash or tribute, which appears to have been now, for the first time, imposed on Oman in addition to the zakat.

Soon after the conquest of Oman by Mujaah, which had caused the emigration of so many Azdite families from that country, the Khalif Abdul Malik, at the request and instigation of Al-Hejaj, began to extend his aggressions towards India. Most of Mekran had been subdued some time before, and Al-Hejaj now sent Saeed bin Aslam bin Zuraa al-Kelali as Wali to Mekran and the frontier with orders to carry on the war. In Mekran, Saeed put to death one Safhni bin Lam al-Hamami, belonging to the powerful Omani family Alafy, of the Beni Asamat. Mohammed and Moawiyeh, sons of Al-Haras al-Alafy, rose in revolt, attacked and killed the Wali Saeed bin Aslam, and seized the government. Al-Hejaj, on hearing of this insurrection, immediately beheaded one Suliman al-Alafy at Busra in retaliation, adopting at the same time stringent measures to recover his authority by despatching Mujaah bin Seer al-Temeemi with a strong force to Kirman. Abdul Rahman, with the advance guard of this army, was waylaid and killed by the Alâfies, but the latter, feeling themselves unable to oppose Mujaah, then fled to Sind and took service with Dahir the Hindoo, King of Dabul, with a following of 500 Arabs in 85 A.H. [704 A.D.].

Mujaah was succeeded by Muhammed bin Haroon bin Zuraa al-Mamari, in whose time the pirates of Dabul plundered eight Moslem ships which had been despatched with presents from Ceylon for the Khalif. Al-Hejaj, trusting to arrange matters amicably, at first sent an embassy to Dahir, to demand satisfaction. This was haughtily refused, and Al-Hejaj, smarting under the insult, and perhaps glad of an opportunity to begin hostilities with the Kafir, who had given an asylum to the rebellious Alâfies, sent an expedition against him under Obaid Ullah bin Nebhan, equipped at enormous expense and to which a reluctant consent had been wrung from the Khalif. Obaid Ullah, however, was defeated and slain by Dahir with the help of his Omani allies. Notwithstanding this disaster the expedition was not abandoned, and the officer appointed by Al-Hejaj to replace Obaid Ullah as its head was Budail bin Tahfa al-Bujali, who was holding a command in the army of occupation in Oman at the time he received his orders. Some say that Budail took his troops with him by sea, but according to others he proceeded to Mekran alone, where the Wali Muhammed had instructions to supply him with a force of 3,000 men, a further reinforcement being sent from Oman to join him under Abdullah bin Kahtan Aslam. The Alâfies were subsequently pardoned by Muhammed Kasim, the famous conqueror of Sind.

This family is conspicuous in the history of Sind at this period, and is doubtless only one of the many Omani families that sought their fortunes in Sind, Hind, and Zanzibar.

We have seen that on the subjugation of Oman by his troops, in 78 A.H. [697 A.D.], Al-Hejaj bin Yusof, with the sanction of the Khalifeh, appointed Al-Kheyrai bin Sirah al-Mujashai Ameer over the country.

In 86 A.H. [705 A.D.] Abdul Malik died and was succeeded by his eldest son Waleed, the "Pharoah of the Ommiades," under whom the Moslem Empire attained the highest point of its power and the greatest extent of territorial dominion to which it ever reached.

Al-Waleed, though he confirmed Al-Hejaj in the government of Irak, changed some of the minor governors under him, and amongst others that of Oman, over which province he now placed Salih bin Abdul Rahman al-Leithy. These changes and transfers, so common in the Eastern Khalifate, were no doubt designed to prevent Governors from becoming too powerful and independent by maturing intrigues and courting popularity with the inhabitants of the province over which they ruled; but the changes must also have been attended with the salutary effect upon the governors themselves of removing prejudices, suggesting comparisons, imparting knowledge and enlarging the general sphere of their observations.

Al-Hejaj was followed in Irak by Yezeed bin Abi Aslam, who

then caused Yezeed bin Saif bin Hany al-Hamadain to be placed over Oman. The Kashf al-Ghummeh, it may be noted, gives this appointment to Saif bin al-Hany himself.

Suliman bin Abdul Malik succeeded his brother Al-Waleed in the Khalifate in 96 A.H. [A.D. 714], and at once removed all the nakims of districts in Oman, making Salih bin Abdul Rahman responsible for the whole Government, but he subsequently saw fit to reinstate those officials, leaving, however, Salih as Ameer over the country.

Salih bin Abdul Rahman did not enjoy power long, for when the famous Omani Yezeed bin Muhallib became Governor of Irak in 98 A.H. [A.D. 716], he took the opportunity to replace Salih by Ziyad, his own younger brother, and as the Muhallibites were renowned for their magnanimity and generosity, it is not surprising to learn from the local historians that the people of Oman were highly contented under his rule.

Soon after the accession of Omar II. as Khalif, Yezeed bin Muhallib fell into disgrace and was imprisoned at Damascus, his brother Ziyad being replaced as Ameer of Oman by Adi bin Artah al-Fezari. The latter deputed another officer to act for him, and this deputy behaved so tyrannically that the people complained to Damascus and had him removed. Omar II., though a mild and just prince, was uncompromisingly bitter against the Muhallibites and would not reinstate Ziyad, whom the Omanis would doubtless have preferred. The new Ameer, who was now appointed, was Omar bin Abdullah bin Sabihah al-Ausary, who was respected and approved of by the inhabitants as a just and good ruler, and who continued as Ameer during the remainder of the reign of Omar II.

This Khalif was poisoned in 101 A.H. [A.D. 719] and was followed by the voluptuous Yezeed II., whose animosity drove Yezeed bin Muhallib into revolt.

Supported by many of the Irakis, Yezeed seized Busra and proclaimed himself Khalif, at the same time recalling Omar bin Abdullah al-Ausary from Oman, and reappointing his brother Ziyad as Ameer over that province.

Yezced bin Muhallib was slain in the following year by Muslama, but Ziyad appears to have held his own in Oman for a time, as the chroniclers state that he continued to rule even to the rise of the Abbasides in 132 A.H. [A.D. 749].

There are difficulties about accepting this statement, but we may take it that Ziyad, who did not dare to return to Irak after the proscription of his family in 102 A.H. [A.D. 720], obtained the adherence of all the Azdite tribes in Oman and remained there unmolested until the commencement of Oman independence, about fifteen years later, when the Ommiade Khalifs ceased to interfere with the province.

In the account of the Battle of Dibba, which took place in 12 A.H. [A.D. 633], I have mentioned that one of the young captives carried off after the sack of that town was Abu Sofra al-Azdi.

The appointment of his grandson Ziyad as Ameer of Oman permits one to offer a slight sketch of this illustrious Omani family, whose virtues and magnificence were as renowned in Islam during the Ommiade dynasty as the Barmekides afterwards became under the Abbasides. The full name of Abu Sofra was Zalim ibn Sarrak al-Atecki al-Azdi, and he appears to have resided at Busra and to have had three sons, Muhallib, Sofra, and Mowarak.

Muhallib was a man of commanding talents and became one of the greatest captains of his time. He was born about twenty years after the death of the Prophet and brought himself to notice at an early age.

In one of Muhallib's early campaigns against the Kharejites, their leader, Obaid Ullah bin Beshir, succeeded in capturing Mowarak, who was slain and crucified by him. Soon after, in 65 A.H. [A.D. 684], a battle took place at Sulaf, where Muhallib was encamped, in which this general was outnumbered and worsted. Subsequently, when Muhallib tried to invent a saying about the strength of the Moslems and the weakness of the Kharejites, the Nidab, a subtribe of the Azd, used to say, " Here comes Muhallib to tell lies." These Nidâbiyeen still form a small tribe in Oman.

The Azdite tribes played a not unimportant part in the Kharejite wars and took opposite sides, some fighting with and some against the imperial troops. In the Battle of Sidlabra, which occurred the following year, 66 A.H. [A.D. 685], the Khowarij had the best of it at first, but Muhallib gathered a band of 3,000 Omanis, each of whom took ten stones and pelted the Kharejites, wearied with victory, and put them to flight.

In 67 A.H. [A.D. 686] Abdullah bin Zoheir made Muhallib Governor of Mosul after the siege of Koofa, in which Mukhtar had been killed. In 68 A.H. [A.D. 687] the Kharejites revolted again and invaded Irak, and Muhallib was ordered to march against them. In 71 A.H. [A.D. 690] they defeated the army of the Khalif Abdul Malik, and once more Muhallib, this time in conjunction with Khaled, took the field, expelling them from Farsistan and Kirman.

In 75 A.H. [A.D. 694], when Al-Hejaj bin Yusof was made Governor of Irak, he perceived the absolute necessity of crushing the seceders, who had now become so numerous and audacious as to menace the stability of the empire. He accordingly set to work to organize a great campaign against them, and wisely entrusted the command to Muhallib. After eighteen months of severe and incessant fighting, Muhallib completely vanquished and broke up that sect, and was henceforth called the conqueror of the Kharejites. Muhallib returned to Busra in 78 A.H. [A.D. 697], and was then made Governor of Khorasan, where he died in 82 A.H. [A.D. 701], leaving four sons—Yezeed, Mojira, Ziyad, and Mufadhal. He was succeeded by his son Yezeed in the Government of Khorasan, but in 84 A.H. [A.D. 703] Al-Hejaj replaced Yezeed by his brother Mufadhal. The Khalif Suliman, who detested Al-Hejaj and all his works, then appointed Yezeed bin Muhallib to the governorship of Irak, but Yezeed preferred Khorasan, and on his return to that post proceeded to reduce Georgia and Tabaristan. Before he had been long on the throne the Khalif Suliman began to grow jealous of Yezeed's great reputation and success and to cherish resentment against him, but he was absorbed in his campaign against the Greeks, and died too soon to execute his vindictive projects. His successor, however, Omar II., was equally rancorous against the Muhallibites, and summoning Yezeed to Damascus threw him into prison with his son

Mukhallid. Soon after they were sent as exiles to Dhalak in the Red Sea, but in 101 A.H. [A.D. 719] they escaped and sought refuge in Irak, where they had numerous supporters.

Omar II. died in Rajab 101 A.H. [A.D. 719], and the first care of the new Khalif, Yezeed II.—for by this time the envy and hatred of the whole Ommiade race had been aroused against the Muhallibites—was to carry on the persecution, and orders were sent to the Governor of Irak to seize all the members of Yezeed's family, with the view of destroying them utterly. The Khalif's order was ruthlessly obeyed, and Yezeed bin Muhallib, now driven to desperation, raised a revolt, took Busra and proclaimed himself Khalif. He was well supported, and in order to extend his power, as well as to secure an asylum in the event of defeat, sent expeditions against Farsistan, Ahwaz, Kirman, Mekran, and Sind, and was gathering a very formidable party when, early in 102 A.H. [A.D. 720], Muslama, the Khalif's brother and general, who had been sent to oppose him, attacked and totally routed his force at Akr near Kerbela. Yezeed was slain in the fight and the cause was lost, whereupon Mufadhal and several of his brothers embarked with the remnant of the Muhallibi family at Busra in a number of vessels and set sail for Hormuz, from whence they proceeded on to Kandabeel, a fortress which had been specially selected by Yezeed as an asylum for himself, but the Kiladar—to whom he had entrusted it, Wadda ibn Hameed Al-Azdi—proved traitor, and Hilal al-Tameemi, who had been sent in pursuit, put the male fugitives to the sword and sold the women and children into slavery.

This famous and powerful Omani race, the Muhallibites, which possessed the provinces of Laristan and Hormuz in Persia, had rendered great services to the Moslem Empire and were celebrated in Arab poetry for their valour, virtues, and generosity, regained some of their pristine power and position in the time of the Abbasides, but, by the later Ommiades, were regarded with bitter jealousy and persecuted to death with a pertinacity almost unparalleled.

About fifteen years after the Ibadhi doctrines had been generally accepted by the people of Oman, the Ommiade dynasty collapsed, and Abdullah bin Mohammed, generally called Abul Abbas al-Saffah, having been proclaimed Khalif at Koofa, became the founder of the Abbaside dynasty and took up his residence at Hashimiyeh.

The first measures of Abul Abbas were directed towards the extermination of the Ommiade family, an object which was accomplished in the most ruthless and cruel manner. Merwan II. was pursued and murdered in a Coptic church in Egypt, and ninety of the family were, according to some writers, treacherously massacred at a banquet to which they had been invited, while others were slain in the various provinces. These sanguinary persecutions and atrocities caused deep indignation among the faithful, which manifested itself in the many serious insurrections that arose in different parts of the empire, and which were not put down without difficulty, but when Abul Abbas had quelled these revolts, he turned his attention to the internal administration of his vast territories and began the consolidation of his power by appointing the principal members of his own family to the provincial governments, from which the officers installed by the former dynasty were systematically removed.

In 133 A.H. [A.D. 750], Abul Abbas gave the government of Busra, with the dependencies of Bahrain and Oman, to his uncle, Suliman bin Ali, who appointed one Jenah bin Abbadeh bin Kais bin Omar al-Hinai as his delegate over Oman. A great number of the friends and supporters of the Ommiade dynasty having escaped from Busra, where they had suffered defeat at the hands of an army from Khorasan, had sought refuge in Oman and had been sheltered by the people. With these fugitives the new court at Hashimiyeh did not, for the present, attempt to interfere and awaited a more favourable opportunity.

Oman had now been free from the imperial yoke for some years and, glad as the Azdites were to see an end of the Ommiades, at whose hands they had suffered so much and from whose resentment they had so much to dread, it cannot be supposed that they were eager to welcome an Ameer from the new dynasty, but the moment was not propitious for rebellion, and they were not disposed to wantonly incur the wrath of "The Bloodshedder." For the time, therefore, the signs of discontent were suppressed and the new delegate was allowed by the Omanis to assume office quietly and to collect the tribute.

Jenah bin Abbadeh seems to have been a discreet and sagacious man and understood the uncertainty and delicacy of his position, for he ruled mildly and took care not to arouse popular irritation. He appears, indeed, to have had much in sympathy with the Omanis, and we are plainly informed that it was not long before he began to imbibe the Ibadhi doctrines himself. This conduct could not, of course, be countenanced at Hashimiyeh, and soon led to Jenah bin Abbadeh's dismissal, his son, Muhammed, being appointed as Ameer in his stead.

The assumption of power by Muhammed threw the whole country into a ferment. Jenah bin Abbadeh, alienated from the Khalif by his disgrace, declared himself an Ibadhi and immediately began to fan the flame of disaffection and revolt among the Omanis.

The Sunni portion of the community sided with the new Ameer, Muhammed bin Jenah, but the Ibadhi tribes, which formed by far the stronger party of the people, threw off the yoke of submission and withheld payment of the tribute, on which the Ameer, Muhammed, finding his position untenable in face of the threatening attitude of the schismatics, quitted Oman and proceeded to the court of the Khalif to report the state of affairs.

A period of disorder and internecine strife now commenced, in which many of the old tribal feuds were strengthened and embittered by religious animosity. Jenah bin Abbadeh, though he had thrown in his lot with the Ibadhis, does not appear to have taken a leading part in the coming struggle, and it became necessary for the national party to select a new chief. A shaikh named Julanda bin Mesood became the object of their choice and was accordingly proclaimed Imam by the Kadhis.

The election was a notable one in this history, as Al-Julanda bin Mesood was the first Imam of the Ibadhis in Oman, and he is called in consequence "the First of the Rightful Imams." He soon showed himself to be an able and energetic ruler as well as a just and popular one, and he was as successful in repressing disorder as in stimulating the martial zeal and enthusiasm of his adherents.

The Khalif Abul Abbas had now obtained the opportunity he had been watching for, and resolved on taking measures without delay to effect the two-fold purpose of re-establishing his power and of gratifying his resentment.

Towards the Ommiade refugees he was still implacable, and they were to be taught that, although they had gained a temporary asylum, they were not beyond the reach of Al-Saffah's avenging hand; while as regards the Omani Kharejites, it was a maxim of Al-Saffah that when forbearance is mischievous, to pardon is weakness, and he deemed it necessary to inflict chastisement on them for harbouring these fugitives as well as for their rebellious and insulting conduct in expelling the imperial delegate. A military expedition was, in 133 A.H. [A.D. 750], accordingly ordered to be prepared and despatched forthwith, and was placed under the command of a shaikh named Shiban, but Al-Saffah repeated the mistake that had been committed by Abdul Malik of despising his enemy, and the force was too weak for the purpose. This force was to be transported by sea from Busra (and was to be met on arrival by an Omani contingent of the Sunni and Nizar tribes, under Hilal bin Atiyeh al-Khorasani and Yahia bin Najih).

The landing of the army from Busra and its junction with the local contingent were duly effected, and the two hostile armies encountered each other at Towwam, and Julanda sent Hilal and Yahia against them.

The result of the battle was indecisive; the first that was slain on the part of the Ibadhis being Yahia bin Najih, while the Khalif's general, Shiban, was the first to fall on his side.

The death of Shiban prevented any further operations by the Khalif's troops, who now remained quiet until the matter had been reported to Abul Abbas.

Enraged at the defeat of his troops and determined to punish the rebels, the Khalif equipped another rèinforcement, which was transported to Oman under the command of Khazim bin Khozaimah.

On arrival in Oman, Khazim was allowed to disembark his troops without opposition, and being confident that he had now a sufficient force with him to overcome all resistance, he sent to inform the Imam Al-Julanda bin Mesood, that he had come to repair the former disaster and to establish the Khạlif's authority, and he counselled the Imam, in order to avert hostilities, to make immediate submission and to surrender the members of the Ommiade family and their adherents, who had sought refuge in Oman.

These demands Al-Julanda, after holding a council of war with the leading shaikhs, firmly rejected. Further demands made by Khazim for the sword and seal of Shiban were also refused by the Imam. A contest between the imperial troops and the Omanis now became inevitable, and in the fight that ensued at Julfar, Hilal bin Atiyeh and a great number of others were slain and the Omanis completely defeated. The Imam Al-Julanda was captured, and to the great grief of his people was put to death by Khazim bin Khozaimah, after a notable reign of two years and one month.

The tribes, now leaderless, could offer no further resistance, and the victor commenced to execute with brutal severity the orders he had received at Hashimiyeh for the extermination of the Ommiades who had escaped the fury of " The Bloodshedder " three years before in Irak. Incredible numbers of these unfortunate political refugees are said to have been now massacred or burnt to death.

This was in the year 135 A.H. [A.D. 752], and thus it was already the fifth time Oman had suffered invasion by the Moslems since Abd and Jeifar had accepted Islam in the Year of Deputations, a century and a quarter before.

The Sunni party in Oman had now obtained their turn of power and did not fail to take advantage of it, under the ægis of Khazim bin Khozaimah and his troops, to indulge their resentment and pay off old scores by pillaging and oppressing the Ibadhis. These oppressors are termed " Al-Jubabareh " or " Tyrants " by the local chroniclers, and they are spoken of with horror and disgust for the way they maltreated and stripped the Kharejite inhabitants.

It is related that Khazim returned to Irak with the imperial troops soon after the Battle of Julfar, apparently without leaving an Ameer in Oman as representative of the Khalif, and the country in consequence fell a prey to lamentable anarchy and confusion.

Among those who now took the lead were the Julandaites, Muhammed bin Zaidah and Rashid bin Shathan bin al-Nadhr.

Soon after these princes had seized power, Ghassan al-Hinai, of the Beni Muharib, in Shaaban 145 A.H. [A.D. 762], plundered Nezwa and attacked the Beni Nafa and the Beni Hameen tribes there, expelling them from the town with great slaughter. Ghassan al-Hinai was then murdered in retaliation by a party of the Beni Harth tribe, who had proceeded to Al-Ateek, between Sohar and Dibba, for that purpose, and the latter were attacked at Ibra, in their turn, by the Julandaites, but the Beni Harth repulsed them with a loss of forty men. This occurred in the reign of the Khalif Al-Mansoor, who at this time had destroyed Al-Madain or Selencia, and transferred the seat of government from Anbar on the Euphrates, to Baghdad on the Tigris, a site which had been selected and on which the foundations of a city had been commenced by that sagacious and energetic monarch Nebuchadnezzar, thirteen centuries before.

During the reigns of the Khalifs, Al-Mehdi and Al-Hadi (158-170 A.H.) [A.D. 774-786], we have but a meagre record of the events that transpired in Oman, and it is even uncertain whether the Imperial Government was able to supervise authoritatively the administration and to collect the mokataah, *i.e.*, the yearly sum fixed to be paid by the province in lieu of poll tax and tithes, or whether the country retained its entire administrative independence. It seems more probable that the former was the case, and that the suzerainty was enforced by the annual despatch of an imperial agent from Baghdad for that purpose.

But we are in no uncertainty as to the internal condition of the country. The bitter sectarian quarrel that had arisen between the orthodox party and the Kharejites for the mastery, and was to last

To face p. 65.

AN ARAB GROUP.

[See p. 85]

during a century and a half, was at this time raging hotly and was destined to produce the usual fruit of religious dissension in an increasing course of bloody strife and turmoil. The struggle, indeed, was not confined to Oman but was, at this period, agitating the whole Muhammedan Empire. The great Khalif, Haroon al-Rasheed, had not long been seated on the throne of Baghdad, and had hardly begun to exhibit those qualities which have made his name imperishable, before the heretics began to raise their rebellious heads in various parts of his dominions and almost to threaten its disruption. In most quarters where they essayed to plant their flag fortune proved fickle, but in Oman the Ibadhi tribes were for a time, at least, successful in asserting their supremacy again, and in once more establishing their predominance over the Sunnis as we may see by their being able to elect a new Imam of their own sect at the capital.

This election took place at Nezwa in 175 A.H. [A.D. 791] under the auspices of the Shaikh Moosa bin Abu Jabir al-Askani, who appears to have exercised a leading influence in the matter and who, in spite of much opposition, caused the preferment of his own nominee, Shaikh Mohammed bin Abu Affan, to be ratified by the general voice.

For two years the Imam Mohammed ruled the country with firmness and with the help, no doubt, of his powerful supporter, Shaikh Moosa. He seems to have held also the military command of the Ibadhi camp at Nezwa, a position for which he may have been well fitted. But his arrogant disposition, want of tact, and imprudent conduct led to a conspiracy being formed against him, and the feeling manifested was so strong that he was compelled to withdraw from Nezwa. Another assembly was convened and Mohammed bin Abu Affan was deposed and the Shaikh al-Warith bin Kaab al-Kharoosy al-Shari al-Yahmady was elected Imam in his stead in 177 A.H. [A.D. 793].

At this period the relations between the province and the supreme government at Baghdad, which had for a long time been on a by-no-means harmonious or satisfactory footing, became strained, and the attitude of the Ibadheer in withholding payment of the mokataah became so insubordinate and uncompromising, that the active intervention of the Imperial power to enforce obedience became necessary. Though the precise circumstances that led to this rupture have not come down to us, it is not altogether impossible perhaps, to guess at the causes underlying the general situation and dictating the national policy.

It is to be remembered that this was the third or fourth time that the Kharejites had hurled defiance at their sovereign, the Khalif, and that their temerity had been not unaccompanied by signal success in the field. We may assume, therefore, that these haughty and refractory heretics deemed the troubled state of the empire a fitting occasion to assert their independence; and, indeed, they reckoned, as the result proved, not unskilfully. Their only weakness was their disunion—engendered by their sectarian fanaticism.

There can be little doubt that if the warlike tribes of Oman could only have laid aside their religious animosities and put out of sight the *odium theologicum*, and coalesced in one solid and united army against the invader, they might have retained their independence and kept at bay the power of Baghdad for ever. The mountain chain offers such superb natural defensive features that, entrenched in their strongholds, ravines, and fastnesses, they could have maintained a most stubborn resistance and have defied any invading army unprovided with a commissariat.

One of the most trustworthy of the Arab historians—Al-Baladzory—has stated that the people of Oman discontinued paying the mokataah in the reign of the Khalif Haroon al-Rasheed, who despatched Eesa bin Jaafar with a strong force from Busra to reduce this recalcitrant province and to restore his authority therein; and that the troops on their arrival began to commit outrages, upon which the people resisted them, killed Eesa and declared their own independence. Al-Baladzory's account is supplemented by the local annalists, who furnish us with further details regarding this expedition, which ended so disastrously for the prestige of the Khalif. Eesa bin Jaafar bin Abul Mansoor's army consisted of 1,000 cavalry and 5,000 infantry, and having been embarked in a large flotilla of transports, arrived in Oman, probably about 187 A.H. [A.D. 802], and news of it was at once sent to the Imam by Daood bin Yezen al-Muhallebi. At first no resistance was encountered; the army was disembarked and the coast occupied without hostility being manifested by the inhabitants, and it is possible that had the commander, whose full name was Eesa bin Jaafar bin Suliman bin Ali bin Abdullah bin al-Abbass (and who was a scion of the royal house ?), conducted the affair with a judicious moderation and maintained a firm discipline among his own soldiery, he might have brought the people back to their allegiance and re-established his master's authority without bloodshed or severe exercise of power. But Eesa did not attempt to win over the people of Oman by tact and prudent conciliation, while at the same time he failed to perceive the military weakness of his own position. Unmindful of the smallness of his force, he permitted his soldiers, in a warlike and disaffected country to indulge in licentious excess and thus to goad the people to exasperation and frenzy. When the invader landed a deceptive calm prevailed, but the fires of rebellion were smouldering—not extinct—they were soon kindled into flame and blazed from one end of Oman to the other.

Oman rose suddenly in revolt and, with their usual secrecy and rapidity in war, the tribes flocked to the Imam's standard and then hurried to the Batineh to place themselves under the leadership of the Shaikh Faris bin Mohammed, whom the Imam Warith had appointed as their general.

The Imperial fleet had anchored at the north-west end of the Batineh coast, between Sohar and Shinas, and Eesa bin Jaafar had occupied with his troops the Wady Hatta and its vicinity without apparently pushing on much further into the interior.

Misled by their passive attitude, he had begun to treat the natives as already terrified into subjection, but in a wild and warlike land like this, where the sword and dagger never long rest sheathed, no desolator's foot stands firm, no foreigner can reign, and he suffered the usual fate of those who despise their enemies.

We are left to conjecture the details of the invaders' overthrow.

Perhaps the Khalif's troops were dispersed on detachment duty or were engaged in ravishing and plundering, and thus, taken unawares, were summoned to the battlefield in haste. The fortune of war soon declared itself. The invaders, unable to withstand the furious onslaught of the Omanis, who wielded their long double-edged swords with great effect, gave way, and a dreadful carnage ensued. A few of the fugitives succeeded in reaching the ships and put to sea. Eesa bin Jaafar was among them, but Faris bin Mohammed immediately despatched three ships in pursuit of him, under Abu Hameed bin Feleh al-Salooni and Amru bin Omar, who overtook him and brought him back to Sohar where he was imprisoned in the fort. Here he lingered but a short time, as he was murdered in his dungeon soon after by a party of Ibadhis, headed by Yahia bin Abdullah Azeez, whose act was probably in retaliation for the atrocities committed on the natives by the Imperial troops, though it is to be noted that the local annalists exonerate and absolve the Imam Warith and the Wali from any participation in the crime, though they extol Yahia as a man of high character and one who obtained great credit for his deed.

Haroon al-Rasheed heard with bitter disappointment and chagrin of the disastrous termination of the expedition, and he was especially incensed at the death of the Commander, Eesa bin Jaafar. He resolved at once to exact the severest retribution from the audacious rebels, and issued orders for a new and more formidable force to be prepared. But the design was never carried into execution. The cause for this is ascribed by some to the death of the Khalif, but as this did not occur till four or five years later, 193 A.H. [A.D. 808], it is necessary to look for some other cause for Haroon's self-restraint, and there is reason to believe that Oman owed its immunity to the Khalif's wrath being disarmed and turned aside by the immediate, though nominal, submission of the Imam Warith—as the fact that the mokataah was thereafter annually remitted to Baghdad with greater or less regularity points to the assumption that the Imam despatched envoys with presents and promises of allegiance.

Whatever may have been, however, the reasons which induced

Haroon to forego the intention of further molesting the independence of Oman and vindicating the defeat and death of Eesa bin Jaafar, the decision was one unquestionably for national congratulation, especially by the Azdite section, as the Khalif's immediate successors, Ameen and Mamoon, were too much engrossed with their own quarrel to entertain warlike projects against this comparatively insignificant province, which for nearly a hundred years was thus spared from foreign invasion.

The life of the Imam Al-Warith was advantageous to his country, which he continued to rule with wisdom and justice until he was accidentally drowned while trying to rescue some prisoner in a flood with seventy of his companions in the Wady Kalbuh, down the bed of which a surging body of water pours from Jebel Akhdar after heavy rain. He died in 189 A.H. [A.D. 804], after a reign of twelve and a-half years and was buried at Nezwa.

Political strife now interposed to hinder the election of a successor, and for three years there was an interregnum in Oman. It was not until Rabi al-Thani, 192 A.H. [A.D. 807], that an assembly could be held of the shaikhs of the Ibadhi tribes, and the result of their deliberation was that Shaikh Ghassan bin Abdullah al-Fajhi al-Yahmadi was installed in the Imamate at Nezwa. The choice was a good one. Ghassan bin Abdullah was a man of firm and enlightened character, and did his best to help his country to ride on the crest of the wave of moral and material progress that distinguished the Arab empire in the age of Haroon and his sons.

The historians indeed do not fail to inform us that the spirit of learning and improvement, which at this time influenced the Khalif's court and which was spreading its ramifications into the most distant corners of the empire, had communicated itself in undiminished radiance and vigour to Oman; that a taste for letters was fostered, that religious precepts were honoured, and that many books were composed in Ghassan's reign.

At this epoch, too, as we shall see further on, maritime trade and expeditions, which had greatly revived among the Moslems, and which were enterprises peculiarly adapted to, and promotive of, the prosperity of the Omani people, were eagerly participated in by them, and tended enormously to increase their wealth and strength. In truth, speaking comparatively, we cannot doubt that Oman had now become a rich, civilized, cultured, and advancing country, populous and luxurious beyond any previous period and rejoicing in its strength, its defensive isolation, and its almost complete independence ; but the land was distraught and racked by an internal cancer which went far to negative the blessings of material prosperity. The bitter religious antagonism between the Sunni and the Ibadhi, and the racial feud between the Yemen and Nizar, prevented the possibility of general tranquillity and repose, and did much to check the progress that might otherwise have added incalculably to the wealth, happiness, and importance of the province.

In the reign of this prince we have the first mention of the creation of an armed navy for the protection of the coast and the merchant shipping from piratical attacks. From much earlier times the Koork or Sanganian pirates in Sind had systematically ravaged the coasts of Western India, but it is not known that they had ever appeared in Arab waters. Attracted, however, by the rich cargoes that now began to traverse the Persian Gulf on their way to and from India, and allured by the wealth that was stored in the bazaars of Sohar, Siraf and Muscat, these sanguinary cutthroats ventured to extend their depredations to Arabia, and their raids had become so grievous and insulting that the Omanis fitted out a fleet of small vessels called *barga* and *zareeka*, and being better and bolder sailors than the Indians, retaliated with such unequivocal success that the pirates meddled with them no more.

After a reign of fifteen years and seven months the Imam fell sick and died of his illness in Dhu' l-Kaadeh, 207 A.H. [A.D. 822], in the reign of the Khalif Mamoon. In the month of Showal in the following year the Shaikh Abdul Malik bin Hameed, who derived from the stock of Soodah bin Ali bin Amr bin Ameer, surnamed Ma al-Sama, was elected Imam of the Ibadhis at Nezwa.

Abdul Malik appears to have been much venerated for his piety, integrity and justice, but after some years his growing senility, for he was beyond middle age when elected, enabled the crafty, ambitious Kadhi Moosa bin Ali to usurp the exercise of temporal power, and eventually (without, however, depriving the Imam of his spiritual functions) to snatch the entire control of political events from his hands.

We may fairly conjecture that Moosa intrigued busily for his own election, but if it were so, his wily schemes were frustrated by the shaikhs who knew him well.

The Khalif Motassim, who succeeded in the year 218 A.H. [A.D. 833], removed his residence from Baghdad to Samarra, and thus, unfortunately, threw the whole power of the Khalifate practically into the hands of the Turkish guard, a body which he had himself created.

The decadence of the empire began from this time and its fall was continuous. It was in the reign of this Khalif, that the Imam of Oman, Abdul Malik, died after ruling his country for eighteen years. His successor was the Shaikh Muhenna bin Jeifar al-Fejhy al-Yahmady, who was elected in Rajab, 226 A.H. [A.D. 840].

The Imam al-Muhenna possessed much firmness and decision of character, and was a strict Ibadhi. During his time the Mahrahs revolted and refused to pay the sadakat or poor rate, which was then levied in kind.

The Imam ordered the Governors of Adam, Senow and Jaalan to endeavour to arrest the Mahrah chief, Waseem bin Jaafar, if possible, and this was effected by the Wali of Adam. Waseem was imprisoned and remained in durance until the Mahrah procured his liberation, through the intercession of the Yahmadi tribe, by whose mediation it was arranged that the Mahrahs should bring the camels allotted for the payment of sadakat to Oman themselves for the future, instead of the Imam having to send a collector to fetch them. The narration of this little episode is useful as showing that at this time the Mahrahs acknowledged the suzerainty of Oman, and it would not be difficult to show that this dependence of the southern coast to the court at Nezwa continued for centuries afterwards.

Another event recorded in the reign of Al-Muhenna tends to throw much light on the political condition of Oman as well as on the obscure history of the Julanda tribe. This time the rebellion broke out among the Sunni tribes in Al-Dhahireh, among whom were the Beni Julanda. Led by Al-Maghaira bin Roosin al-Julandai, the Sunni confederation marched to Al-Beraimi, which they attacked and carried; the governor there, Abdul Wadhdhah, who was appointed by the Imam, was killed in the fight. The news soon reached Sohar, which was then in possession of the Imam, and the governor there, Abu Merwan, immediately set to work to stem the tide of revolt and he soon started for Towwam with Al-Mattar, shaikh of the Al-Hindi tribe, and an overwhelming force, the strength of which, doubtless greatly exaggerated, is stated at 12,000. Encountering the rebels, Abu Merwan inflicted so severe a defeat that their power in Al-Dhahireh was broken and the Julanda tribe itself almost annihilated, their village or settlement was burnt to the ground, and their families cruelly driven into the desert to starve. From this date we hear nothing more of the Julanda family, which soon became extinct by absorption. We see from this event that the Julandaites had never accepted the Ibadhi doctrines but had remained true to the Sunni faith. We also learn that the Imam's power was paramount in Oman, and that the agent of the Baghdad Government was not able to offer any aid to the rebels.

Al-Muhenna's conduct was not approved by all his adherents, but he was allowed to reign until his death, in Rabi al-Akhir, 237 A.H. [A.D. 851], in the time of the cruel and debauched Khalif Motawakkil, after a rule of ten years and some months.

In this year, 237 A.H. [A.D. 851], we are informed by Kodama, who wrote on the financial condition of the empire at this period, the mokataah or fixed yearly sum paid by Oman to Baghdad was reckoned at 300,000 gold deenars, equivalent to 4,500,000 dirhems, according to Von Kremer's *Kultur Geschichte*, and the statement is corroborated by the Roll of Ibn Modabbir. This vast sum is a proof of the flourishing state to which Oman had arrived by its industry, arts, and commerce, and eloquently testifies to the wealth, populousness, and activity of the land, which had now arrived at the climax of its national existence.

On the very day that Al-Muhenna died, the leading shaikhs of the Ibadhi tribes swore allegiance to Al-Salt bin Malik, who governed uprightly for many years, until he had outlived his contemporaries and chief supporters, and had become bodily incapacitated by the infirmities of age, although his mental powers continued unimpaired. In 273 A.H. [A.D. 886] he was then driven from Nezwa by an intriguing and officious kadhi named Moosa bin Moosa, and took refuge in Fark, where he passed away in Dhu' l-Hijrah, 275 A.H. [A.D. 888]. The rule of this Imam extended over a longer period than that of any of his predecessors, having covered a period of thirty-seven years and seven months, during which time no less than six Khalifs had sat on the throne of Baghdad. The political atmosphere of Oman appears to have remained undisturbed by stormy currents, at least no internecine troubles are recorded by the annalists. Subsequent events, however, show clearly that deep and burning questions were agitating the minds of the people below this surface, and that during the apparent lull and calm of prosperity the way was being prepared for a period of strife, anarchy, civil war, and all the horrors of foreign invasion and subjection. For though no allusion is made to the fact by the Omani historians, it was during the reign of Al-Salt or his successor that allegiance to Baghdad was thrown off, and that the tribute ceased to be remitted. This information we owe to Ibn Ghordadbeh, who wrote about 270 or 275 A.H. [A.D. 883 or 888], and who, while omitting any return for Eastern Arabia, states expressly that it was then in possession of the Kharejites and not in fealty to the Khalif Motamid.

Al-Salt, having been deposed, the Shaikh Rashid bin Al-Nadhr was, in Dhu' l-Hijrah, 273 A.H. [A.D. 886], put up by the Kadhi Moosa bin Moosa as a puppet Imam, but he proved incompetent to wield power and maintain it at so critical a period; the passive timidity of his disposition, in fact, alienating him from an ambitious life, and he seems to have been throughout the dupe of the Kadhi, who used him to further his schemes of religious fanaticism and persecution.

The result was that dissensions everywhere broke out, and the evils, which are the usual concomitants of priestly rule, so completely permeated the land and divided the people that they became plunged into civil war, which lasted for seven years. The Kadhi Moosa appears to have formed a coalition to oppose the Sunnis or Nizar party and to have used his influence to incite the Ibadhi people against them.

The immediate cause of the discord and the particulars of the quarrel between the parties, which led to such important consequences, are not narrated by the Ibadhi chroniclers, but their eloquent silence on certain points makes it tolerably certain that Moosa bin Moosa was the *fons et origo mali*, and must be regarded as the real author of the internecine war that brought so much misery and ruin on his country and led ultimately to a foreign mission, though it is by no means improbable that the emissaries of the Kharejites in other provinces had not a little to do in fomenting religious animosity.

That the Sunni party were not the aggressors in this struggle may be fairly inferred from the fact that they were at this time decidedly in the minority and were consequently not likely to have commenced an unequal contest. At all events, in two of the fights that took place during the ensuing three years, the Nizar were worsted, viz., at Al-Raudha in the Tanoof Valley, in which the latter were led by Fahm bin Warith and Musaab bin Suliman, and again in the battle that occurred near Rostak, when Shazan bin al-Maan al-Salt was defeated and driven off by the Ibadhis.

It was soon after these occurrences that the Kadhi Moosa and the Imam Rashid fell out, the latter probably not proving so pliant a tool in the Kadhi's hands as he had hoped.

The influence of Moosa was accordingly exerted to depose Rashid bin al-Nadhr as it had already been to depose the Imam al-Salt, and having succeeded in getting rid of Rashid, he nominated his friend the Shaikh Azzan bin Temeen al-Kharoosi to the Imamate in the month of Safar, 277 A.H. [A.D. 890].

At first all went smoothly but it was not long before the

relations between the new Imam and the Kadhis began to change. Azzan observed with increasing jealousy and anger the encroachments of Moosa on his authority and the invidious attempts made to undermine his power, and he determined to bring the matter to an issue. A rupture ensued. Moosa was deprived of the Chief Kadhiship and fled to Zikki, where he took refuge with the faction he had so long and so bitterly opposed. Moosa's reception at Zikki did not fail to inspire the Imam with some alarm, and the apprehensions thus created naturally tended to increase the animosity between the two factions.

Hostilities now broke out afresh, and in Shaâban, 278 A.H. [A.D. 891], eighteen months after the accession of the Imam Azzan —an Ibadhi force was despatched to Zikki and siege laid to the walled enclosure or fortlet at that town, inhabited by the Nizar, in which the ex-Kadhi Moosa had obtained sanctuary.

The attacking force was too strong to be resisted, and after a short struggle the enclosure was carried, sacked and burnt to the ground. The slaughter was great, the devastation and the triumph were complete, and the *teterrima causa belli*, Moosa bin Moosa, was amongst the slain.

The town of Zikki, where this massacre occurred, is situate at the south end of the Jebel Akhdar clump, at an elevation of about 2,000 feet above the sea, and on the banks of the Wady Halfain which rises not far off. On the right bank stand the great fort and the two walled enclosures occupied respectively, as of yore, by the Yemen and Nizar, who still remember the terrible Yom of Shaaban and continue to cherish their ancient feud with undiminished vigour, diverting themselves occasionally with skirmishes and fights.

The Imam Azzan received those who brought him the intelligence of the success of his expedition with honour, and liberally rewarded his troops, feeling, doubtless, much relieved at the death of his quondam associate and supporter, Moosa bin Moosa. There are not sufficient materials at hand to enable us to judge with certainty of Moosa's character. His policy seems to have been guided by arrogance and ambition, but the inculpating inferences of history are not actual evidence and do not justify us in pronouncing positively on him; he may have had good reasons for deposing Al-Salt and Rashid and in quarrelling with Azzan, but such schemes are more probably selfish promptings of an insidious and crafty mind worked by cupidity and the lust of power.

The acrimony between the parties was aggravated tenfold by this event and the Nizar tribes thirsted for revenge. It was the most salient and sanguinary of all the conflicts that had taken place in the five years during which the civil war had lasted, and yet deep and wide-spreading as was the misery of the inhabitants they had only begun, as it were, to taste the cup of affliction.

Hitherto the Nizar, being numerically inferior to the Azdites, had been almost invariably worsted in the campaign and were unable to cope with their enemies in the open field, but they resolved, nevertheless, to continue the struggle and even to undertake offensive operations against the Imam.

The man who now took the field as their leader was Al-Fadhl bin al-Howari al-Koreishi, who was supported by Shaikh Abdullah of the Beni Haddan, by Al-Howari bin Abdullah al-Salooni, by the Beni Harth of the Batineh, and by others of the Nizar. Al-Fadhl proceeded first to Al-Beraimi to collect adherents and then returned to his home in Al-Dhahireh. Having arranged his plans with the shaikhs, he next moved down with his force upon Sohar, where he arrived on the 23rd Showal, 278 A.H. [A.D. 891]. In the meantime the Imam Azzan bin Temeem was not idle.

The month of Ramzan, which comes next before Showal, had put a truce to hostilities, and he had employed it in gathering his forces, at the head of which he placed the Shaikh of the Beni Hina, Al-Aheef bin Hamham. This general being informed of Al-Fadhl's movements, marched his army along the Batineh to oppose him and was joined on the way by Fahm bin Warith al-Yahmadi (apparently the same person as the shaikh who was defeated at Eaudheh three or four years previously).

The two armies met at Al-Majiz, not far from Sohar, on the 26th Showal, and the battle that took place ended in the total rout of Al-Fadhl and the Nizar army. This affair brought the war practically to a conclusion and left the Yemenite faction masters of the situation. The meagreness of the accounts that have come down to us leave us much in the dark as to the true position of parties, but it is evident that the character of the war had entirely changed since the rupture between Moosa and the Imam. At that time the war was a religious one between the Sunnis and Ibadhis; it had now become one of race between the Yemen and Nizar, as Fahm bin Warith and the Sunni Beni Hina and others, who were formerly in opposition, were now ranged on the Imam's side.

Although Azzan still reigned as Imam, the chroniclers inform us that the Imamate became to the Omanis a thing to sport with and an object of ambitious design; so much so, that in one year, 386 A.H. [A.D. 996], they set up sixteen different Imams, each of whom failed to retain the allegiance of the people. This was subsequent to Bin Noor's invasion. This crowd of clerical rulers must have been of a class not gifted with the qualities requisite for leaders of men and must have hurled one another, in very rapid succession, from the movable throne.

It is manifest that the Omanis were now in a state of ruinous division and that they had fallen into constant feud and warfare with each other to indulge their jealousies and revenges. Though the shaikhs were at times sufficiently politic and patriotic to combine their efforts, the Imams were generally obliged to meet the successive invading armies of the Khalif with a partizan, not with a national following, and consequently with little cohesion and unity of spirit. The envious, selfish or vindictive minds of the various shaikhs often saw and gloated over the misfortunes of each other, and thus facilitated in a very great degree the encroachments and victories of the Imperial delegates.

In Rajab, 279 A.H. [A.D. 892], the Khalif of Baghdad, Motadhid, died and was succeeded by his nephew, Abban, whose father, Mowaffik Nasir al-Din, had compelled the feeble Motamid to nominate to the succession, to the exclusion of the latter's son and rightful heir. Motadhid Billah, as the new Khalif was styled, had been (like his father) the *de facto* ruler of the empire ever since his father's death, and had proved himself a capable and crafty statesman. He retained his grasp of power with firmness, and the tightening of the rein was soon felt in every province of his dominion.

Oman did not escape his notice. Indeed it was not likely that the rebellious attitude of the Kharejites in this province towards the Khalifate would be suffered by so strong and jealous a sovereign to pass without an effort to chastise and reduce it.

For ten years no mokataah had been remitted to Baghdad, neither had any delegate been permitted to enter Oman to collect it. The new Khalif, doubtless, had long nurtured feelings of resentment against the Omanis on this account, but it is not probable that the storm of imperial rage would have burst so soon on this luckless land if it had not been precipitated by the events occurring in the country itself. The continual bloody and internecine strife that had so long convulsed the country had so envenomed the attitude of the Yemen and Nizar, and had rendered the factions so implacable, that the land was now divided into two hostile camps, and the deep hate engendered thereby was the true cause of the revolution that had been silently rising up in their midst. For though the events we have described as transpiring in Oman must have helped to attract the attention of the court of Baghdad to the disloyal province, the oppression of the Sunnis by the Kharejites had, we may be sure, roused much indignation among their co-religionists, it does not appear that any project of interference had been entertained until the arrival of the deputation to beseech the protection of the Imperial power.

It seems to have been after the Battle of Al-Majiz in 279 A.H. [A.D. 892] that the Nizar chiefs in conclave, despairing of maintaining their prestige by force of arms, and thirsting to wreak their vengeance on their persecutors, determined to invoke the intervention of the Khalif and to solicit his aid to enable them to recover their position.

Notwithstanding the unquestionable provocation that the Nizar had received at the hands of the Yemen faction, this invitation to invade the country, the main object of which was to secure their own political and religious ascendency, sent by one part of the nation to a superior and aggressive power, was as unpatriotic and ill-judged as it was ineffective in furthering the objects of permanently uprooting the Ibadhi heresy in Oman and of giving the political predominance to the Nizar, while the devastation, cruelty, and bloodshed brought on the land in this the greatest, wickedest, and most unnatural invasion that ever assailed it are traditioned by the people to have exceeded all previous and subsequent experience and have brought undying odium on the faction to which the responsibility attaches.

We learn from several Arab historians that the envoys selected to carry the grievances of the party and the invitation to invade Oman were the Shaikhs Mohammed bin Abul Kasim al-Sami and Basheer bin al-Munthir—both belonging to the tribe Beni Sama bin Lawa bin Ghalib, which was one of the most powerful of the Nizar clans in Oman. Whether this mission was despatched secretly, or whether any attempt was made to effect a reconciliation before resorting to foreign aid, does not appear, but, from no mention having been made of any general assembly of shaikhs, we may conclude that the Yemen tribes were not made aware of the Nizar's intention to invite Imperial succour. However this may be, it seems clear that the envoys proceeded first to Bahrain, where the Ameer of Eastern Arabia, which included Oman, then resided.

The name of the Ameer at this time, who was subordinate to the Wali or Governor-General of Irak Arabi, was Mohammed bin Noor, of whose career we know nothing but this one notable and successful episode which, while it has stamped him as a good general, has branded his name with infamy as a monster of cruelty.

With attentive and indignant ears Mohammed bin Noor listened to the story of the civil war in his rebellious district, and of the sufferings endured by the Sunnis at the hands of the heretical Yemenites, and he inwardly resolved to seize, without delay, the opportunity now thrown open to him of reclaiming his lawful authority over Oman, and of putting his foot on the neck of those who had hitherto trampled his dignity under foot and had oppressed the orthodox Moslems. Doubtless he had long had in view the reduction of Oman, and had only been biding his time until the wished for chance should favour his scheme and fulfil his desire to emulate the career of the famous Muhallib as a conqueror of the Kharejites. The promise of the co-operation and support of the Maaddic tribes strengthened Bin Noor's resolve to embark if possible in the enterprise, and the discussion of the details with the envoys enabled him to prepare the plan of campaign previous to laying his project before his Imperial master for consideration and decision.

Retaining Basheer with him, the Ameer sent Mohammed bin Abul Kasim on to Baghdad with a letter addressed to the Khalif, representing how Oman had been cleft asunder into two great factions by the hatchet of discord, the wisdom of aggravating these discussions in the Imperial interest, and urging the immediate despatch of a punitive expedition to chastise the insolence of the Kharejites at so favourable a juncture.

Armed with this letter, Mohammed bin Abul Kasim had no difficulty in procuring admission to the presence of the Khalif Motadhid Billah, whose strong mind quickly grasped the force of the arguments used by the Envoy and the Ameer of Bahrain, and who, knowing that the Kharejite wars of previous reigns had deepened and intensified the feeling between the schismatics and the orthodox, and that Oman was now the chief, if not the only stronghold of the former party, at once perceived the necessity of seizing the opportunity to strike at the heart of the mischief, and thus extinguish the flame of heresy throughout Islam. Recognizing, therefore, the claims of the Sunni and Nizar tribes to protection and that the bond of creed could not be ignored, Motadhid Billah decided not to reject the overtures of the Envoy and the advice of the Ameer, but to issue speedy orders for the organization of an expeditionary force, and mindful of th: fate of Haroon al-Rasheed's small army, he determined that it should be of overwhelming strength.

The news of the war soon spread and the Maaddic tribes poured forth their quotas to rally under the standard of the army of retaliation against the heterodox Azdites, who had persecuted the Nizar, and so popular was the expedition against Oman, so eager were the northern tribes for the spoliation of the land, and so expeditiously did the Ameer Bin Noor and Shaikh Abul Kasim employ their time, that within five months from the date of Al-Motadhid's accession the preparations for the invasion were complete.

The Sunni and Nizar gathered from every corner of Northern Arabia, Syria, Mesopotamia, and Irak, and threw themselves into the struggle with enthusiasm, bound by a common nationality in the hope of extirpating the heretics and of enriching themselves by the plunder of a wealthy province.

Hundreds of shaikhs with their slaves and fierce Bedouin followers volunteered for the new crusade and swelled the total of the force; one of the most notable contingents being a body of the great Tai tribe, which came from Al-Sham to join in the religious war—and altogether an army of about 25,000 men, including 3,500 cavalry in chain armour, raised principally from the warlike tribes of Maaddic stock, assembled under the white banner of the imperial general. This large and well equipped expedition appears to have been divided in two divisions, one of which set sail from Busra with the impedimenta and stores in a flotilla of transports and disembarked at Julfar, while the other, comprising the main body under Mohammed bin Noor, marched by land from Lahsa and crossing the Sabkheh reached Abu Thubi, from whence, engaging on the way with the tribes of Al-Sirr in skirmishes and desultory warfare, after the fashion of Arabia, he moved on to Al-Beraimi in Al-Jow or Towwam, as it was then called, where he arrived on the 24th Moharram, 280 A.H. [A.D. 893]. Here a junction was probably effected with the second division from Julfar, and the whole force then prepared to cross Al-Dhahireh and attack the capital, which is situate in the heart of Oman.

The approach of an army of this magnitude, designed expressly for their subjugation and chastisement by the Khalif, could not fail to cause the utmost consternation and dismay throughout Oman, and it became evident to all that their country was menaced by a calamity of the first order and that little hope of escape, save by a miracle, from the yoke of Baghdad, remained. Oman, indeed, had never before this day, nor has she since, been threatened by an expedition so formidable, so resentful, or so highly organized.

Distracted as the country was by the bitter feuds and sanguinary contests between the rival factions, all possibility of a united force and combined resistance to their powerful enemy was out of the question, as the Nizar tribes, now thoroughly estranged and hostile, had themselves invited the evil and had little to fear, while the national party, though comprising the major portion of the population, was hardly strong enough to cope with it. Paralyzed at the impending weight of an overwhelming force on their frontier, the chiefs appear to have lost heart and to have retained insufficient energy to sustain the strain of such a struggle. It is therefore not to be wondered at that the first feeling was one of hopeless terror and despair, instead of a vigorous and unanimous effort to coalesce against the foe. The Ameer, Mohammed bin Noor, had, it must be admitted, entered with peculiar advantages on his campaign against the Omani Kharejites and their ruler, the Imam Azzan bin Temeem, whose resources were small, whose election was recent, and who was recognized by and held sway over only a section of the nation which, torn by internecine feuds and at a most critical juncture, he was now suddenly called on to guide and defend.

The Imam Azzan does not appear to have been gifted with the talent and character needful to weld his people together and to inspire them with full confidence, but he was not unworthy of the trust reposed in him, and he did his duty manfully. Knowing well that his people had everything to dread from the resentment of the Nizar, and might expect the most vindictive retaliation at their hands, he exerted himself to smoothe the troubled waters of discord among the Yemenites, to raise their drooping spirits and induce them to join patriotically in trying to stem the torrent of invasion, but the response to his efforts was not great, though he certainly succeeded in inducing some of the Sunni tribes to remain loyally on the side of the national party. A number of wealthy inhabitants and some influential shaikhs, who had taken a leading part against the Nizar faction in the late troubles, fled from Oman without waiting to strike a blow. We are told of one named Suliman bin Abdul Malik bin Bilah al-Saleeni who emigrated with his family, slaves and retainers to Hormuz; of many who went with their families and property from Sohar and the Batineh to Shiraz and Busra, and of others who sailed off to East Africa.

These emigrants were doubtless those who formed the most wealthy part of the community and intended to remain with their riches in security until the storm had passed and they could venture to return in safety.

In the meanwhile Mohammed bin Noor, having marshalled his forces, struck his camp at Al-Beraimi and began his march across the district of Al-Dhahireh towards the capital Nezwa, which lay in the heart of Oman; his army, swollen by the adhesion of the disaffected Nizar tribes, having now increased probably to more than 30,000 men.

The Imam's endeavour to arrest the invaders' progress proved unavailing, for the Omani tribes had in but few instances obeyed their leaders' summons. Deserted by so many, and in face of so much treacherous despondency, the Imam deemed his capital untenable, and undismayed by the heavy odds against him, fell back with the few thousand troops he had been able to muster round him to Semed al-Shan, where he resolved to make a stand for liberty. However hopeless the resistance and inadequate the national means may have been to cope with the tidal wave of aggression, which they had to a great extent brought on themselves by their domineering and oppressive conduct towards their fellow-countrymen, the Nizar, the Ibadhis were certainly bound by all the ties of humanity and manliness to strike a blow for the defence of their homes, and are worthy of just censure for not having loyally supported the Imam in adopting a vigorous, patriotic and united system of opposition to the despoiling host. Their pusillanimous and wavering behaviour on this occasion has ever been felt as a stain by the Omanis, and it is to be regretted that the names of the tribes that gallantly stood by the Imam in the forlorn conflict at Semed are not mentioned.

Passing by Senaina, Obre, and Bahila, Mohammed bin Noor occupied Nezwa without opposition, and having established there his headquarters, continued his advance on Semed al-Shan. Here on the 25th of Safar, 280 A.H. [A.D. 893], an obstinate battle was fought and maintained by the two armies throughout the day; but the Imperial troops, superior in numbers, in weapons and in discipline, were victorious and cut down the Omanis, notwithstanding their desperate valour, with irremediable slaughter.

The storm had now burst over Oman; the blackening cloud that had threatened to deluge the land had fallen, and the people were soon to learn the full extent of their misfortunes. Mohammed bin Noor sent the head of the Imam, Azzan bin Temeem, who had been slain in the battle,* to the Khalif, Motadhid Billah, and returned with his elated and triumphant army to his camp at Nezwa. He signalized his victory by a series of brutal and savage massacres, and, according to tradition, cruelty and lust ran wild throughout the land. When the pursuit of the fugitives, the ravage of the country with all its horrors and the collection of booty was over, each kor or district of Oman was then systematically brought under subjection and garrisoned and the conquest of Oman was then complete.

The Nizar tribes, formerly so despondent, were now in the ascendant, and we may be sure lost no time or opportunity in taking their revenge and recouping themselves for the losses they had sustained at the hands of their Yemenite oppressors.

Since the death of Zizad bin Mahallib in Rabi al-Thani, 117 A.H. [A.D. 735]—a period of 163 years—Oman had succeeded in maintaining its virtual independence, having defeated the attempt made by Haroon al-Rasheed to subjugate it.

But, as is remarked in the following passage of Ross's *Annals*

---

* Ibn al-Atheer only says of this invasion that in 280 A.H. [A.D. 893] Mohd bin Noor conquered Oman and sent the heads of its chief inhabitants to the Khalif.

of Oman: "They had fought among themselves for power and supremacy, each one aiming at having the authority in his own hands or in the hands of those he favoured, so God delivered them into the power of one more unjust than themselves, and since they had become corrupt in their religion therefore God deprived them of the kingdom and set an enemy over them to rule them."

Among the causes that led to the almost passive surrender of their independence and the easy grasp of absolute sway by the Khalif's lieutenant, were the universal desire to engage in commercial pursuits by the Omani Arabs, and the spread of effeminacy, luxury, and indolence, following in the wake of the revival of trade. This revival, which was so sudden and extensive that it might almost be called a new birth, had taken place in the Persian Gulf about two centuries before, and the riches amassed for themselves by the community through this commerce and industry, had tended to greatly alter the social aspect of their lives. By this change of occupation the Hadhr or settled Arabs had become less inured to war and less capable of, as well as less inclined to undertake, military hardships, while the Bedouin tribes who had been the chief combatants in the incessant strife and turmoil of civil war, were naturally less fitted to meet the trained and experienced troops of imperial Baghdad in the field of Mars.

While Bin Noor was ravaging Oman the great Alfred of England was lying on his deathbed. By a curious coincidence an almost parallel circumstance occurred about the same time in the two countries, which then held probably a very similar population. The ninth century had seen England invaded and overcome by the Danes, unchecked by the infructuous attempt of Alfgar, and their depredations continued until the turn of fortune came and Alfred's victory at Bratten Hill or Ethandune on May 15th, 878 A.D., changed the position of affairs and drove the northmen from the land. Oman, like England, had its Alfgar and similarly failed, through want of skill and prudence, in an attempt against the aggressor.

This Alfgar, or Hereward, appeared in the person of the Shaikh of Beni Hina—Al-Aheef bin Hamham, who took the lead in an insurrection to drive the hated invaders from the country. The Beni Hina was one of the most powerful tribes in Oman and were, it is to be observed, Sunnis. Its Temeemeh, or Head Shaikh, Al-Aheef, is traditioned to have been a man of bold and firm character, sagacious and wily. On him, therefore, fell naturally the burden of confronting the storm and of guiding the people after the Imam Azzan's death, though he does not appear to have been suitable for the Imamate.

From the disastrous day of Semed he had never ceased to watch his opportunity and keep alive the spirit of revolt against the tyrant. It was not long before a favourable moment presented itself, and the people, now chastened and united by adversity, and still bleeding from their wound, saw with savage joy their enemy lulled into false security, and, conscious of superior strength, disdaining precautions, oblivious of danger and bent only on rapine and pleasure.

Loaded with booty and intoxicated with pride, a large portion of the Northern tribes, who had flocked to Bin Noor's standard with the sole object of plunder, had returned to Busra, while from the main body that remained, many detachments had been sent out to garrison and overawe the various towns and districts. Scattered, diminished and negligent as Bin Noor's army thus was, there must have been nevertheless a strong force of some 12,000 or 15,000 men still encamped at the capital, where their general had fixed his residence.

The shaikhs of the Yemen and Ibadhi tribes were called on by circular letters despatched to all parts of Oman, to rise and crush their oppressors or expel them from the land, and all the chiefs who had not fled the country or made submission to the conqueror answered the appeal with greater enthusiasm and alacrity than they had shown towards that of the Imam Azzan. Oman soon became a seething cauldron of conspiracy and insurrection. Bound by common sympathy the people coalesced rapidly for the great object in view, and Al-Aheef soon had a numerous and valiant army at his disposal. With a sudden spring through the mountains he made a dash at Nezwa, and the Ameer bin Noor, taken by surprise and unable to repulse the attack, quitted the capital and retired with his troops towards the sea. Passing by Zikki, the Khalif's general entered the Wady Tyeen and retreated through the Thaika pass to the coast near the town of Kuriyat, whither he was pursued by the Omani force. Here, Bin Noor, being brought to bay, was compelled to make a stand and prepare for the inevitable conflict, as, hemmed in by the mountains and the sea, he could retreat no further.

After a fierce struggle, in which both sides behaved with desperate valour and suffered heavy loss in killed and wounded, the fortune of war began to declare in favour of the Omanis, whose hearts were brightened and encouraged by the hope that the land would soon be swept clear of its enemies. But at this critical point of the battle, while the combat was still raging furiously, and the imperial troops were being beaten back, a reinforcement of the Nizar, despatched by Abu Abaideh bin Mohammed, Shaikh of the Sama—Bin Noor's own tribe—came hurrying up, on camels, and having dismounted, charged at once, pell mell, into the thick of the fray. This unlooked for and welcome addition to the strength of the enemy made them redouble their efforts, the tide of triumph was turned and the victory that had seemed within their grasp was snatched from the hands of the Omanis.

Al-Aheef bin Hamham was slain on the field, fighting valiantly, together with many of his relations, and but few of the Ibadhi host escaped the carnage.

Mohammed bin Noor once more, and this time unexpectedly, a victor, returned in haste to Nezwa, and smarting from the shame of his ignominious terror and retreat, wasted no time in taking steps to slake his thirst for vengeance on the inhabitants.

With Al-Aheef's death, the insurrection entirely collapsed and no national force remained to dispute supremacy in the field, but this did not suffice to turn the bloody purpose of Bin Noor, who gave orders for the cruel and inhuman treatment of the people and the devastation of the land. Such of the shaikhs and leading inhabitants as were not sentenced to be killed outright were sentenced to mutilation. With revolting barbarity he caused their hands, feet, and ears to be cut off and their eyes put out. Their property was seized and transferred to the Nizar, and their women and children enslaved.

The felejes or water conduits, on which the people depended for the irrigation of their fields, were destroyed; the books were burnt, and destruction and desolation were spread around. The horrors of this retribution, the most humiliating and complete that Oman ever underwent, can only be described by the words—murder, rape, pillage, enslavement, and beggary. These atrocities swept away at one blow the progress and improvement that the civilization of the new Arab empire had spread over the land and reduced it to a condition that inflicted untold misery on the wretched survivors. In fact such a depopulation ensued from the fury of this ruthless tyrant that many years elapsed before Oman began to recover from the calamities he inflicted. The Omanis mention Mohammed bin Noor's name to this day with the utmost abhorrence and detestation, and repeat many tales of his iniquities. He is universally spoken of now in Oman as "Bin Boor" or the "Reprobate."

The Omanis have never thought of attempting to minimise the magnitude of their disaster and humiliation at this time; on the contrary, it is constantly talked of at the present hour, and the name of Bin Noor has probably not lost anything in the way of hatred and loathing during the thousand years through which it has been handed down.

How long the Ameer continued to rule over Oman and distress the people with his rod of iron we do not know, but it is not likely that he remained long away from the superior post he held as Governor of Bahrain. On his departure he appointed Ahmed bin Hilal bin Okht al-Kuttah in 304 A.H. [A.D. 916] to succeed him as Ameer of Oman, and appears to have withdrawn the major portion of the imperial troops, as Ahmed deemed it prudent to at once quit Nezwa and fix his residence at Bahila, an ancient town situated in a valley under Jebel Koor, and at that time, and for long subsequently the central point and chief town of the Sunni and Nizar faction. Ahmed, however, did not venture to leave the capital of the Ibadhi tribes altogether unwatched, but placed as deputy there a shaikh named Bahareh Abu Ahmed. The selection was not a good one. Bahareh was bigoted and tyrannical and soon made himself so obnoxious to the inhabitants that they rose up and slew him, dragged his corpse outside the city and buried it in a dung heap.

During the remainder of the reign of Motadhid Billah, Oman was firmly held in subjection, and the spoliation of the country that had been commenced by Bin Noor was systematically continued, a heavy annual tribute or mokataah being exacted and extorted from the Kharejites for remission to Baghdad, and this grievous oppression must have tended to drain the country of its wealth and to ruin the inhabitants, for it goes without saying that the Imperial Government gave nothing in return for the taxes it levied in the provinces.

It was in the reign of Motadhid that the Carmathians of Bahrain struck their first blow at the power and faith of the Imperial Government and spread the fame of a sect, which was to be a terror to Islam for nearly a century, and it is to M. de Goeje we are indebted for all the information we possess about them. The rise of the Carmathians was due to a man of Persian origin, who, actuated by an intense, deep-seated animosity against Islam and the Arab race, founded a sect that shook the throne of the Khalifs to its foundation and for nearly a century continued to devastate a great part of the Moslem Empire. This was Abdullah al-Kaddah. Subsequently the Grand Dai at Koufa, Hassan Carmath, nominated Abu Saeed as Dai in Southern Persia and afterwards transferred him to Bahrain where, by the year 286 A.H. [A.D. 899], he had brought a large portion of the territory under his sway, and had captured Kateef. Bahrain had been well selected by the Dai for his purpose.

Occupied to a great extent by Bedouin Arabs and people of Persian descent, the anti-Islamic doctrines preached by these fanatics spread rapidly, while still more fortunately for them large numbers of negroes, who had escaped the massacres after the suppression of the servile insurrection in Irak, flocked to join them and recruited their forces with splendid fighting material. In 287 A.H. [A.D. 900], their insolence and daring rose to such a pitch that they soon began to march on Busra. Motadhid, with his usual energy, at once despatched a force of 2,000 men under Abbass bin Amr to meet them and the encounter between the armies took place in Rajab, 287 A.H. [A.D. 900]. In this battle the rout of the Imperialists was complete, the carnage was frightful, and Abbass with 700 others was taken prisoner. Abu Saeed returned in triumph to Bahrain and massacred all his prisoners except Abbass, whom he sent to Baghdad. The noise of this event resounded and reverberated throughout Islam, but the Khalif, though mad with anger, did nothing to repair the disaster. It was followed by the siege of Al-Hajar, the capital of Bahrain, which was taken by Abu Saeed in 290 A.H. [A.D. 902] after a two years' siege by turning off the water supply of the town. Abu Saeed then took up his residence at Lahsa, and the fall of Al-Hajar, which consolidated the power of the Carmathians, led practically to the subjection of the whole province of Bahrain, though Ibn Bauon, who had succeeded Mohammed bin Noor as Governor, had some small successes and retook Kateef for a time.

Their attention was now directed to the neighbouring countries of Yemen and Oman, which they determined to subdue.

Among those who had fled from Oman to escape the persecutions and cruelties of Bin Noor were many Ibadhis, who turned their steps to Bahrain and imitated the example set them by the Nizar in imploring the aid of the Dai in driving the hated Imperial troops from their land. Abu Saeed had given a ready ear to their appeal and resolved, after disposing of Yemen, to take advantage of the opportunity offered by the feuds and dissensions in Oman to invade, subjugate, and annex that country.

In thus invoking the help of Abu Saeed it is certain that the Ibadhi refugees were actuated solely by desire of revenge and freedom, and were not drawn to him by any sympathy for the Carmathian doctrines, which they, as much as the Sunnis, held in the utmost horror and detestation. Al-Islam indeed, orthodox and

Kharejite alike, accounted the Carmathians as infidels, for the latter allowed the free use of wine, abrogated the religious precepts of the Prophet, and gave allegorical interpretations to the Koran; they called their Imam Al-Massoom or "the Preserved of God," and with the greatest inconsistency claimed a prophetic mission for their founder, while denying, absolutely, the existence of divine revelation.

The Khalif Al-Moktafi Billah, who succeeded Al-Motadhid in 289 A.H. [A.D. 901], was a strong and able ruler and had striven to revive the glories and prestige of the Khalifate; but his reign was too short to allow him to achieve much in the way of reform. It was in the last few years of this vigorous sway—perhaps in 293 A.H. [A.D. 905] that Abu Saeed made his first attempt to conquer Oman. Several accounts are extant of this Oman expedition, but in none of them are we informed of the precise year in which it took place. Al-Mowairy and others state that the invading force consisted of 600 men and was almost completely annihilated.

Al-Balkhy Istakhey, however, indicates that the Carmathians were so far successful that on reaching Oman they gained possession of one of the forts in the country, which we may guess to have been either Towwam (now Beraimi) or Julfar. This repulse of the Carmathians was entirely due to the gallantry of the Imperial garrison and the Nizar tribes under the leadership of the Ameer Ahmed bin Hilal, who had been able to muster a sufficient force to overawe the Ibadhis and prevent their rallying while he crushed the invaders. Abu Saeed made no further attempt on Oman where he had been so completely foiled by the Ameer, and in 301 A.H. [A.D. 913] was assassinated in his house at Lahsa.

In 295 A.H. [A.D. 907] the Khalif Al-Moktafi was succeeded by his brother, Al-Moktader Billah, who assumed the reins at the age of thirteen and lived for a quarter of a century on the throne. He was a feeble and dissolute prince, guided entirely by his eunuchs and women, and under him the decay of the empire sped a rapid course.

In 305 A.H. [A.D. 917] the Carmathians under Saeed, who had succeeded his father, Abu Saeed, as Dai at Lahsa, made another attempt to subdue Oman. Al-Mesoodi does not mention this event, though that famous traveller and historian tells us that Ahmed bin Hilal was still Ameer of Oman when he (Mesoodi) visited Sohar in this year; but Al-Jauzi relates that the Ameer Ahmed bin Hilal sent costly presents to Moktader in 305 A.H. [A.D. 917], accompanied by a request for a military force to aid in repelling a threatened invasion by these enemies of Islam who were marching down from Lahsa. Among the presents sent to the Khalif, says Al-Soyuti, was a talking Mynah, which repeated Indian and Persian words better than a parrot. The Khalif despatched the troops asked for without delay, and the result was that the Carmathian operations, which were directed by Saeed's younger brother, Abu Tahir Suliman, then only a youth of twenty-two, were as abortive as those of Abu Saeed had been, and the conquest of Oman had again to be abandoned. In this fruitless expedition Abu Tahir appears to have spent two years, that is, until 307 A.H. [A.D. 919], when he was recalled by Obaidullah, who sent him to Irak.

Owing to the pressure of political events occurring at Baghdad at this period, the Khalif Al Moktader now decided to withdraw his Governor and troops from Oman, and to allow it to regain partial independence on the conditions that it was to acknowledge allegiance and to pay a certain annual tribute to the Imperial treasury. To maintain Oman as a conquered province had evidently proved a great expense and a heavy drain in soldiers, and it suited the central authority at Baghdad to substitute an arrangement by which Oman could be made profitable without being a military incubus.

It was therefore ordered that an official should be sent yearly to the province, supported by a sufficient escort to enforce the collection of the stipulated mokataah and bring it back to the capital, and that this system continued to prevail for many years we learn from the local annalists.

Relieved for a time from the apprehensions of Carmathian incursion and held in restraint no longer by the presence of an Imperial Government, the inhabitants were now left to dwell together in unity or to resume, if they pleased, the old order of antagonistic faction as it existed before Bin Noor's invasion. For a time matters went smoothly. Without a single date being given or a single event in the concurrent history of Oman being recorded at this period by the chroniclers, a number of Imams flit before us in rapid succession, and we may fairly suppose that no important occurrences took place. Of one of these Imams—Abdullah bin Mohammed—we learn that he was nicknamed Abu Saeed al-Karmati, possibly on account of his personal resemblance to the famous flour merchant, or some such reason. Of another Imam, the Shaikh Al-Hawari bin Matraf al-Haddani, who came seventh in succession after the recovery of independence, we are told that when the agent of the Khalif was deputed from Baghdad to collect the annual tribute, he used to vacate the official residence allotted to the Imam and resign the functions of the Imamate, thus leaving the agent to extort what sums he pleased from the people without venturing to expostulate with the rapacious tax gatherer or shield his subjects in any way, however grievous the burden may have been. When the agent and his myrmidons quitted Oman to return to Baghdad with the treasure he had amassed, the Imam returned to his public quarters and resumed charge of his office. This proceeding could hardly have tended to increase the people's respect for their Imam, but Al-Hawari is spoken of, nevertheless, as being very strict and just, and as one who repressed the licentious and evil-doers with rigour.

In view of the impoverishment of Oman by the ruthless ravages and robberies of Mohammed bin Noor and his Nizar followers, we cannot for a moment suppose that the amount of the tribute now extorted approached the large sum levied from it in the height of its prosperity, an amount which is said to have reached, as we have seen, in the days of the Khalif Motawakkil four and a-half million dirhems, or about £180,000. The agent on returning to Baghdad did not leave his master the Khalif wholly unrepresented in Oman, for we learn that a small detachment of the Beni Assameh, a Western Maaddic tribe, was posted at Nezwa to attend upon, and of course at the same time to be a check on the Imam.

On the death of the Imam Al-Hawari his nephew, Omar bin

Mohammed bin Matraf, was elected to the Imamate, and it is recorded of him that he followed the same policy as his uncle, that is, he withdrew from office when the Khalif's agent came for the tribute and resumed his functions after the agent's departure.

The author of the Kashf al-Ghummeh, according to Ross, expresses the opinion that none of these Imams after Salt bin Malik was universally recognized and that their rule did not extend over the entire country. It would appear that, unable to bury the past in oblivion, embittered by religious hatred and divided by factious quarrels, the people could not agree in selecting an Imam to govern the nation, so consequently the power of the shaikh nominated was extremely precarious and fluctuating and restricted also to certain districts only of the country.

In 311 A.H. [A.D. 923] Busra was attacked by the Carmathians who slew, ravaged and ravished the inhabitants without mercy and gutted the city. The courage and ability displayed by Abu Tahir Suliman, who commanded in this campaign, led to the deposition of his brother Saeed from the post of Dai, and the appointment in his place of Abu Tahir by the Ikdaniya and Obaidullah.

The next few years were spent by Abu Tahir in constructing a massive fortress at Lahsa, which was completed in 315 A.H. [A.D. 927] and was called Mooriniya and also Dar al-Hijrah.

Soon after this came the preparations for the most daring and notorious enterprise the Carmathians ever undertook; this was nothing less than an attack on Mecca al-Shereef itself, and in this achievement they perpetrated a sacrilege that staggered Islam and made every true Moslem tremble with consternation, horror, and indignation.

It is probable that Obaidullah had long contemplated the design of this hazardous expedition and had warily waited to seize the most opportune moment for thus inflicting so mortal a blow on the prestige of the Khalifate; and it may be judged that he could not have selected a more fitting hour for executing his plan.

In 316 A.H. [A.D. 928] the Khalif Moktadir appointed Mansoor the Dailamite as Ameer Al-Kafila, and despatched the pilgrim caravan in his charge on its overland journey to Mecca.

Abu Tahir Suliman was well apprised of its movements and permitted it to reach its destination in safety; but a little later he was on the march too across Arabia and with the same objective.

On the 8th Dhu 'l-Hijrah, 317 A.H. [A.D. 929], he fell with a sudden swoop on the Holy City and drove the frightened crowds of citizens and pilgrims into the kaaba or temple. Panic-stricken and unresisting the people huddled together like sheep and the pavement of its spacious precincts was soon reddened with their blood as they were knived, daggered, and mown down by the sword. Thirty thousand victims were the hecatomb offered on that day according to the historians.

The sacrilegious Abu Tahir appropriated and carried off to Bahrain many precious trinkets and relics, some of which had been robbed from Christian churches. Among these were the famous pearl Yateema, the Rod of Moses, the horn of the Ram that saved Isaac or Ishmael from the sacrificing knife of Abraham, and the gold earrings of the mother of Mohammed's son, but, greatest crime of all, he took away the Hajar al-Aswad, the venerated black stone to which the whole Moslem world turns in prayer.

With an incredible amount of booty and a long weary train of captives, men, women and children, Abu Tahir crossed the desert and the Nejd and entered Lahsa in triumph.

Elated by the glory of this exploit, enriched and strengthened by the vast spoils they had acquired in that memorable expedition, Obaidullah allowed his troops but little rest to recover their fatigues, and in the following year, 318 A.H. [A.D. 930], resolved to complete the conquest of Arabia by sending the Ikdaniya across the Sabkheh into Oman, that fertile and isolated province whose subjugation the grim warriors of Bahrain had so many times essayed in vain.

The attempt this time was crowned with success; the tribes, both Yemen and Nizar, dismayed and humiliated by the great disaster which had befallen Islam the year before, offering but little, if any, opposition. All the rest of the Peninsula for some time submitted to the arms of the Carmathian and now Oman had fallen. But as it was the last to yield, so, as we shall see, it was the first to throw off the yoke.

By this event the bonds which had so long, though so intermittently linked Oman to the Imperial throne were snapped asunder, and the annual tribute which the Khalif had received was diverted from Baghdad to Lahsa for a long period, the duration of which, however, is uncertain. The incidents accompanying this irruption have not been circumstantially narrated by any historian, and we are merely informed that the Khalif's agent fled to Persia, but there can be little doubt as regards the date.

Ibn Khaldoon refers to the event, but his account is too confused to be of much service, though he states explicitly that the reduction of Oman took place after the expedition to Mecca.

That it occurred at latest early in 319 A.H. [A.D. 931] is clear from the fact that early in this year Abu Tahir led his troops to Koofa.

Abul Mahasin has been thought to refer o this campaign in Oman when he relates that in 319 A.H. [A.D. 931] the enemies of the Wazeer al-Hoossani ibn al-Wasim advised the Khalif Moktadir Billah to send Abu Tahir an exile to Oman. The native annalists do not give any date and refrain from furnishing any details of the campaign and confine themselves to the remark that when the Keramitah invaded Oman the Imam Omar bin Mohammed, in whose reign the event happened, resigned office, and that when they returned to Bahrain he did not resume it.

There is much reason to believe that the Carmathian conquest did not entail undue interference on their part with the institutions of the country nor molestation of the Ibadhi inhabitants, who, indeed, probably welcomed them as liberators. Some resistance may have been offered by the Nizar tribes, who had opposed them so stoutly and effectively before, but there are no traditionary accounts in Oman, so far as I can gather, of sanguinary contests, and it seems to have been, on the whole, a comparatively bloodless victory.

In 320 A.H. [A.D. 932] the Khalif Moktadir Billah was slain outside the walls of Baghdad in a contest with the Eunuch Moonis al-Mudhaffer, his general, whom he had called to his aid from Mosul and whom on his approach he insanely moved out to attack. Moktadir was succeeded by his brother, Kahir Billah, the last but one of the Khalifs who ruled as well as reigned, and next to the Khalif al-Motadhid, the most cruel and inhuman wretch of them all. In his reign much religious excitement was caused in Baghdad by the proceedings of Ali bin Beleek, who cursed Moawiya in the pulpits and attacked Burbahari, the Chief of the Hanbalites. To quell the disturbance Ali bin Beleek and his companions were imprisoned, put on board vessels at Busra and shipped off to Oman.

The retirement of the Imam Omar bin Mohammed, consequent upon the Carmathian conquest, was followed by an interregnum of short duration during which no Imam was elected, but as the Carmathians appear to have been satisfied with the payment of tribute and did not oppose the Imamate, the Ibadhis proceeded to confer that office on the Shaikh Mohammed bin Yezeed al-Kindi in whose reign the unhappy country was again desolated by warfare. The paramount power at Baghdad had seen with undisguised disquietude another of its provinces torn from its grasp, its rich tribute, which it could ill afford to lose, annexed, and its Ameer or Agent put to flight by the accursed Carmat, and it resolved on an energetic effort to dispossess him. A strong force of Imperial troops was accordingly sent which, in conjunction probably with the Sunni tribes, pushed the Carmathians back to the hills forming two corps of observation—one at a town on the pirate coast and the other at Nakhl under Jebel Shaibeh. Further operations resulted in the flight of the Imam Mohammed bin Yezeed, who, finding his capital no longer tenable, sailed from Oman and sought refuge probably at the Yemen or Zanzibar. Nezwa was then occupied in force and the turn of fortune's wheel again placed the Ibadhis at the mercy of the Nizar faction. This may possibly be the expedition of Yusof bin Wajih, about whom we read in Ibn al-Atheer, but it is unlikely that Yusof was in Oman at so early a date, and we may more safely conjecture that this force was despatched by Kahir Billah and that it gained a temporary success, until the Carmathians, being reinforced from Bahrain, expelled the invaders and re-possessed themselves of the country.

The return of the Carmathians permitted the election of another Imam by the Ibadhis, and this time the choice fell on the Shaikh al-Hakam bin al-Moalla al-Bohri, who is spoken of contemptuously by some writers as an imbecile. He died soon after his installation as Imam.

That the Ibadhis preferred the Carmathian suzerainty to the yoke of the Imperialists cannot be doubted, as they not only recovered through the former their old political predominance, but enjoyed a respite for a time from the business of war, and were thus able to turn aside to the arts and pursuits of peace, and to look forward to a fresh tide of prosperity and wealth. But the changed condition of affairs and the deliverance of the people from oppression were not alone sufficient to produce this happy result—it needed a strong and wise leader to guide them through the perils, confusion, and troubles by which they were beset, and they appear to have found one in the Shaikh Abul Kasim Saeed bin Abdulla bin Mohammed bin Mahbool bin al-Rabaid bin Saif bin Hobairah, the Horseman of the Prophet, to whom they vowed allegiance, as their next Imam immediately on the death of Al-Hakam. On this prince, Saeed bin Abdulla, unstinted praise is lavished by the annalist, who extols him as a monument of erudition, piety, and uprightness.

It is asserted that his attainments surpassed those of any previous Imam and that he was superior even to Julanda bin Mesood, who was the most distinguished of the earlier princes.

Under his sway the fires of faction are said to have burnt feebly, while the moral improvement and other advantages which invariably result to a people when their ruler is devoted to and encourages literature and industry, give prominence to the reign of this Imam, under whom Oman began to rise in power and civilization, and would have regained probably much of its former trade and opulence had his reign been prolonged and peace preserved.

Allowing that the panegyric of the chronicler has been inspired by a too partial religious bias, it is certain that the Imam Saeed bin Abdulla must have been a capable and sagacious ruler. We have no mention of the further advent of Imperial troops in his time, and we may conclude that the Carmathians remained peacefully masters of the position. The beneficent and prosperous rule of this prince was brought to a premature close by his accidental death, for he was slain in trying to quell a tumult at Rostak in the year 328 A.H. [A.D. 939] in the reign of the Khalif Radhi Billah. The date given in Ross's *Annals of Oman* is 323 A.H. [A.D. 934], but this would only allow five years from the date of the Carmathian conquest, to include an interregnum, and the reigns of three Imams. I think, therefore, that the other date, given by Ibn Keisar, may be accepted as more probable.

The Khalif Radhi Billah had succeeded his uncle Kahir in 322 A.H. [A.D. 933], the latter having made his rule so insupportable, by reason of his bloodthirsty cruelty during his two years of office, that he was deposed and blinded. Al-Radhi was mild and well-meaning and his conduct was in striking contrast to that of his predecessor Kahir; but it is not to be forgotten that the Khalifate, which had been for years on the downward path of degradation and decay, fell by a sudden drop on to a still lower stage of disintegration and servility by the appointment in 324 A.H. [A.D. 935] of Mohammed bin Raik as Ameer al-Omra and the surrender to him of unlimited control over the administration. No good cause has been assigned for this step, which brought the Khalifate to a more abject condition than any other single event. Whether Radhi was of so indolent a disposition that he was glad to hand over the reins of power to another or whether he was actuated by a consciousness of incapacity to rule is not apparent, but whatever the cause, the effect was disastrous, —not only to the Khalif and his capital but to all the provinces of the Empire. Having summoned Ibn Raik to Baghdad he gave him supreme power over the finances of the state and the army, abolishing the treasury and other offices and even superseding the Grand Wazeer himself, who was now reduced to the more humble position of Secretary. From the slough of despond in which Radhi had thus deliberately cast the Khalifate, no one could extricate it, nor could the chains by which the Turkish mercenaries had bound it be burst, and the disintegration of the empire, which had already begun, proceeded more rapidly than ever.

In Oman it was not long before the iron shoe of the Turk trod the ground and trampled over the wretched inhabitants.

The Imam Saeed bin Abdulla had administered affairs with so much discretion and had exhibited so much tact in conciliating all parties that his untimely death was universally felt to be a real misfortune to his country. His had been a reign of peace. But though the busy occupations of commerce had given a serene and placid air to the country, they had not so entirely engrossed the attention of the tribes as to make them forget their mutual feuds and jealousies; it soon became apparent that the slumbering elements of discord existed in full strength and that they only awaited an opportunity to spring into full activity. This was afforded at the election of the next Imam, when the animosities engendered by rival claims brought on a new tide of disunion and decay.

At the meeting held at Nezwa for the purpose the three shaikhs who took a leading part agreed to nominate Rashid bin Waleed, but this selection found many dissentients, and in view of the strong divergence of opinion among the representatives of the various parties it was deemed expedient to summon a general council. This took place in the house of Rashid bin Waleed himself, and was probably attended almost exclusively by his own supporters, by whose votes the confirmation of his election was easily assured. From the laboured defence, however, of these proceedings by the Ibadhi historian we may conjecture that the council was fully alive to the weakness of its position, and we learn that in order to disarm opposition it passed a resolution adopting a policy of toleration for the new Imam's government and of oblivion towards the post in connection with the dissensions that had resulted in the death of the Kadhi Moosa bin Moosa in the days of the Imam Azzan bin Temeen fifty years before, and which had caused such terrible internecine strife and brought such misery on the country.

At a council so constituted the decision could not long be doubtful, and when the point was carried the shaikh proceeded to the open space by the Wady Kalbuh, where a great multitude had gathered together from all parts to hear the result. The choice was proclaimed to the people by Abu Mohammed Abdulla bin Saihnah, who called upon them to ratify it by giving the new prince, Rashid bin al-Waleed, their allegiance. The Ibadhi portion of the population granted their fealty unhesitatingly and the assembly dispersed quietly. The Imam Rashid at once despatched his governors and agents to all the districts and villages in Oman, where his authority was likely to be respected, directing them to collect the sadakat or poor rate, the mokataah or tribute, and other taxes. He also re-garrisoned the forts, assuming all the powers of a patriarchal government, and acted beyond doubt as an independent prince whose rule was undisputed and uncontrolled, save and except by the Carmathian agent at Nezwa, who was there to exact tribute.

Rashid is much belauded by the chroniclers for his virtues, and he is represented as a just, courteous, and benevolent prince. It is to their admiration for the high character he bore that we may perhaps ascribe the tacit acceptance of his rule, in the early days of it, to the Nizar and Sunni tribes, who if they did not actually swear allegiance, at least offered no overt opposition to him. His reign began auspiciously and there was a fair prospect to his country of continued peace and prosperity.

But a change was at hand. The machinations of his rivals for the Imamate, who, busy with slander and calumny, had been watching for opportunities to injure him, had their effect, and it was not long before sedition, dissension, and evil passion took the place of harmony and loyal devotion. Many of the more powerful Ibadhi tribes withdrew from their adherence and loyalty and the Imam Rashid grew in unpopularity and disfavour.

His good qualities and virtues failed to sustain him in the eyes of his subjects, and he seems to have lacked the energy and ability requisite for the task of curbing the unruly and dissipating the dark clouds of enmity and disaffection that had gathered around him, and his efforts to throw oil on the troubled waters of discord were altogether unavailing.

At this juncture of affairs, news reached Oman that an expeditionary force of Imperial troops had been prepared at Baghdad for the re-conquest of the country, and that the Sultan was already on the march towards Al-Sirr. This intelligence turned the thoughts of all in a new direction and local squabbles and politics were again set aside in the consternation and dismay produced by it. The Imam Rashid appears to have resolved at once on his course of action and endeavoured to rally round him the great tribes of the land in the defence of their country. He summoned them to his standard in vain. The Ibadhis, embittered perhaps by their late quarrels, held aloof and decided to remain neutral; while the Sunni and Nizar tribes did not hesitate to declare their intention of welcoming the invader, and lost no time in gathering round a chief of their own at Bahila. Rashid bin al-Waleed proceeded to Bahila to induce them to forego this intention and tried his utmost to dissuade them from deserting their country's cause. But religious animosity and their resentment against the Kharejite hegemony were stronger than their patriotism and he pleaded in vain.

Meanwhile the Turkish army, under Yusof bin Wajih, had advanced from Abu Thabee to Beraimi and the Imam fearing to remain longer among his rebellious Nizar subjects at Bahila retired, first to Kadam and then to the Wady al-Nakhr.

Of the previous history of the race and kindred of this Yusof bin Wajih, who was destined to govern Oman for so many years and to perish there by the hand of a slave, we know nothing, and the precise date of his conquest has not been given either by local or by general historians, but as Ibn al-Atheer mentions him as already Lord of Oman in 331 A.H. [A.D. 942], it must have taken place before that year.

At this period, Mesopotamia was in a sad state of confusion and disorder. Khalif was succeeding Khalif and Ameer al-Omra was succeeding Ameer al-Omra in rapid succession.

The all-powerful Ameer ibn Raik had given place in 326 A.H. A.D. 937] to Bajkam, a Turk, who on the death of Al-Radhi in 329 A.H. [A.D. 940] practically put the Khalifate up for sale and was himself slain soon afterwards. The purchaser, Al-Muttaki, had a short but a very chequered and eventful career and had more than once to flee his capital. He gave the post of Ameer al-Omra first to Al-Baridi and after a few weeks to a Turk named Kuttekin. After a few months he was replaced by Ibn Raik, who on the reappearance of Al-Baridi carried the Khalif off to Mosul in 330 A.H. [A.D.. 941]. In the same year Al-Muttaki, supported by the Hamdanis, returned to Baghdad, and Al-Baridi is driven back first to Wasit and then to Busra.

In the following year Toozoon, the most insolent, cruel and despotic of all the Ameers al-Omra was appointed and soon made his own power absolute, reducing the Khalif to the most abject condition. During these years the city of peace, Baghdad, was a prey to all the horrors of civil war, Turkish brutality and licence of every description that anarchy alone can sanction. It does not seem probable that in all these vicissitudes and revolutions the central Government can have found time or means to organize an expedition to Oman, and I am inclined to think that Yusof bin Wajih was selected and despatched under the orders of Toozoon in Showal, 331 A.H. [A.D. 942]. Toozoon entered Baghdad on the 25th Ramzan, 331 A.H. [A.D. 942], and was then made Ameer al-Omra by Muttaki Billah.

While Yusof bin Wajih, the tyrant Sultan, as he is called, was marching unopposed through Dhahireh to the capital Nezwa, the Imam Rashid bin al-Waleed was making strenuous exertions to collect more adherents, and having succeeded in mustering a sufficient force, moved up in conjunction with his allies, the Carmathians, and took up a position between Manh and Nezwa. As the object of the Imperial general was not so much to crush the Kharejites as to expel the Carmathians and divert the Oman tribute from Al-Hajar to Baghdad, we may take it that the Carmat warriors intended to fight bravely, as they invariably had done, and that the small guard of Ikdaniya, left behind by Abu Thubi, constituted the backbone of the defending army.

The Imam perhaps would have acted more wisely had he placed himself at the head of his troops and led them against the enemy, but he preferred to station himself at the Akbat al-Feeh, a small gorge to the eastward of Manh, and send his force on under the command of Shaikh Abu Mohammed Abdullah bin Abul Madther to the attack.

No particulars of the action have come down to us, but the result was what might have been expected from an encounter between the mixed army, which, organized in haste and uncheered by the presence of the Imam, went forth to battle, and the well equipped and trained Turkish troops of Yusof bin Wajih.

The fight took place at Ghasb, not far from Nezwa, in Dhu'l-Kaadeh, 331 A.H. [A.D. 942], and though a gallant stand was doubtless made by the allies, the contest was an unequal one and they were completely routed. Abu Mohammed was slain and but few either of the Omanis or Carmats survived the field.

With the Battle of Nezwa all resistance ceased. Every tribe, every town, and fort submitted without condition or reserve. The people indeed eagerly yielded their necks to the foreign yoke, while the conqueror, Yusof bin Wajih, wisely restrained his soldiers and seems to have done his best to restore order and tranquillity to the country.

Oman was now once more a province of Baghdad, but our knowledge of it at this period is too superficial to allow us to understand the cause of this tame and abject submission to the Imperial arms.

The Imam Rashid had maintained his post at Al-Feeh until the fugitives of his army, escaping the carnage of the field, apprised him of his disaster, when, quitting the place, he fled down the Wady Semail to take refuge in the mountains and there, friendless and alone, hunted by his enemies and denied an asylum by all, he wandered for some time. At length he repaired to Nezwa and was pardoned by the new Lord of Oman, but was compelled to do personal homage and service at Court.

He died shortly afterwards, shunned, neglected, and scorned by his people.

For a time the Carmathians were expelled from Oman, but they persisted for many years afterwards in their efforts to maintain a footing there and to impose tribute. That scourge of Islam, Hamdan Carmath or Obaidullah, had not long survived his crowning triumph, the conquest of Oman, for his death had taken place in 322 A.H.

[A.D. 933]. He had been succeeded as Grand Dai by Al-Kasaim who, ten years later, was besieged in Lahsa by the Khalif's general, Al-Yezeed, an event which foreshadowed a change of fortune, and in Ramzan of the same year, 332 A.H. [A.D. 943], died Abu Tahir Suliman, the most brilliant warrior and leader the Carmathians produced, and a successor to whom could not easily be found.

Weakened by the fall of the stoutest pillar of the State, the Grand Dai's influence began to decline, and to the same cause we may ascribe the relaxation and gradual paralysis of his power at the extremities of his dominion. But the disappearance of Abu Tahir enabled Yusof bin Wajih to maintain his grasp on Oman for a long time to come.

Yusof bin Wajih, after completing his conquest, was not allowed much leisure to consolidate his power and had not been many weeks in Oman before he received orders from the Ameer al-Omra at Baghdad to undertake an expedition against Al-Baridi. Yusof had, however, by this time so overawed and conciliated the inhabitants that all the resources of the country were already at his disposal and he had little fear of an insurrection. Having collected a large flotilla of ships and transports at Julfar, which was almost invariably made use of by the Arabs in those days as a military port in preference to Sohar or Muscat, owing to the dread they entertained of rocks and currents at Cape Mussendom, he embarked his troops and war material in the last days of the year 331 A.H. [A.D. 942].

The Persian adventurer, Abu Abdulla Ali bin Mohammed, against whom this enterprise was directed, had obtained his cognomen of Al-Baridi from having formerly held the office of Postmaster-General at Baghdad. Not satisfied with the independent rule of Wasit and Busra, which he had torn from the hands of Ibn Raik, he raised his ambitious hopes, on the death of Bajkam, to the office of Ameer al-Omra, and marching on the capital, entered it in triumph, but was soon compelled to evacuate it. Undaunted by reverse, however, and still formidable, he renewed his attack after a few months and was again successful. The Khalif Muttaki Billah sought refuge at Mosul with the Hamdanis, and with their aid Baridi was again expelled and driven back to Wasit. This happened at the close of 330 A.H. [A.D. 941] and in Dhu'l-Kaadeh of the following year, 331 A.H. [A.D. 942], the Turkish Ameer Toozoon, moving down from Baghdad, pushed him back to Busra, which city he had barely occupied when another enemy was at his gates, and he had to meet the assault of the armament from Oman.

Yusof's operations were marked by great vigour. Ibla fell to him at once, and he prosecuted the siege so actively that he nearly got possession of Busra. Baridi would have been lost had he not had recourse to a stratagem. An expert seaman in his service was summoned and promised a reward to carry the hazardous plan into effect. Two boats were filled with dry date leaves and other combustibles and floated down the river at night as fire-ships. Yusof's flotilla moored at night, side by side, across the stream and fastened together to form a bridge of boats and for protection, could not be disengaged in time to avert a catastrophe. The blazing boats struck them full and ignited them, and the flames spreading, the wind soon completed the destruction. The fire attracted crowds from the city, who added to the confusion and disaster of the armada by pillage. The spoil they collected is said to have been immense.

Leaving his ships and stores a prey to the flames and spoilers, Yusof bin Wajih escaped back to Oman with the broken remnant of his force as best he could.

The stability of Yusof's regime in Oman does not appear to have been affected by this untoward event, which took place in Moharram, 332 A.H. [A.D. 943]. He is styled the Lord of Oman by Ibn al-Atheer, and doubtless returned to find the people in the same state of subjection as when he had left them two months before; there is at least no record of any revolt having taken place.

In 332 A.H. [A.D. 943] the Khalif al-Muttaki, finding the insults and tyranny of Toozoon intolerable, quitted Baghdad and repaired to Tekreet, where he began negotiations with the Hamanis. He then proceeded to Ricca and wrote to the Ikhshidite Sultan of Egypt, but these schemes came to nought, and the Khalif deemed it best to effect a reconciliation with Toozoon, who confirmed his promise of loyalty by the most solemn oaths. Al-Muttaki returned to the capital in the beginning of 333 A.H. [A.D. 944] and was met a long distance off by Toozoon, who treated him with the greatest deference and homage and preceded him on foot to the palace, where the treacherous Turk changed his attitude and deposed and degraded him and destroyed his sight by hot irons.

He was succeeded by Mostakfi, the son of Moktafi, who was then forty-three years old and who became as helpless and insignificant a puppet in Toozoon's hands as his predecessor had been.

Toozoon, however, did not long survive his perfidy. Finding his disease incurable, he nominated his secretary and deputy, Abu Jaafar bin Sheerzad, as his successor and apprised the Khalif of the appointment. Toozoon died in Moharram, 334 A.H. [A.D. 945], and Abu Jaafar's assumption of the office of Ameer was submissively confirmed by Mostakfi. But Abu Jaafar's rapacity and insolence were as insufferable as those of Toozoon and his hateful conduct paved the way for a new and more powerful dynasty, which, though hardly less pernicious, was now about to sweep away the detested rule of the Turkish guard.

Abu Jaafar was not only a tyrant but was incompetent to deal with the enemies of the state. Anarchy and distress reigned supreme in the capital. The legions of Ahmed ibn Buwaih, who had marched from Kirman to Ahwaz and had thence been secretly invited by some of the citizens, encompassed the great metropolis, devastated the country around and cut off supplies.

The Khalif and Abu Jaafar fled from their palaces. The Turkish Guard would not strike a blow but abandoned the city and marched off to Mosul. The Khalif then returned and received an envoy from the Buwaih, with whom a concordat was soon arranged.

Ahmed ibn Buwaih then entered Baghdad in state and was invested with a robe of honour and the office of Ameer al-Omra, with the title of Muiz al-Dowla—the Khalif at the same time formally abdicating his temporal authority and conferring full powers as sovereign on Ahmed, whose name was henceforth to be struck on the coinage with the Khalif's and to be associated in the public prayers.

As Muiz al-Dowla was soon about to play a part in the drama of Oman history it may be suitable to add that he was the son of a Dailamite chief. His two elder brothers, Ali and Hasson, who received the titles of Imad al-Dowla and Rukn al-Dowla, had spread their conquest in Persian provinces, and Ahmed had joined them in their attack on Shiraz in 322 A.H. [A.D. 933]. The military success of the Bowides had now culminated in the acquisition of the Imperial capital and the absolute control of the central government.

Al-Mostakfi soon fell under suspicion of intriguing to bring back the Turkish Guard and was seized in open durbar, dragged on foot to the Ameer's house and deposed in Jemadi 2nd, 334 A.H. [A.D. 945]. He was succeeded by Muthi Billah, Mostakfi's rival and enemy, who took a vindictive pleasure in blinding his wretched cousin. Al-Muthi was reduced to an even more humiliated position, if possible, than his predecessors, and for all his Court and household expenses was given an allowance of 100 deenars a day. The spiritual authority and influence of the Khalif alone remained intact.

We have no particulars from any source as to what was happening in Oman during the next few years, but there is reason to suppose that the Carmathians did not tamely acquiesce in their expulsion from the country, and that they made more than one attempt to recover this lost ground and exact some portion of the tribute.

Ibn Haukal, according to de Goeje, informs us that the Oman tribute was among the ordinary revenues, and he narrates an expedition under Abu Ali or Hassan bin Asem, in which the Ikdaniya marched together in a phalanx but were routed by the valour of Yusof bin Wajih's Turkish troops. This attempt probably took place between 332 and 339 A.H. [A.D. 943 and 950]. That the Carmathians did not relax their efforts to retain Oman we learn also from Ibn Khaldoon, whose statement is to the effect that the endeavours of the Grand Dai to keep his hold on Oman were pertinacious and unceasing, and that they did not terminate until the year 375 A.H. [A.D. 985].

In 339 A.H. [A.D. 950] the Carmathians were in the service of Muiz al-Dowla and had by this time perhaps recovered part of their authority in Oman and a share of the tribute from the Turkish Governor Yusof, who was inimical to the Bowides and entirely independent. Indeed, he seems to have omitted no opportunity of striking a blow at the Bowide Dynasty, for about the end of the year 340 A.H. [A.D. 951] he took occasion, when Busra was undefended and a rupture had taken place between Muiz al-Dowla and the Carmathians, to plan and lead an expedition against that city.

Muiz al-Dowla had summoned the Carmathians to join him on his march to Busra, and their refusal to do so had become known to Yusof bin Wajih, who immediately opened negotiations with Lahsa for an alliance. By offering the Grand Dai the temptation of the sack of Busra he induced him to promise his co-operation on the land side, while the Oman fleet was to enter the Shat al-Arab and lead the attack by sea. The news of Yusof's intentions, however, had somehow reached the ears of the Wazeer al-Mohallebi who had been employed in settling the affairs of Ahwaz, and he lost no time in setting his troops in motion and was able to occupy Busra in force before Yusof's fleet was in sight. Meantime Yusof had set sail from Oman early in 341 A.H. [A.D. 952], and in anchoring off Busra learned not only that the Wazeer had stolen a march on him but also that Muiz al-Dowla was rapidly moving down to its support. He was further disappointed to find that the Carmathian contingent, commanded by a brother of Abu Tahir named Abu Yakoob Yusof al-Hassan al-Jenabi,* which had been despatched by the Grand Dai, had been compelled to retire and was unable to co-operate, as had been agreed upon.

Yusof bin Wajih and his Turks were nevertheless indisposed to retreat without an effort to dislodge the Wazeer and carry the city, and for two days the battle raged between them, but it was in vain.

* Abu Yakoob was probably the Grand Dai himself.

Disaster again attended Yusof's arms, and he was put to flight with the loss of his ships and all the army and stores that were in them.

It was probably in the following year (342 A.H. [A.D. 953]) that Nafi, the black slave of Yusof, took revenge on his master for some injury or affront and assassinated him. Ibn al-Atheer puts this event in the year 332 A.H. [A.D. 943], but as Yusof bin Wajih was alive, as we have just seen, in 341 A.H. [A.D. 952], his death could not have taken place until after his return from Busra. Regarding the cause of the tragedy we have no information, but it is recorded that Nafi took possession of the government and remained undisturbed ruler of Oman until the invasion of Muiz al-Dowla.

We have now to pass over ten years, during the lapse of which the chroniclers maintain an unbroken silence on the history of this land, and during which no change in the office of Khalif or in that of Ameer al-Omra took place at Baghdad.

Though we know nothing of the character of their rule, except that it did not partake of the nature of a titular government, as the Omanis wished for nothing so much as to be left alone, and probably groaned heavily under the grinding heel of the Calmuk, it is certain that Nafi and his Turks were still in possession of Oman or of the greater part of it.

In 352 A.H. [A.D. 963] the Ameer Muiz al-Dowla, being tolerably free in Irak, determined to attack his hated enemies, the Turks, in Oman and, with this object, despatched his Wazeer, Abu Mohammed al-Hassan bin Mohammed al-Mohallebi, with a powerful army in Jemadi 2nd. For the transport of this expedition by sea to Julfar a flotilla had been assembled at Busra and was waiting there to embark the troops. In the organization and despatch of this force Al-Mohallebi may have over exerted himself. He started to accompany it from Baghdad but was struck down by illness on the way, and by the time he had reached the coast his condition had become so critical that he was compelled to abandon the enterprise and return to the capital. But the hand of death was upon him, and in Shaaban, two months after he had received the Ameer's commands to lead the Oman expedition, he succumbed to the disease he had contracted. His coffin was carried to Baghdad and interred there. As a recompense for his long and distinguished career in the public service, for he had succeeded to the Wazeerate thirteen years before, his master, Muiz al-Dowla, with true Persian rapacity, immediately confiscated all his wealth and property and disposed of his women and slaves.

Two years elapsed before Muiz al-Dowla found himself sufficiently at leisure to be able to concentrate his energies afresh upon the conquest of Oman, and this time he resolved to take the command in person. We have no data as to the strength of the armament that was embarked at Busra on this occasion, but Muiz al-Dowla had no intention of hazarding a reverse, and took care that the army destined for the invasion should be strong enough to overawe the Turks and put any attempt at resistance out of the question. The landing of the troops appears to have been effected without opposition, and Nafi, perceiving that hostilities would probably result in the extermination of his party, made a virtue of necessity and tendered his submission, which was accepted by Muiz al-Dowla. The names of the Khalif and of Muiz al-Dowla were now ordered to be read in the prayers in the mosques and to be struck on the Omani coinage, and the country became once more a province of the Eastern Khalifate.

What the inhabitants thought of this change in their foreign tyrants, what treatment they experienced, and what attitude they assumed towards them does not transpire, but as there is no mention of the tribes offering any resistance we may conjecture that the transfer and pacification of the country were effected without much violence, rapine, or bloodshed.

Muiz al-Dowla did not remain long in Oman. Nafi had so well ingratiated himself with him and won his confidence to such an extent that he was appointed Governor and Collector of Tribute by the Ameer al-Omra, who, leaving him in charge, embarked his army and sailed for Busra. Nafi had played his game adroitly and had gained his object. He had obtained sovereignty in 342 A.H. [A.D. 953] by the treacherous murder of his master, Yusof, and he had now

(354 A.H. [A.D. 965]) succeeded by cajoling the Ameer in retaining the supreme power over the land on the departure of the invaders. Of pure African descent, Nafi is described as being very black and his character seems to have been of the usual negro type.

Scarcely had the Bowide legions returned to Busra than the Ibadhi tribes, being apprised of the approach of a strong Carmathian force, seized the opportunity to throw off their subjection to the Ameer and proclaim themselves independent. Before Nafi could take any steps to suppress this revolt, the Carmathians were at the frontier and entered the districts of Al-Jow and Dhahireh. Here the Turks, no longer allied with and strengthened by the Sunni tribes, met and opposed them, and endeavoured to bar their further progress. Fighting between these rivals for the mastery took place incessantly, the Carmathians skirmishing during the day and retiring to their camp at night. The Turks fought desperately to retain their hold and the Carmathians pressed on with stubborn and unabated vigour, but the latter, finding at length that they could not advance, wrote to Al-Hajar, informing the Grand Dai of their position and asking for reinforcements. Incensed at the conduct of Nafi and his Turks in so readily accepting the yoke of Muiz al-Dowla, for the Omanis, both Kharejite and Sunni, held the Shaikhs in intense and deeply-rooted detestation, the tribes appear to have held aloof in this contest and not to have assisted either party, as had the Nizar sided with the Turks at this juncture, it is probable that the Carmathians might have been easily routed and expelled. But the nation was united in its hatred to the Shaikh Ameer al-Omra, and with the arrival of fresh reinforcements to the Carmathians, all hope of success on the part of the Turks vanished.

The Carmathians soon penetrated as far as Nezwa and occupied the greater part of the hilly districts. Defeated and broken, Nafi fled the country and sailed for Mesopotamia, to carry the tale of the Carmathian incursion and his own disaster to Muiz al-Dowla.

His conquest of the land being now almost complete, the Commander or the Carmathians or Hajarites, whose army seems to have numbered from 8,000 to 10,000 men, proceeded to make heavy exactions and to oppress the people until the latter lost their temper and took retribution.

On the Commander leaving Oman he appointed one Ali bin Ahmed as Katib or Deputy to control the affairs of the country and collect the tribute. This man appears to have been a tax gatherer of the worst sort, and he is said to have seized a tenth part of the produce from the inhabitants for himself in addition to the usual tribute. His rapacity at length led to an arrangement being come to by which a native of Oman, named Ibn Toghan, was to act as arbitrator or agent for the public. Ibn Toghan was one of the small Kaids in the country, and his appointment caused so much jealousy and ill-will against him among the others that he became fearful of their enmity. He accordingly seized upon eighty of the Kaids, some of whom he massacred and some he caused to be drowned. In Arabia such crimes seldom pass unpunished. The blood feud was taken up by two nephews of one of the murdered men and they soon found an opportunity for revenge at a reception held by him and at which they slew him.

He was succeeded by another Omani named Abdul Wahab ibn Ahmed bin Merwan, who ruled as Katib for a time but was soon intrigued against by the ex-Katib, Ali bin Ahmed, who devised a stratagem to gain over the negro portion of the Carmathian army. These Africans numbered 6,000 and formed the main strength of the force. When issuing the allowances to the troops Ali bin Ahmed paid the Arabs and Persians, or *white* troops as they are described, the full amount, but gave the blacks only half their due, declaring that he did so under the orders of Abdul Wahab. The negroes rose indignantly and steadily refused to receive anything less than the full allowance. Whereupon Ali bin Ahmed promised to pay them in full on condition of their serving him and supporting his claim to replace Abdul Wahab. This innovation, however, was vigorously protested against by the white portion of the Carmathian army, who appear to have always received double the pay given to the negroes. The dispute grew fierce, and as neither party would give way, the final arbiter, the sword, was called in to decide the point.

In the collision that took place the negroes, who were numerically much superior, proved victorious and drove the whites off the field. Abdul Wahab was then dismissed and fled the country, to escape the enmity of Ali bin Ahmed, who now resumed his former position as Katib.

The main result of Ali bin Ahmed's intrigues was the expulsion of the Carmathians from Oman. The people had had sufficient experience of Ali's character as ruler, and had no desire to be ground down again by his excessive greed and rapacity. Taking advantage, therefore, of the disunited and weakened conditions of the Hajarites, the Omanis rose against them, and the nation acting once more in unison, they succeeded in overcoming and expelling them from the country. The occupation of the Carmathians could have lasted only a few months as the interval between the first and second invasions of Muiz al-Dowla occurred between the middle of 354 and 355 A.H. [A.D. 965].

The year 355 A.H. [A.D. 965] had about half expired when the Ameer Muiz al-Dowla raised an army which he destined for the reconquest of Oman. He moved first on Wasit, where he purposed to attack Amran bin Shakeen, who was waiting to oppose him, and on arriving near that city was met by Nafi the Black, whom he received and treated with respect and kindness. By the month of Ramzan he had terminated the war with Amran bin Shakeen and was then able to move on to Ibla near Busra, where he busied himself for some time in collecting ships, men, and material and in organizing the expedition against Oman. The Ameer al-Omra entrusted the command to Abul Faraj Mohammed bin Abbas bin Fasany, who having embarked his army in 100 ships set sail from Busra in the middle of the month of Showal. Sailing down the Persian Gulf he fell in with the army at Siraf, which had been collected in Fars by Adad al-Dowla to reinforce that of his uncle, the Ameer at Baghdad, Muiz al-Dowla. Having consulted what was best to be done, the two commanders determined to join forces and sailed on in company to Julfar, where they cast anchor on the 9th day of Dhu'l-Hijrah, the last month of the year 355 A.H. [A.D. 965].

As the result showed, the Omanis had been ill-advised in

quarrelling with and expelling the Carmathians before they were done with Muiz al-Dowla, as, allied with the valiant Hajarites, the tribes might perhaps have successfully resisted the combined Bowide armies and driven them back into the sea. But, unsupported, they were powerless to offer effective opposition, and soon found themselves prostrate before a ruthless enemy.

Whether the Omanis did in fact make any effort to defend themselves we are not told, but Abul Faraj had no sooner disembarked his troops and made good his position than he began an indiscriminate massacre of the inhabitants, the slaughter of whom was terrible—fire and blood, lust and rapine again raged through the land, and Oman was left writhing in indescribable misery by these savage barbarians. But we learn that eighty-nine Omani ships were destroyed and that the Khutba was again ordered to be read in the name of Muiz al-Dowla.

In the following year, 356 A.H. [A.D. 966] the General, Abul Faraj Mohammed bin Abbas, who was engaged in settling the affairs of Oman, received news that the Ameer al-Omra Muiz al-Dowla had died in the month of Rabi 13th; and handing over charge of affairs to the Nawab Adad al-Dowla he hastily prepared for departure and returned to the capital.

Muiz al-Dowla had been Ameer for twenty-two years when he died in 356 A.H. [A.D. 966]. He was a man of strong character and abilities and was indeed, next to Saiful Dowla al-Hamadani, the greatest man of his age in the Moslem Empire; he was probably the most exalted personage who ever visited Oman. He was succeeded as Ameer by his son Bakhtiyar, who took the title of Izz al-Dowla, but the latter was of inferior calibre to his father, and it was not long before jealousies and rivalries tore the Bowide family to pieces and created such disorder that the effect of them was felt even in the remote province of Oman.

No sooner had Abul Faraj quitted the scene of his triumph than the Nawab Adad al-Dowla appears to have also taken his departure for Kirman, leaving his Wazeer Abul Kasim al-Mathhar bin Mohammed in charge of the Persian troops, while the supreme command devolved on the Naib of Abul Faraj, named Omar bin Nahban al-Tai, who ruled the country for six years in the names of the Khalif and the Ameer al-Omra. This position of affairs, however, at length drew the attention of Adad al-Dowla, who seeing his cousin Izz al-Dowla losing his power, considered that Oman should belong to himself, and claimed it as part of his own territories.

At this juncture an event occurred which brought the whole question to an issue and precipitated the action of Adad al-Dowla in forcibly annexing the country.

The Dailamite army of occupation in Oman under the Naib Omar bin Nahban al-Tai was composed, as the Imperial armies always were at that time, to a very large extent of negroes, originally imported as slaves from the East Coast of Africa, and spoken of by the Arab historians as Zenj. In 362 A.H. [A.D. 972] this body, probably numbering some thousands, mutinied and were joined by several divisions of the White or Dailamite troops. They chose as their leader a man named Al-Hellaj and under his guidance began their revolt by the murder of their Governor, the Naib Omar, whose death placed the entire country at their disposal and mercy.

The news of this revolt soon reached Irak, but Izz al-Dowla, the Ameer, was, as the mutineers had doubtless well calculated, too much engaged in securing his own position to be able to pay any attention to this province.

The Prince of Fars, Adad al-Dowla Abu Sharja Khusra, however, viewed matters differently. He had long been watching his opportunity to invade and conquer Oman, and he had no sooner received intelligence of the outbreak among the Ameer's troops and the anarchy that had followed than he commenced at once to organize an expedition to be despatched thither.

Over this force he placed Abul Harab Tughon in command, and having provided transports for their embarkation at Siraf, directed Abul Harab to cross the Persian Gulf and land the army at Julfar. Having disembarked his troops on the pirate coast, Abul Harab sent the flotilla round Cape Mussendom to Sohar to attack the Imperial fleet there, which was in the hands of the mutineers.

The Zenj and the Dailamites, on hearing of the advent of the Persians, moved down at once from the interior to meet the enemy, and a great battle ensued in which the Zenj were routed and dispersed with great slaughter. About the same time the two fleets engaged off Sohar, the victory in this case also remaining with the Persians. After the fight with the Zenj, which had probably taken place near Sohar, Abul Harab put the people of that city to the sword and gave it over to his soldiers to sack, an event which is also alluded to by Ibn al-Mojawir.

After their defeat the mutineers retired up the Wady Jezza, along which they were pursued for two days as far as Beraimi by Abul Harab. Here the dispirited but still formidable Zenj made a stand, and another desperate conflict occurred, the result, as before, being a victory for the Persians over the mutineers, who were now finally broken and cut to pieces. A large number of prisoners was taken by Abul Harab, who by this campaign had annexed Oman to the dominions of his master, Adad al-Dowla, Sovereign of Fars.

The destruction and dispersion of this formidable band of lawless banditti, the Dailamite mutineers, who had been a curse and terror to the land, were hailed with joy by the inhabitants, who had suffered much from their brutal violence and depredation.

But the invading host under Abul Harab, which had rid them of the pest, brought still greater evils in its train, for its coming was dictated by the lust of conquest and subjugation, not inspired by the desire for the deliverance of the people from oppression. It is therefore not surprising to learn that a national movement now commenced against their new oppressors, whose Shihr doctrines were condemned and abhorred by all parties, ranks, and sects alike in Oman.

Among the Ibadhis especially great enthusiasm appears to have prevailed. They assembled at Nezwa and elected as their Imam and General the Shaikh Ward bin Ziyad, appointing as second in command the Shaikh Hafs bin Rashid. Such numbers flocked to the Imam's standard that the national force was soon able to take the field successfully and to hurl the invaders back to the coast or even to expel them from the land altogether.

We have no particulars of this campaign as the orthodox historians are not fond of chronicling Kharejite victories, and the local annalists, as said before, are silent on this period of Oman history.

The tribes had made a gallant struggle for freedom and had for a time recovered their independence. But they had not yet attained their final deliverance; indeed, their success, as we shall see, only resulted in bringing about a fresh inroad of their barbarian tyrants and a renewal of the horrors and humiliations of conquest.

It seems to have been early in the year 363 A.H. [A.D. 973] when tidings reached Adad al-Dowla, Malik of Fars, of the rising against his authority in Oman and the disasters to his troops at the hands of the Kharejite inhabitants. He lost no time in organizing a strong body of troops to reinforce his discomfited army in Oman and embarked them in transports under the chief command of his Wazeer, Abul Kasim al-Mathar bin Mohammed bin Abdulla. The fleet sailed first to Khor Fakan, a town in the Shemal of Oman, which was attacked and carried with a loss to its inhabitants of many killed and many prisoners.

At Sohar, the Wazeer re-embarked his army and sailed on to Dhamar below Kuriyat, which is about 200 miles from Sohar, and is described as four days' journey. At this part of the coast there is a small maritime plain at the exit of the Devil's Gap or Wady Thaika, and here the national force of Oman was concentrated under the two Imams Ward and Hafs. The Wazeer Abul Kasim again disembarked his troops and a great battle was fought between the contending armies, in which the Omanis were completely worsted and put to flight. The carnage is described as terrible and many of the Omani shaikhs were taken prisoners. This affair practically decided the fate of the country below the hills and gave the Persians an immense advantage and a base of operations for prosecuting the campaign. The Imams Ward and Hafs, with the remainder of their following, retired up the Wady Tyeen to Nezwa, whither they were pursued by the Wazeer in the month of Rabi 1st, 363 A.H. [A.D. 973]. Quitting his capital on the approach of his enemies, the Imam Ward made another stand and gave battle in the plain beyond. But the same disastrous result happened as before—the Wazeer Abul Kasim al-Mathar was again victorious and routed the Omanis after a sanguinary contest. The Imam Ward bin Ziyad was killed, while Hafs bin Rashid succeeded in effecting his escape to the coast, from whence he sailed for the Yemen, where he became a schoolmaster.

Undaunted by their successive defeats at Kuriyat and Nezwa, the Omanis, probably on this occasion mostly Beni Riyam, again mustered in strength near Bahila at a wide plain known as Shoraf* near the Jebel Akhdar and prepared to receive the onslaught of the Persians.

Ibn al-Atheer mentions the national army at about 10,000, but this is perhaps an over estimate.

The Persians were certainly less numerous, but elated with the tide of victory, and besides being better armed, offered a more solid formation to their antagonists, and made a resistless attack on the Beni Ryam and completely routed them.

This ended the campaign. The Wazeer al-Mathhar met with no further obstacle to his progress and soon brought the whole land under subjection to the Prince of Fars, not a single district, it is said, remaining unsubdued.

The pacification and settlement of the country, the appointment of prefects and the disposition of the troops composing the garrison, occupied the attention of the Wazeer al-Mathhar bin Abdulla until he was recalled to Kirman by Adad al-Dowla in the following year 364 A.H. [A.D. 974].

While these events were transpiring in Oman, changes were taking place in the Central Government at Baghdad, where the Khalif al-Mutti, having been struck with paralysis, abdicated the throne in favour of his son, Al-Tai Billah, in Dhu'l-Kaadeh, 363 A.H. [A.D. 973], after a reign of twenty-nine years.

* Shoraf is ten hours north of Nezwa near the Akaba Shash above the Wady Beni Khaross and on the plateau of the mountain.

The post of Ameer al-Omra was also about to change hands, owing to the inability of Izz al-Dowla to control events. Being at variance with his Chamberlain, Sabuktegin, who had sought the aid of the Turks, he was compelled to quit the capital and retire to Wasit. Hither Sabuktegin, taking the Khalif al-Tai Billah in his train, followed him, and having the superiority drove the Ameer to Ahwaz in Persian Irak. But here the tide of fortune changed, for Izz al-Dowla was soon joined by his cousin, Adad al-Dowla, Malik of Fars, to whom he had applied for help, and the united forces, now too formidable to be opposed, marched to Baghdad, where Izz al-Dowla was reinstated by the pliant Khalif in his former post.

The campaign, however, had served to teach Adad al-Dowla his own power, and he began to covet the proud position of his cousin as absolute ruler in the City of Peace, a position which so far outshone his own humble Court at Shiraz. Reft asunder by mutual distrust and jealousy war soon followed. The Malik of Fars was the aggressor and in 366 A.H. [A.D. 976] defeated Izz al-Dowla, who fled to Syria, the following year witnessing the usurpation by Adad al-Dowla of the post of Ameer al-Omra of the Khalif's empire. This prince was the greatest of the Bowides and perhaps the most powerful and splendid king of his time in Asia. He is extolled for his wise administration and munificence, and had he reigned longer might have done something to prop up the crumbling empire.

Doubtless Oman participated in the benefits of his sway, but the Persian Governor, Ustad Hormuz, he set over the land appears to have been chiefly intent on enriching himself at the expense of the people.

When Adad al-Dowla died in 372 A.H. [A.D. 982] at the age of forty-seven his dominions were partitioned among his sons, Oman falling to the lot of the Malik of Fars, Sharaf al-Dowla Abul Fowaris Sheerzaid, who confirmed his father's governor, the Ustad Hormuz, in his post. The bitter animosities and rivalries, however, that now raged among the brothers and distracted all the territories of the Bowides, were soon felt in this distant province. In 374 A.H. [A.D.

984] the second brother, Samsam al-Dowla Abu Kaleejar Marzban, intrigued for the possession of Oman and succeeded in gaining over the Governor, Ustad Hormuz, and the garrison, who appear to have perfidiously deserted their master, Sharaf al-Dowla, without striking a blow. The usurper's triumph, however, was short lived, for Sharaf al-Dowla, directly the news reached him, despatched a strong force to Oman, which routed Ustad Hormuz and speedily restored Oman to its former master, Sharaf al-Dowla. Ustad Hormuz was taken prisoner and thrown into one of the fortresses, where he probably met his death, after being relieved of the great stores of ill-gotten wealth he had acquired during his long tenure of office in Oman.

Whether Samsam al-Dowla obtained possession of Oman on the death of Sharaf al-Dowla in 379 A.H. [A.D. 989] we do not know.

Although we have had no mention of them for a long time, the Carmathians, according to Ibn Khaldoon, held a precarious position in Oman until the year 375 A.H. [A.D. 985], after which year they came no more, and indeed soon disappeared from the stage of history. Their last stronghold in Oman was, we may safely conjecture, at Al-Beraimi.

The history of the Bowide Dynasty is so confused, intricate, and conflicting that it is difficult to say to which prince Oman belonged from 379–388 A.H. [A.D. 989–998]. In the former year Sharaf al-Dowla had been succeeded as Ameer al-Omra at Baghdad by his younger brother, Boha al-Dowla Abu Nasr Firooz, and the latter was at war with his brother, Samsam al-Dowla of Fars, and had just sustained a severe defeat at the hands of Ustad Hormuz's son, Abu Ali, when Samsam al-Dowla was assassinated at Shiraz at the hands of his nephew in 388 A.H. [A.D. 998].

Boha al-Dowla then added Fars to his former possessions, and in 390 A.H. [A.D. 999] appointed Abu Mohammed bin Mukrim to rule over Oman. Of this person's antecedents we may glean something from Ibn al-Atheer, but of the character of his rule in Oman we have no information, except that it appears to have been of a very tolerant nature, as we read in Ross's *Annals of Oman* of an Imam named Khalil bin Shathan, elected by the Ibadhis (in his reign) in the beginning of the fifth century. That this Imam exercised merely spiritual and not temporal powers we may take for granted, but considering the religious antagonism between the Shihrs and Ibadhis at that period, the circumstance is a noteworthy one.

In 401 A.H. [A.D. 1010] we learn that the Khalif Kadir Billah, who had succeeded Al-Tai Billah in 381 A.H. [A.D. 991] sent the Kadhi Abu Bekr al-Bakalain to the Ameer al-Omra Boha al-Dowla to warn him that the Alyites and Abbasides were fighting with each other from Koofa to Baghdad. The services rendered by the Kadhi at this period were rewarded by his being appointed chief Kadhi for Oman and the East Coast of Africa.

Boha al-Dowla, Ameer al-Omra, died in the year 403 A.H. [1012 A.D.] and was succeeded by his eldest son, Sultan al-Dowla Abu-Shujra, in whose reign the Governorship of Oman passed from Abu Mohammed bin Mukrim to his son, Abul Kasim, who retained for many years the control of this province.

Sultan al-Dowla died at Shiraz in the year 415 A.H. [A.D. 1024] and the succession to his throne was disputed by his brother and his son.

The latter, Imad al-Din Abul Kaleejar Morzaban, then quite a youth, was residing at Ahwaz and had been summoned at once by the late ruler of Oman, Abu Mohammed, to come and take his father's place. But he was not ready. His uncle, on the contrary, Kawam al-Dowla Abul Fowaris, Malik of Kirman, was prepared for the event and determined to profit by it. He immediately marched to Shiraz, occupied it and took up the reins of Government unopposed. Abu Mohammed endeavoured to escape to Oman but was seized and put to death by Kawam al-Dowla. Abul Kasim, on hearing of his father's death, at once declared against Kawam al-Dowla and offered the resources of Oman to Abul Kaleejar, who accepted them. About a year later, Abul Kaleejar, having gathered his supporters and organized his army, took the field against his uncle, Abul Fowaris, whom he utterly routed and drove back to Kirman; he then took possession of the Government of Fars.

The liberal and praiseworthy Abul Kasim Ali bin Hoosain bin Makrim, Lord of Oman, died in the year 428 A.H. [A.D. 1036] and was succeeded by his eldest son, Abul Jaish bin Mukrin.

Where the Bowide Governors fixed their residence and held their Court is not mentioned, but I have reason to think it was at Rostak. Abul Kasim's commandant of troops was a man named Ali bin Hattal, and he had a Naib or deputy stationed at Nezwa, named Al-Murtadha.

Abul Jaish appears to have been of feeble constitution and his reign was short, but it was not uneventful. He had three brothers, viz., Al-Mohathib, Abu Mohammed, and another who at this time was an infant.

The second, Al-Mohathib, took offence at the unbecoming marks of consideration and favour heaped on the General, Ali bin Hattal, by Abul Jaish, who used to rise from his seat on his approach and show other signs of respect, and he (Al-Mohathib) made known his displeasure by openly reviling and disparaging Ali bin Hattal. The wily general soon heard of this and conceived a scheme to bring about Al-Mohathib's ruin. He invited him to a feast, treated him with mock servility and courtesy and plied him with wine until he had lost the power of judgment. Ali then proposed that they should join in a revolt against Abul Jaish, whom Ali represented as being feeble and unfit to rule, and that after he had been deposed, Al-Mohathib should reign in his place. Al-Mohathib, too dizzy from drink to perceive the snare, agreed to the plan and gave Ali a letter authorizing him to act, and conferring dignities and honours on him in the event of success. The next morning Ali bin Hattal went straight to Abul Jaish, informed him that his brother was hatching a conspiracy against him, revealed the sham plot and exhibited Al-Mohathib's letter. Abul Jaish was furious; he at once had Al-Mohathib arrested and bound, and, with the usual precipitation and recklessness of Oriental despots, ordered him to be strangled. Ali bin Hattal obtained his revenge.

This event happened in 431 A.H. [A.D. 1039], and a few months later in the same year Abul Jaish died.

Ali bin Hattal found himself at this moment master of the position, and conceived a project for further aggrandizing himself.

He resolved to put up Abul Kasim's third son, Abu Mohammed, as ruler, to keep him in tutelage as long as suited him, and then having disposed of him in some way, to assume the lordship of Oman himself.

The scheme, however, was thwarted by the boy's mother, who refused to entrust her son in Ali bin Hattal's hands, intimating to him that he might govern the country if he chose to take the responsibility, and that her son, Abu Mohammed, would not attempt to interfere in the affairs of State, but that he was too young to leave her.

If Ali bin Hattal had been a sagacious and prudent man it is probable that he might have retained power in his hands for a considerable time, but he had no sooner tasted the sweets of rule than he began to abuse it, oppressing the people, and seizing the property of the traders.

It was not long before the news of what was going on in Oman, and the attitude of Ali bin Hattal towards the sons of Abul Kasim, reached the Court at Shiraz and astounded Abul Kaleejar and his Wazeer. Prompt chastisement of Ali's insolence and presumption was decided on. The Naib Al-Mustadha was written to by Al-Adil Abu Mansoor bin Mafanneh to undertake operations against Ali bin Hattal, and was promised that an army would be organised and despatched from Busra to his assistance. The people of Oman responded with alacrity to Al-Mustadha's summons to them to join him, as they had had enough of Ali bin Hattal's tyranny, and, with the aid of the Dailamite troops sent him, the Naib soon recovered possession of the greater part of the country, but for the rest Ali bin Hattal appears to have retained his hold over his soldiers, and having occupied a strong defensive position to have held the Naib in check.

Al-Mustadha then had recourse to assassination, which was accomplished with the aid of a slave who had formerly belonged to Ibn Makrim, but had been appropriated by Ali bin Hattal, and with the death of this usurper tranquillity was restored.

As soon as Al-Adil Abu Mansoor heard that Ali was dead and that the danger had passed, he set out for Oman, and having obtained the young chief, Abu Mohammed bin Abul Kasim bin Mukrim, from his mother, confirmed him as Governor of Oman in the year 431 A.H. [A.D. 1039].

The rule of Abu Mohammed did not please the Omanis; being inexperienced, he no doubt entrusted all affairs to his Naibs and officials, who, like all Persians of that class, were rapacious, unjust, and extortionate.

Two years had not elapsed before the country was in revolt, and so serious was the complexion of affairs that the King of Fars, Abul Kaleejar, was forced to proceed thither himself.

He embarked with an army at some port in Fars and sailed to Sohar, where he landed his troops and took possession of it. How far he advanced or how long it took him to reduce his rebellious province we are not told. We only know that he succeeded in subduing it, and then, having appointed his own son Governor, re-embarked his soldiers and returned to Shiraz.*

But the end of the Persian occupation of Oman was now approaching, and the Bowide Dynasty was about to give place to one far mighty and more durable—that of the Turkish Seljooks. The increasing feebleness and degeneracy of the Dailamites in Oman encouraged insurrection. The last attempt had had only a temporary success; the next effort to rid the land of the hated Shihr was equally futile.

The Ameer Imad al-Din Abu Kaleejar Marzaban, Malik of Fars, had died at Shiraz, and had been succeeded by Abu Nasr Khusra Firooz Raheem, the last of his line, in 440 A.H. [A.D. 1048]. The son of Abu Kaleejar, the Ameer Abu Modhaffar, was reigning at Nezwa, where, in 442 A.H. [A.D. 1050], six years before the extinction of the dynasty, the storm of rebellion drove him from his throne and put an end to the Persian sovereignty. The proximate cause of the revolution appears to have been the harsh and oppressive conduct

* It is probable that Abu Mohammed was killed during this rising as we hear no more of him.

of a negro slave, to whom his master, Abu Modhaffar, had entrusted the affairs of state, and who practically controlled and ruled the whole country. His exactions and cruelty created discontent, and discontent grew into disaffection. The hour prôduced the man—Shaikh Rashid bin Saeed was the prototype of the Seyyid Ahmed bin Saeed —the founder of the Al-bu Saeedi dynasty. A man of strong and turbulent disposition, he had been foremost since the time of Abul Kasim bin Mukrim in combating the Persian oppressor, in trying to redress wrongs and shield the weak. Having succeeded in raising the tribes and collecting a numerous following, Shaikh Rashid made a hostile movement on Nezwa, and Abu Modhaffar, having advanced with his troops to meet him, they joined battle, in which the Kharejites were defeated and dispersed.*

Undaunted by this reverse, the tribes again assembled in force, and this time determined to strike a final blow for freedom. Despite the ill success of his first attack, the Arabs retained confidence in Rashid as a leader, and, united in a national cause, mustered again at his call from all quarters. In the second battle Shaikh Rashid was victorious and completely routed the Dailamites. He slew the slave of the Ameer who had roused the people's vengeance, and carried Abu Modhaffar himself a captive to the mountains. Such of the Dailamites who escaped the carnage of the field were soon made prisoners and shared the fate of their Ameer. Rashid bin Saeed now took possession of the country and rooted out the Dailamite officials and tax-gatherers in all directions. He razed the palace of the Bowide Ameers to the ground, saying it had been a house for the ruination of the people and for the degradation of justice rather than a palace. It is averred by Ibn al-Atheer that Rashid bin Saeed became so arrogant after his success that he styled himself Rashid Billah, that he caused the prayers to be read in his own name, that he took to wearing wool, and that he built a house for himself in the form of a mosque. But the great historian of the middle ages, Ibn al-Atheer, who has rescued Rashid's deeds from oblivion, was

* This rebellion was Rashid bin Saeed's first failure.

an orthodox Sunni, holding schismatics and heretics in abhorrence, and exhibits throughout a strong bias against the Omanis.

We learn from Ross's *Annals of Oman* that Rashid bin Saeed was elected Imam by the people, and that he died in Moharram, 445 A.H. [A.D. 1053]. His election to the Imamate probably succeeded the expulsion of the tyrants, and was the expression of the people's gratitude for his services in having liberated the land from a foreign yoke. The annalist, without recording his exploits, quotes a verse which testifies to and appreciates the high character of Rashid bin Saeed as a ruler.

From the Persian work of Mohammed Ibrahim we are led to infer that the Dailamites did not accept their defeat and expulsion by Rashid bin Saeed as terminating their grasp on Oman, as a fresh army was despatched by the Malik of Fars to reconquer Oman and avenge the death of Abu Modhaffar. This expedition was commanded by Shahriyar bin Tafeel, and must have been successful in reducing the country in whole, or in part, as Shahriyar was in power at the time of the Seljookian Conquest. It is quite possible that the Imam Rashid may have met his death in battle during Shahriyar's invasion or at his hands after victory.

Although seventy-five years had elapsed since their final evacuation of Oman, the amicable relations which continued to subsist between the Carmathians and the Ibadhis were illustrated by an event which occurred about the year 450 A.H. [A.D. 1058].

A serious revolt having occurred in the Island of Awal against the impost of an extraordinary tax by the Government at Lahsa, the Carmathian Wazeer, then Abu Abdulla Sinbar, despatched one of his sons to Oman to entreat assistance in arms and money from the Ibadhi tribes. The appeal was generously responded to, and the Wazeer's son quitted Oman with 5,000 deenars and 3,000 spears as a contribution to the military resources at Lahsa. The gift, however, did not reach its destination for the party was intercepted on the way by the insurgents, who killed the Wazeer's son and forty of his comrades, and plundered their baggage.

The horizon of Baghdad had been for a long time darkening.

Under the intolerable and impotent rule of the Bowides, the Khalif's provinces had passed into other hands, anarchy reigned supreme, and the once world-wide Arab Empire had so dwindled and sunk into so low a condition of impoverishment, degradation, and decrepitude that it was at death's door when, in 447 A.H. [A.D. 1055] the son of the conquering Seljook, Toghrul Bey, whose aid had been implored by the Khalif Kasin Bi-Amr-Allah, entered the capital, and having removed the Ameer al-Omra Abu Nasir, took the Government into his firm grasp and inspired the empire with renewed life, vigour, and influence. The dismembered provinces were once more brought together, order and prosperity took the place of tumult and decay, and though Toghrul Bey's Turkomans were savage and bloodthirsty in war, the benefits of his rule far outweighed the drawbacks.

Oman was one of the last provinces to be trodden by the iron heel of the Turk, and it is only recently that the particulars of this invasion have been brought to light by Professor Houtsma.

Ibn al-Mojawir had indeed already informed us in his "Tareekh al-Mustabsir" that, as he learnt from Abu Bekr al-Basrawi, Oman belonged first to the Kings of Kirman of the Seljook Dynasty, that it was then ruled by the Ghuz, and that subsequently Sohar became deserted and was destroyed by the Arabs. And this is still, I believe, the only indication we possess of the Ghuz occupation.

We find that the Seljooks of Kirman held sway there from 433 or 448 to 583 A.H. [A.D. 1041 or 1056 to 1187], that Malik Deenar succeeded to them in power, and that from 621–766 A.H. [A.D. 1224–1364] the Ghuz family of Kara Katayans held possession of Kirman.

These Turkish princes undoubtedly held Oman in subjection during a considerable part of the period left blank by the native annalist, and we may fairly ascribe to the ruthless excesses committed by the savage Turkomans, and the humiliation endured by the people, the cause of his silence, as with Arab pride he disdained to soil the page of history with a recital of their misfortunes.

The first of the Seljook race established in the Government of

To face p. 129.

PART OF THE FORT AT BAHILA.

[See p 203]

Kirman was Kadir Bey or Kaward (the Wolf), the son of Chagar Bey, and grandson of Seljook. He was appointed Governor of Kirman by the authority of his uncle, Toghrul Bey, and ruled it in conjunction with the Bowide prince, Abu Mansoor Foolad, Sultan from 433–448 A.H. [A.D. 1041–1056], when Ab-Mansoor died and Kaward assumed the control of the State. In 455 A.H. [A.D. 1063] he acquired possession of the province of Fars, and in 456 A.H. [A.D. 1063] the further province of Oman.

In 456 A.H. [A.D. 1063], and subsequent to the conquest and spoliation of Garmseer in Fars, Kaward turned his attention, as mentioned above, to Oman, which he understood to be wealthy, filled with treasures of every kind and, withal, defenceless.

He anticipated no difficulty in conquering it and apprehended no danger except from the sea, to which he was a stranger.

He accordingly ordered the Ameer of Hormuz (the city so named being then on the mainland and not on the island) to collect ships and boats and to make all needful arrangements for the embarkation of the troops and their transportation to Oman. The Persian Ameer did as he was bid; the flotilla was prepared, and Kaward boldly trusting himself to the sea, which he probably saw for the first time in his life, set sail for the Oman coast.

The invasion appears to have been entirely unforeseen, either by the Dailamite Governor and garrison or by the inhabitants, and the appearance of the flotilla, followed by the disembarkation of the expeditionary force, consequently took the Omanis completely by surprise. There was no time to muster forces or to organize resistance, and the Ameer Shahriyar bin Tafeel, or as he is also called Tazeek, is said to have had no resource but to conceal himself. The Seljooks spread rapidly over the land, meeting with no opposition, and indiscriminate massacre, enslavement of women and children, fire and rapine everywhere marked the trail of the conquerors. Kaward took undisputed possession of and occupied the country; he then proclaimed himself the righteous and just king, ordered the Khutba to be read, and coins to be struck in his own name, and then set to work to carry out the main object of his enterprise—the plunder of the people.

Meanwhile search was being made for the missing Ameer, and it was made known that his life would be spared if he surrendered. A long hunt took place and Shahriyar was at length found hidden in an oven. On Shahriyar being brought into his presence, Kaward received him with reproaches and treated him with indignity, but subsequently changed his attitude and, according to the Persian chronicler, promised to reinstate him in the governorship of the country under the proviso that a Seljook official should reside at his court in the capacity of political agent. The submission and vassalage of the Dailamites and Omanis having thus been accepted by the victor, Shahriyar (or Tazeek) begged that the life of his young children, who had apparently been seized as hostages on the first advance of the invaders, might be spared, and this seems to have been conceded. But Tazeek was compelled to disgorge the whole of the wealth and treasure he had accumulated during his vice-royalty. During their occupation of the country the main energies of the Seljooks had been employed in sacking and ransacking the towns and villages, and when the plunder of the inhabitants had been focussed at the port of embarkation, Kaward and his Turkomans quitted Oman and sailed for Garmseer.

We have seen that within a period of about 200 years there had been no less than ten successive waves of invasion and incursion by land and sea, with as many changes of alien dominion over this unhappy land. From the time of the conquest by the Imperial legions under Bin Noor, with his relentless persecution of the schismatics, Oman had been swept by an unbroken series of invaders—Arabs, Turks, Persians, Carmathians, Dailamites and Turkomans—who, one and all, incited by lust of power and pillage, and unprovoked by any act of aggression, had wantonly slain the inhabitants, enslaved their women, and robbed their property. Few countries have been so vilely treated by their neighbours; fewer still have shown such indomitable pride under oppression, such valour, and such an elastic power of recuperation. History can hardly exhibit anything more sad than the spectacle of this proud and noble race overcome and trampled upon by the brutal hordes of barbarians of Central Asia.

Kaward, Prince of Kirman, the Sultan Adhdad al-Din Alp Arslan, who had succeeded Toghrul Bey in 455 A.H. [A.D. 1063], and the Khalif Bi-amr-allah, were contemporaries of Harold and William the Conqueror of England, and the Seljook invasion of Oman only antedated by a couple of years one of the most momentous events in English history, the Norman Conquest.

Alp Arslan, the Sultan of Baghdad, was killed in 465 A.H. [A.D. 1072]. He had, previously to his death, set aside his eldest son from the succession and had appointed his second son, Jelal al-Din Abul Fath, who followed him on the throne under the title of Malik Shah. This prince had no sooner assumed the purple than troubles broke out in many parts of his vast dominions, and among others in Kirman, where Kaward had at once revolted and proclaimed himself independent. Malik Shah took the field against him without delay, and in one of the bloodiest battles ever fought in Persia, defeated him and took him prisoner. Kaward was put to death by poison or the bowstring immediately afterwards, and for two years the provinces of Fars and Kirman were administered by Malik Shah's lieutenants.

In 467 A.H. [A.D. 1074], however, Malik Shah pardoned Kaward's son, Sultan Shah, and conferred on him the Government of Kirman with its dependency Oman, which he governed probably in the same way as his father had done, with a resident Seljook Ameer at the capital to control events and receive the revenue.

In the same year (467 A.H. [A.D. 1074]) the Khalif Kamin Bi-amr-allah died at Baghdad after a long reign of forty-five years, and was followed by his grandson, Moktadi Bi-amr-allah, who, with the tacit permission of Malik Shah, began to exert some of the prerogatives of the throne, and attempted to reform the corrupt administration of justice at Baghdad.

Oman, or part of it, appears to have continued under the peaceable subjection of the Seljooks of Kirman during the subsequent reigns of Toorun Shah (477–489 A.H. [A.D. 1084–1095]), and Iran Shah (489–494 A.H. [A.D. 1095–1100]). But we begin to hear of troubles in the time of his successor, Arslan Shah bin Kirman Shah, who enjoyed a long reign of forty-two years, as we read in the *Kamil* that in the year 495 A.H. [A.D. 1101], the Ameer Abu Saeed Mohammed bin Madhar bin Mahwood had taken possession of that half of Oman which had become a dependency of Busra. Indeed, at this time Islam was in peril from without and within. The great Seljooks had passed away, and the Empire had now again become one vast arena of internecine strife. While already in 488 A.H. [A.D. 1095], Pope Urban, instigated by Peter Gautier, had started the first crusade and Godfrey de Bouillon had entered the Holy Land.

That the Seljook hold on Oman had by this time become precarious, and that the tribes had to some extent regained their independence, is to be inferred from the mention by the local annalist at this period of several Imams, of whose reigns, however, no details are given. The first Imam named in Ross's *Annals* is Mohammed bin Habees, who was elected in 510 A.H. [A.D. 1116]. The next may have been Rashid bin Ali, who was appointed in 513 A.H. [A.D. 1119], but as we also find the dates 446 and 476 A.H. [A.D. 1054 and 1083] given to him, his position in the list becomes uncertain and confused. Another Imam was Moosa bin Jabir al-Muali bin Moosa bin Nejad, who died in 549 A.H. [A.D. 1154]. After whom probably came the Imam Mohammed bin Khanbash, who died in 557 A.H. [A.D. 1161]. The death of this Prince is said to have occasioned greater sufferings to the people of Oman than that of any previous Imam, but we have no clue to the troubles in Oman at that period.

We must now go back a little to the real sovereigns of Oman, the Seljooks of Kirman. Arslan Shah had died in 536 A.H. [A.D. 1141], and had been succeeded by Malik Mogheth al-Din Mohammed, who, being a Turk and too fond to rule alone, could not endure a brother near the throne, and began his reign after the amicable fashion of his race, by blinding or murdering his brethren, one of whom, however, Seljook Shah, was fortunate enough to escape and to find a refuge in Oman.

Here he appears to have been well received by the garrison, and perhaps also by the people, who were not sorry to give him their allegiance, and thus to break away from the grinding tyranny of the Kirman Government. It is certain, at all events, that the

Kirman Agent thenceforward ceased to reside at Nezwa and control the Government.

Malik Mogheth al-Din died in 551 A.H. [A.D. 1156], after a reign of fourteen years. There is no record of any attempt on his part to recover Oman from his brother, Seljook Shah, and we may conjecture that his sway over Oman terminated about the year 538 A.H. [A.D. 1143], which gives a period of eighty-two years to the predominance of the Kawardian Dynasty of Kirman over Oman.

What took place on the death of Seljook Shah, and in what year this event took place, are matters that have passed into oblivion, but we may assume that it preceded that of Shaikh Mohammed bin Khanbash, who then took up the control of affairs.

The last of the Kawardian Princes—Sultan Mohammed Shah—was expelled from Kirman in 583 A.H. [A.D. 1187] by Malik Deenar. This chieftain made himself absolute master of that country and ruled it; he was succeeded by Abul Kasim al-Zuzeny.

In Oman, Mohammed bin Khanbash was succeeded by his son, Hafs bin Mohammed, and we then come to the rule of the Nebhani, of which we are afforded very little information. Of the origin and rise of this family the annalists relate nothing, and the names and dates of the Maliks or Chiefs are almost entirely wanting. It appears, however, that the authority of the Nebhanis was strongest in Al-Dhahireh, and did not extend over all Oman, and that their chiefs were called Maliks, who possessed temporal power only.

Oman, however, was not independent at this time, but had passed from the subjugation of the Seljooks, after a short interval, to that of the Ghuz of Kirman. These Ghuz were a predatory horde of Turkomans, who, under their leader, Boraik Hajab, had, in 619 A.H. [A.D. 1222], invaded Kirman and taken it from Abul Kasim al-Zuzeny, and soon after subdued Oman, which probably remained under their sway till about 766 A.H. [A.D. 1364].

In 656 A.H. [A.D. 1258] the Mohammedan world was paralyzed by the destruction of the Eastern Khalifate; the metropolis of the Empire, Baghdad, having been captured by Hulagu Khan (the grandson of Jenghis Khan), who massacred Al-Mustassim, the last of the Khalifs, with all his family. The fall of Baghdad, while causing the disruption of the Empire, had a very important effect on commerce, as it diverted the course of trade, flowing from East to West, into a new channel, and thus, while Sohar and Busra fell, Aden and Egypt rose.

The next occurrence we hear of in Oman history is the encroachment of Hormuz on the Arab littoral, an event which took place in 660 A.H. [A.D. 1261].

This Hormuz Dynasty was founded, according to Texeira, on the coast of Kirman by one Shah Mohammed of Mogestan, and became, probably, tributary to the Ghuz of Kirman. In 660 A.H. [A.D. 1261], as already observed, Rukn al-Deen Mahmood, the twelfth King of Hormuz, an enterprising and warlike prince who began to reign 641 A.H. [A.D. 1243], took an expedition of combined Hormuz and Ghuz troops to Kilhat and demanded tribute from the Nebhani Chiefs, Abul Maali Kahlan bin Nebhan and his brother, Omar bin Nebhan, who refused compliance and began to procrastinate. Rukn al-Deen, not being able, apparently, to attempt the conquest of the interior, proceeded by sea to Dhofar, leaving a garrison of the Ghuz at Kilhat. Part of this garrison moved down to Taiwee with the intention of plundering it, but were attacked and driven off with heavy loss by the Beni Jabir, and the graves of these Turks are still shown at Taiwee by the Arabs. Probably very few of the Ghuz returned to Kilhat.

In connection with the date of this occupation of Kilhat by the ruler of Hormuz, it must be remarked that Yakoot, who died in 626 A.H. [A.D. 1228] states that in his time Oman was subject to Hormuz.

In 675 A.H. [A.D. 1276] we learn that Oman was the scene of an incursion of the Moghuls of Shiraz, when the sons of the Governor or Reis, whose names were Fakhr al-Deen and Shahab al-Deen, with a force of 4,500 horse landed at Sohar and marched to Nezwa, which they plundered and burned. The bazaars, mosques, and books were destroyed and the women carried off. This happened in the reign of Hilal bin Omar bin Nebhan, who attacked the Persians and their allies, the Beni Haddan, but were defeated with a loss of 300 men. Fakhr al-Deen Ahmed bin al-Daya then besieged Bahila but was repulsed. The death of Fakhr al-Deen put an end to the campaign, and the Persians quitted Oman after a stay of four months.

We are told by Yakoot that in his time Sohar was the capital of Oman; but Abulfeda, writing nearly a century later, tells us that Sohar was in ruins.

It was about the year 700 A.H. [A.D. 1300] that the capital of the Hormuz Dynasty was removed from the Kirman Coast to the Island of Jeroon at the mouth of the Persian Gulf, which island thenceforth became known as Hormuz.

In 731 A.H. [A.D. 1330] Oman was visited by the Oriental traveller, Ibn Batuta, who found that Kilhat was in the hands of Kotub al-Deen, King of Hormuz. Ibn Batuta tells us that the Sultan of Oman was Abu Mahommed bin Nebhani, and that Abu Mohammed was the name among them of all the Sultans who rule over Oman.

In 749 A.H. [A.D. 1348] occurred the universal plague or Black Death, which is said to have originated in China in 742 A.H. [A.D. 1341] and spread to Europe. Though not mentioned by the annalists, it doubtless devastated Oman.

As it was somewhere about the year 766 A.H. [A.D. 1364] that the Ghuz dynasty of Kirman came to an end, we may suppose that Oman recovered her independence at that time, and that on the departure of the Ghuz the Nebhanis resumed their undisputed supremacy and sway.

For about forty years we hear of no rivalry between the Nebhanis and Ibadhi Moollas, but in the year 809 A.H. [A.D. 1406] we find that an Imam was appointed in the person of Malik bin Ali al-Howari, who resided at Nezwa and exercised power over the greater part of Oman.

Malik bin Ali al-Howari died in 833 A.H. [A.D. 1429] and seven years later was succeeded by Abdul Hassan bin Khamis bin Amr, who was elected in 834 A.H. [A.D. 1430]. This Imam died in 846 A.H. [A.D. 1442] and was followed by the Imam Omar bin Katab bin

Mohammed bin Ahmed bin Shidan bin Salt in 855 A.H. [A.D. 1451], or, according to Ross, 885 A.H. [A.D. 1480].

In the year 845 A.H. A.D. 1441] Abdul Rizak bin Ishak, ambassador from Shah Rookh to India, set out on his journey and reached Muscat, from whence he proceeded to Kuriyat and Soor. He was too engrossed in his own health to give any information about the politics or state of the country. This Imam Omar was not destined to remain in peace, for about a year after his election he was defeated and deposed by Suliman bin Suliman bin Muzhaffer al-Nebhani at Himat in the Wady Semail. Omar, however, appears to have been re-elected Imam, and in the year 887 A.H. [A.D. 1482] he seized in retaliation, apparently for his own defeat, the property of the Beni Nebhan and confiscated it.

Omar was succeeded by the Kadhi Mohammed bin Suliman bin Ahmed bin Mofarrij in 894 A.H. [A.D. 1488]. This Imam, however, was soon deposed and the Imam Omar bin Sherrif was elected and remained in office for one year, after which he retired to Bahila. Mohammed bin Suliman was then re-elected at Nezwa.

The next Imam appears to have been Mohammed al-Ismaili, who began to reign in 906 A.H. [A.D. 1500] and in whose reign, seven years later, the great Conquistador, Affonsod' Albuquerque, appeared on the scene and laid waste the whole coast from Ras al-Had to Mussendom.

CHAPTER III.

THE PORTUGUESE IN EASTERN ARABIA.

THE transference of the possession of the great Indian trade from the hands of the Venetians to the Portuguese, from the Portuguese to the Dutch, and from the Dutch to the English during the sixteenth, seventeenth and eighteenth centuries, is a matter of much interest and importance, and it may be as well to give a slight sketch of the earlier events before proceeding to the transactions of the Portuguese in Arabia.

At the middle of the fifteenth century Venice was at the zenith of her power—enriched by the monopoly of the commerce between the East and West. She had by her wealth and maritime strength become one of the chief powers of Europe, and her ships were the merchant navy of the Christian nations. But here her progress was stayed, and having crested the eminence of her glory, she began to feel her influence decline and to suffer the humiliation of her increasing weakness and decay. The first severe blow was the conquest by the Turks of Constantinople in 1452, from which city the Venetians had previously been driven by the Genoese. This gave the victors the command of the Levantine trade, and put an end for a time to the Persian Gulf and Syrian trade. The wars of the Venetian Republic with Genoa and the ambitious extension of territory on the Italian mainland occupied her attention fully and tried her strength, but she could, no doubt, for a lengthened period have withstood all rivals and maintained her supremacy in commerce almost unimpaired had it not been for the enterprise and courage of a smaller and far weaker state in the West of Europe, viz., Portugal.

It was in August of the year 1498 that the great discoverer, Vasco da Gama, first cast anchor in the waters of an Indian port, viz., Calicut, after doubling the Cape of Good Hope, effecting by this notable voyage a revolution in Oriental commerce which not only brought wealth and fame to its promoter, but brought ruin to three rival and powerful states, viz., Egypt, Venice and Turkey. Egypt fell within twenty years, Venice may be said to have closed her marts in 1573, after the capture of Cyprus by the Turks, though the Republic was only finally extinguished by the hand of the great Napoleon in 1796. The fall of Turkey has been more gradual, but has been none the less sure, and for many years he has been the Sick Man of Europe.

At the period we are speaking of the sea-borne trade from India up the Persian Gulf to Busra and along the Red Sea to Suez was in the hands chiefly of the Muscat and Yemen Arabs, who had maintained the profitable intercourse uninterruptedly in their own hands from remote ages, and these Arab merchants at Calicut, therefore, not unnaturally offered a most strenuous opposition to Vasco da Gama's dealings with the Zamorin, as they instinctively felt the deadly nature of the blow that had been struck at their trade, and saw at once that the cumbrous and complicated system in Egypt and Syria, in which the profits were divided by so many, was doomed to speedy ruin.

On the arrival of da Gama at Calicut, therefore, they lost no time in transmitting news of the event to Egypt, and informing the Sultan at Cairo of the unexpected interference of the Portuguese, so that in all probability he became acquainted with the momentous tidings of the change before the King of Portugal, as there was ample time during the twelve months that had elapsed between August, 1498, and September, 1499, when da Gama returned to Lisbon and imparted to the King the joyful news of his successful voyage. The significance of the news was fully understood by the Venetian merchants on receiving it from Egypt, and caused the utmost dismay. The Republic, however, did not immediately succumb to the blow struck by her rival, and made more than one vigorous though ineffectual effort to ward off the danger and recover her commercial supremacy. She pointed out the peril to Egypt and Turkey, and urged them to aid her in her attempts to avert it. The appeal she made was not only fully appreciated, but was at once responded to. By their united action a powerful fleet was equipped at Suez and despatched to the Arabian Sea to overwhelm the Portuguese.

In 1501 the Doge of Venice sent an ambassador, Signor Pietro Payualigo, to Lisbon to see how matters were progressing, and on his arrival, the King, Dom Manoel, though receiving him courteously, told him that if it pleased him to send ships to Lisbon to trade in spices they would be made welcome, and that the merchants would be given every facility and protection. The ambassador, Signor Payualigo, seeing that the Venetian monopoly of the Indian trade was obviously now at an end, and that the dangerous Red Sea route could no longer compete with that round the Cape, causing the inevitable ruin of his own State, resolved at once to return home.

Dom Manoel's invitation to open the harbour to the Venetian community to trade was not, of course, accepted by the Doge, as he had already engaged with the Sultan of Egypt, who was at that time independent of the Porte, to attack the Portuguese in the Arabian Sea, and did not dare to play a double part lest the depôts of merchandise at Cairo and Alexandria might be pillaged and destroyed, in which case his friends and allies, the Egyptians, would be turned into bitter foes, and he would be entirely isolated. The Doge was, moreover, doubtless influenced by considerations of pride and dignity, as well as those of policy, in refusing to purchase spices from his former customers. Besides these considerations it was natural that the Venetians, who had never attempted to join in the explorations of the West African Coast, should be averse from participation in the newly-discovered sea-borne trade to India after da Gama's first voyage. In their arrogance and disdain they contented themselves with trying to frustrate the Portuguese in their efforts to create a new commerce for their own country, but in these endeavours the Venetians had as little success as the Arab merchants at Calicut had in opposing Vasco da Gama.

The Sultan of Egypt, instigated by Venice, sent an imperious message to the Pope and to King Dom Manoel, requiring them to command all Christians to abstain from navigation or trading in the Arabian Sea, threatening otherwise to kill all the Christians in Egypt and to destroy the Holy Sepulchre. As, however, this *brutum fulmen* was treated with contempt, the Levantine confederacy despatched a fleet to the Indian Sea, which, after a long cruise, encountered a Portuguese armada in 1508, and was completely annihilated. As fleet after fleet left Lisbon for the East, the new-born trade rose rapidly and soon eclipsed the old-fashioned system. The diminution in the cost of freight alone was so marked, being about 60 per cent., that the Arabs could not attempt to compete, and thus the old routes through the Persian Gulf and Red Sea fell by degrees into desuetude.

In one of the earliest fleets that was despatched to India in the sixteenth century by the King was to be found the most commanding genius that Portugal ever sent to the East, Affonso d'Albuquerque, who sailed from Lisbon on February 6th, 1503, in charge of a squadron of three ships for Cochin to help to build a fort. During his stay in India he made good use of his time in collecting notes and in maturing plans for the future consideration of his King and the guidance of his country. On his return in 1504 he laid before Dom Manoel gigantic schemes of conquest, annexation, commerce, and maritime supremacy, which he considered feasible in view of the comparative feebleness of the Asiatics.

Albuquerque's ambitious plan, after much heated disputation in council, where it was opposed by the Marquis of Saldanha and other influential noblemen, was at length adopted, and the King resolved to entrust its execution to the master mind which had conceived it. The Duke of Almeida had been appointed Viceroy of India in 1505, and was doing good service there; therefore it was not desirable to supersede him, and the policy of Lisbon was a cautious one. It was not until 1506 that Albuquerque again left his native country, but when he did it was with full orders to inaugurate a policy of conquest and territorial aggrandisement in the East that had been determined on in pursuance of his advice. He carried, in fact, a secret commission from the King as Viceroy and Governor-General, which appointment he was to assume three years after sailing from Lisbon in succession to the Duke of Almeida, who was then to return to Europe. A complete account of the Portuguese conquests and subjugation of the coast of Africa and India would, perhaps, form one of the most instructive and entertaining chapters in the history of the world, but it has yet to be written, though we are not without many tentative works on the subject, and there must be rich materials still waiting rescue from oblivion in the archives of Lisbon, Goa, and the Simancas. The native annalists of Oman, as might be expected, maintain a discreet silence respecting the arrival and conquests of the Infidels in their country, but some of the contests that took place at a late period, when the increasing feebleness of the Portuguese garrisons encouraged insurrection, are frequently and exultingly recorded, particularly their final expulsion, as we may read in the pages of Ross's *Annals of Oman.*

In 1506 three fleets were despatched from Lisbon by the King, one of which, consisting of sixteen ships, left the quays of the Tagus on March 6th, and carried with it the illustrious Conquistador, Affonso d'Albuquerque.

The chief captain of this fleet was Tristan da Cunha, who received orders to sail to Socotra and there construct a fort, which, while protecting the Christians supposed to inhabit that island, would also serve as a depôt for the use of the fleet destined to oppose the Egypto-Venetian confederacy and to blockade the Red Sea. On the completion of the fort, da Cunha was to proceed to India with his share of the fleet, leaving Albuquerque with a small squadron to attack Jedda and Aden, and to obstruct the Moorish trade.

After many adventures and some losses, Tristan da Cunha arrived safely at Soko, the port of Socotra, in the middle of the year 1507, having on the way been joined by the *Flor de la Mar*, commanded by Captain Joao da Nova, who had proceeded to India with a former fleet and afterwards proved such a thorn in the side of Albuquerque at Hormuz. At Soko, da Cunha found a different reception awaiting him from what he had expected. The island was in possession of Sultan Ibrahim, son of the Sultan of Kisheen, who resolutely rejected the Admiral's demand for surrender. The fort was accordingly bombarded by the Portuguese, and in spite of a valiant resistance, assaulted and carried, the Mahra garrison being put to the sword. The fort was then repaired and named St. Thomas, and Affonso da Noronha was appointed to the command. It was the end of July, 1507, before affairs were finally arranged at Socotra, and the time then arrived for da Cunha and Albuquerque to part company and to pursue the course of action prescribed for each respectively by the King.

The squadron allotted to d'Albuquerque by the chief captain—da Cunha—consisted of the *Cirne*, the flagship of Albuquerque; the *Ruy Grande*, Captain Francisco da Tavora; the *Flor de la Mar*, Captain Joao da Nova; the *Ruy Peyneno*, Captain Manoel Jules Barretto; the *Sam Jorge*, transport, Captain A. Lopes da Costa; the *Espirito Santo*, Captain A. da Campo.

Having completed his arrangements, Tristan da Cunha sailed away to India on August 7th, leaving Albuquerque free to decide on and carry out his plan of operations against Moorish commerce. There is much discrepancy among the various Portuguese authors as to the instructions given to Albuquerque for his guidance, or it may be that the King's orders were in fact rather vague and indefinite, leaving him to act very much at his own discretion and as circumstances might dictate. According to the text of his own *Commentaries* he was to destroy Hormuz and to do what he could to intercept the tide of Arab trade to the Levant through the alternative routes of Alexandria and Busra, before proceeding to undertake aggressive wars on land. Couto in his *Decadas*, however, asserts that Albuquerque was ordered merely to obstruct the Red Sea and to capture the port of Aden.

Albuquerque had, no doubt, apprehended at once that the flotilla bequeathed to him by da Cunha was too small to attempt the capture of the almost impregnable fortress of Aden, and thought it better, soon after the departure of da Cunha, to deviate somewhat from his instructions and to steer straight for Eastern Arabia, where, after making himself master of Kilhat and Muscat, which, together with Hormuz, were at that time the chief marts in the Persian Gulf and the entrepôts, where the Eastern commerce concentrated itself before re-shipment to the Shat al-Arab, he intended to annex Hormuz and form that island into a depôt for Portuguese trade exclusively.

Before, however, taking any decided action Albuquerque deemed it prudent to call a council of war and to discuss the matter with his captains. At this council it was resolved that as provisions were running short and the south-west monsoon still prevailing, the expedition against Jedda should be abandoned in favour of a short cruise to pick up Moorish vessels coming from the Red Sea, after which the fleet should proceed to Muscat, where the Admiral could decide what to do next. On August 10th, accordingly, the little fleet set sail from Soko for the Arabian coast, intending to commence the cruise at the Kooria Mooria Islands. These islands, however, were passed without being sighted by any of the ships, and Albuquerque then decided to give up the cruise altogether, as he feared to run out of supplies, and he had only agreed to the plan in deference to the opinion of his captains.

Sailing on to the north-east, the fleet appears to have anchored for the first time in Oman waters, near the Island of Maseera, from whence, on the following day, they proceeded on until they had weathered Ras al-Had, under shelter of which Albuquerque anchored in smooth water and began hostilities by firing all the Arab vessels he found lying in Khor Hejareh, some thirty or forty in number. The next place, Khor Jeramah, was explored in the boats by the master of the transports, who sounded seven fathoms in the lagoon; here four more vessels were doomed to the flames. Passing Soor, which is described as a small fishing village, the fleet—sailing close, and followed by a large concourse of people along the shore—next arrived at the city of Kilhat, where Albuquerque ordered his ships to come to an anchor with as much noise and display as could be made. This was the first appearance of European warships in the Gulf of Oman since the days of Alexander, eighteen centuries before, and from the ready submission of the people in Kilhat the arrival of the fleet seems to have created no little terror and dismay, the Persians having doubtless heard of the proceedings of the Portuguese on the Indian coast and of their warlike character and superiority.

At the time of these events the Arab in power in Oman was the Imam Mohammed bin Ismail al-Ismaili, who had been elected in 906 A.H. [A.D. 1500] and who died in 942 A.H. [A.D. 1535]. He held sway over the interior portion of the country, and he usually resided at Al-Rostak, the coast line being still, as it had been since A.D. 1270, subject to the Persian King of Hormuz, whose chief governor on the Arab coast was at Kilhat. No communication was held the first day with the city, but on the following morning a boat was sent on shore with two officers and an interpreter, who were civilly received and were informed that the town belonged to the King of Hormuz and that anything required for the fleet would be willingly supplied.

On the next day further communication took place between the Governor and Albuquerque, to whom a present of fruit, etc., was sent on board by the former. The present, however, was not accepted by Albuquerque, who required the unconditional submission of the town and the transfer of allegiance to the King of Portugal.

The Governor being unprepared for resistance, resolved to temporize, and humbly deprecating the opening of hostilities and the destruction of the town, besought Albuquerque to proceed to Hormuz and make terms with the King, promising that whether peace or war might result there, Kilhat would nevertheless yield subjection to the King of Portugal. This evasive reply was fully understood by Albuquerque, but as he was in urgent need of provisions he took the advice of his officers and accepted the position until a more convenient opportunity. Before leaving, Albuquerque gave a written guarantee of safety from attack by other Portuguese ships in the name of the King Dom Manoel to the Governor, but he did not scruple to make prize of an Aden dhow of 200 tons lying in the harbour, which was held to ransom.

On Sunday, August 22nd, Albuquerque weighed from Kilhat and sailed for Taiwee, which he had supposed to be a large port, but on finding it merely a watering-place, he passed on to Kuriyat, where he anchored for the night. The next day no boat came off from the shore, and it was seen that the inhabitants had prepared for resistance; Albuquerque accordingly reconnoitred the place in his boat and arranged his plan of attack for the following morning. It was ascertained that the Arabs had two batteries, on one of which they had mounted four mortars, and the attack was consequently concentrated on these points. The struggle was long and severe, but the natives were ultimately driven out of their defences and pursued half a league by the Portuguese, who slaughtered indiscriminately all the men, women, and children they could reach. Some prisoners taken in the town had their ears and noses lopped off to signalize the victory, and Kuriyat was plundered and set on fire; twenty-five firelocks, besides spears, bows and arrows, etc., were captured, and thirty-eight vessels, large and small, lying in the port were burnt.

Muscat, the next scene of destruction, was reached in four days after leaving Kuriyat, and was found to be a very formidable and well fortified place. It is also described as being the principal port on that coast. The inhabitants had heard of the fate of Kuriyat, and were disinclined to expose their city to a similar catastrophe; they therefore did not wait for a summons to surrender but immediately on the arrival of the fleet sent off two of their chief men to Albuquerque, offering submission to the King of Portugal and promising to agree to any terms that might be demanded.

Albuquerque, finding that they were unprovided with written power to treat from the Governor, sent them on shore again, desiring them to return on board the following day. In the meantime he sounded the harbour and reconnoitred the fortifications. It was found that the Arabs had constructed a rampart of wood and earth from hill to hill above the beach in front of the town, and had mounted thereon a number of mortars. On the two shaikhs visiting Albuquerque next day they were informed that they were required to pay an annual tribute and furnish his fleet with supplies and water during the operations against Hormuz. Compliance with the requisition for provisions was made at once; but during the night the inhabitants were reinforced by a powerful shaikh from the interior and felt strong enough to withdraw their submission and defy the Portuguese. Albuquerque, therefore, resolved on reducing the town without delay, and having ordered his ships to take up positions commenced to bombard the stockade and batteries. The fire of the guns, however, had little effect, owing probably to the distance of the ships, and Albuquerque thought it best to call a council of war to decide on what was to be done. The captains, who had already begun to get restive under the iron rule of their commander, seeing that Albuquerque had made up his mind as to the course he would pursue and dreading, perhaps, the strength of the place, declined to discuss the plan of operations or express an opinion, and informed him simply that they were ready to obey his orders. Being now free to act, Albuquerque no longer hesitated and gave directions for an assault on the morrow. He divided his force into two, giving command of the right division against the stockade to Captains da Tavora and da Costa, while he himself took charge of the left. The landing was effected under the fortifications, and although an obstinate defence was made, the walls were stormed and carried at both points. A junction was then effected in the streets between the two attacking parties, according to previous arrangement, and the enemy was then gradually driven through and out of the town.

The shaikh, whose arrival had caused such rejoicing and had inspired the people to oppose their invaders, escaped after a long pursuit, but the slaughter of the Arabs was very great, and included the Persian Governor of the town and a number of women and children. In the slaughter of the women the two captains, who subsequently mutinied and deserted their leader, viz., Antao da Campo and Joao da Nova, seem to have particularly distinguished themselves, but Albuquerque's conduct is equally deserving of reprobation, for after the rout of the Arabs was complete and the scattered Portuguese soldiers were collected in the town, he proceeded to massacre most of the remaining inhabitants—men, women, and children—without distinction. After guarding against surprise, the town was occupied and pillaged, and the men were allowed to retain their loot and remove it on board as some compensation for the hardships they had undergone. Among the spoil were thirty guns, bows and arrows, lances and other weapons used by the Arabs. Albuquerque spent eight days here and took the opportunity to refit his fleet and victual it with provisions and water. Having done this he was preparing to evacuate the town and set it on fire when the inhabitants who had taken refuge on the heights above, guessing his intention, despatched an Arab with a flag of truce to beseech him to be content with having slain the women and children and to spare the town and ships from the flames. Albuquerque replied to the envoy that he regretted the destruction of the city, but that the inhabitants had broken faith with him and he could not consequently admit their claim to forbearance. He consented, however, to hold the city to ransom, which he fixed at 10,000 ashrafies in gold, to be paid the next day at noon. This amount the Arabs were unable or unwilling to pay by the time appointed, and the town was therefore destroyed by fire, together with thirty-four dhows and many fishing boats. The mosque, described as a very large and beautiful edifice constructed of wood elaborately carved, also fell a prey to the flames, and it is related that the three Portuguese engaged in hacking at the carved wooden pillars were crushed and buried by the sudden collapse of the building; all believed they had perished, but as they emerged unhurt, the Commander at once returned thanks to the Holy Virgin for her miraculous interposition on their behalf during their pious labour. Albuquerque gives the following curious description of Muscat at that time:—

"Muscat is a large and very populous town, flanked on both sides with high mountains and the front is close to the water's edge; behind, towards the interior, there is a plain as large as the square of Lisbon, all covered with salt pans. Not that the tide reaches there but the springs are salt and salt forms there. Hard by are many pools of fresh water, of which the inhabitants make use, and there are orchards, gardens, and palm groves with wells for watering them by means of swipes and other engines. The harbour is small, shaped like a horseshoe and sheltered from every wind. It is the principal entrepôt of the Kingdom of Hormuz, into which all the ships that navigate these parts must of necessity enter to avoid the opposite coast, which contains many shallows. It is an ancient mart for the shipment of horses and dates. It is a very fine town with many good houses and supplied from the interior with much wheat, millet, barley, and dates, for lading as many vessels as come for them. This city of Muscat forms part of the Kingdom of Hormuz, and the interior belongs to a king called the Ben Jaber who had two brothers; between these brothers was divided the country which extends as far as Aden; on the north it is washed by the Persian Sea, and from thence it stretches as far as the vicinity of Mecca. The Arabs call this country the Island of Arabia, because the Persian Sea turns inwards opposite to the Red Sea in such a manner that the country is circular and is almost surrounded by water, that is by the Red and Persian Seas. It is a very small country and is called on that account the Island of Arabia. It had formerly been all reigned over by a king called the Ben Jaber, and this man had three sons, to whom at his death he left the land to be divided among them, and the eldest afterwards retained the name of Ben Jaber, as the father had done. The other two acknowledged him as their lord. This Ben Jaber has dominions over Fartak, Dhofar, Kilhat, and Muscat, and his boundary reaches to the land of the Shaikh of Aden; the other two dwell on the coast of the Persian Sea, and one of them had taken from the King of Hormuz the Island of Bahrain, where there is a pearl fishery about five days' voyage from the Island of Hormuz, and had also taken Kateef, an island held originally by the King of Hormuz on the Arabian coast.

"In this country of Ben Jaber there are many horses,

which the farmers breed for sale; there is also great abundance of wheat, millet, and barley, and great flocks and herds, and there are many who hunt with falcons about the size of our goshawks and take by their aid gazelles smaller than ours, training very swift hounds to assist the falcons in catching the prey."

Previous to the departure of the fleet from Muscat, the first open rupture took place between the Chief Captain and Captain Joao da Nova of the *Flor de la Mar*. Albuquerque had information that da Nova intended to desert him here and slip away to India, and he therefore summoned him to his ship and convened a council; da Nova did not deny the charge, and the officers having supported Albuquerque, da Nova submitted and was ordered to continue with the fleet under severe penalty.

Passing the Deymanieh Islands the fleet anchored in due course off Sohar. A message was immediately despatched by the Governor to Albuquerque, informing him that the city belonged to the King of Hormuz and intimating that if he landed he would meet with a different reception from what the other towns on the coast had given him; at the same time the messenger pointed to the troops on shore where as much display and parade were being made as possible. Albuquerque replied shortly that the Governor had better reconsider his determination and own allegiance to Portugal, otherwise the fortress would assuredly be taken from him in the morning. The sight of the imposing force of infantry and cavalry on shore had a pacific effect on the other captains in the fleet, but Albuquerque knew his strength better, and as soon as the messenger had gone, commenced his preparations for the attack. All was ready by noon the next day and the boats were about to shove off when a deputation from the town arrived and stated that the Governor had just dismissed a force of 7,000 men, which had been sent by the Ben Jaber to his aid, and that as the King of Hormuz had not sent the succour he had promised, the Governor was ready to submit to the King of Portugal and to deliver up the fort. Albuquerque said he was glad that the Governor had changed his mind, and intimated that he would accept the submission of the town on condition of its paying a yearly tribute. The envoys, alarmed at the preparations they had seen on board, agreed to this, and having concluded a convention, returned to the Governor. Due arrangements having been made, the Portuguese standard was carried to the fort in state and hoisted on the highest tower under a salute.

On seeing the strength of the place Albuquerque was inclined at first to retain possession of it, as he would thereby gain complete command of the Oman coast, but on second thoughts he decided to entrust the fort to the Governor for the present, and accordingly placed him in charge, appointing the yearly tribute fixed for the town for the payment of the Arab garrison. A written acknowledgment of allegiance to the King of Portugal was then executed by the Governor, and a guarantee of protection was given by Albuquerque in return, and matters having thus been adjusted, Albuquerque weighed anchor the next morning, and steered his course for Khor Fakan. The inhabitants of this place had received news of the fleet's approach by a boat from Sohar, and made a great display of horse and foot on the beach, hoping to deter the Portuguese from attack by mere bravado. This continued the whole of the first day, and as Albuquerque received no message or offer of submission from the Governor he determined to attack early the following morning, and made his signal two hours after midnight. After clearing the beach by his guns in the boats, the troops landed and marched up, pursuing the Arabs, who hastily retired to the gates of the fort. As they entered pell-mell, some of the Portuguese, headed by Albuquerque's nephew, Noronha, managed to press in with them, and being soon supported by Albuquerque himself, found themselves after a long and stubborn fight in possession of the town and fortress, which were occupied and guarded. One of the elders of the town, who was too old and infirm to escape, and had concealed himself in a cellar, was captured and brought before Albuquerque, to whom he gave important information respecting the kingdom of Hormuz; he also gave Albuquerque a Persian history of Alexander, and in consideration of this, was honourably treated and released. Some days were spent in getting provisions and water on board (the prisoners being used as slaves in this work), and meanwhile the Arabs made repeated attempts to regain possession of the town, but without success.

As the fleet had approached Khor Fakan, the Portuguese had observed several vessels sailing away in the direction of Cape Mussendom, and they now learned that these dhows contained the Hindoo traders from Cutch, escaping with their property; very little booty, consequently, was found in the town, much to the disappointment of the victors. Numerous captives, however, were taken, who appear to have been released with the customary mutilation of ears and noses.

Khor Fakan is described by Albuquerque as being situate at the foot of a very high mountain, and almost impregnable on the land side. It was a large town with many Banian merchants, and was a dependency of Hormuz. The climate was temperate and healthy, and there was extensive cultivation of wheat and millet, with oranges, limes, dates, plantains, and figs. The harbour was good, being protected by two small islets. Horses were extensively exported hence to India, and the interior belonged to Ben Jaber, like the other parts.

Khor Fakan was the last scene of Albuquerque's exploits on the Oman coast, and he had as little compassion on this as on former places; the town was set on fire and destroyed, and the Conquistador, elated by his victories and confident in his strength, signalled to the fleet, and made his way direct to Hormuz.

The capture of Hormuz was the principal object of Albuquerque's expedition, as before remarked, and his operations and exploits here were characterized by the same distinguished ability, valour, and success that had marked his previous career. Owing, however, to the disaffection of his officers and the desertion of two of his ships, he was compelled to retire before the finish had been put to his conquest, by the completion of the fort which was to overawe the town. He sailed away to Socotra, where his arrival was most opportune, for he found the garrison in great distress from famine and the enmity of the natives. He soon put affairs in order there, and his fleet having been increased by two ships that had arrived from

Portugal to join him, he weighed from Soko on August 15th, 1508, to return to Hormuz, intending on the way to reduce the city of Kilhat in retaliation for the assistance rendered by it to the King of Hormuz in violation of agreement during the war. On anchoring off Kilhat, Albuquerque sent his nephew, Noronha, in a boat to reconnoitre. Near the shore Noronha met an Arab bringing presents from the Governor, on which he turned back and accompanied the man to the flagship, where Albuquerque questioned the Arab as to the Governor's name and the force at his disposal. Having elicited the required information, Albuquerque despatched Noronha to the shore again to see the Governor, Sherif al-Deen, and if possible to entice him on board, which Noronha endeavoured to do by representing Albuquerque as an officer who had just arrived from Portugal with reinforcements to support Albuquerque at Hormuz. Sherif al-Deen was polite, and offered the new commander a hospitable reception on shore if it pleased him to land, but he was too wary to trust himself on board a Portuguese ship.

On his nephew's return from his ineffective mission, Albuquerque made preparations to attack the town, which is situated on a declivity under a high and steep cliff. The struggle for the possession of the place did not last long, for the Persians, terror-stricken by the vigorous onslaught of the Portuguese, were driven in confusion out of the town, and Sherif al-Deen was obliged to retire to the heights behind the city, from whence he watched the proceedings of the invaders. Albuquerque, having posted guards on the gates and ramparts against surprise, gave the place over to plunder, whereon the vigilant Sherif al-Deen, after three days, seeing that the Portuguese dispersed intent on pillage, deemed it a fitting opportunity to attempt to regain the town. Followed by five hundred men he accordingly made a descent from the hills and tried to force one of the gates; at first the guard posted there was driven back, but having speedily rallied, the men closed with the Persians, and, after a valiant fight, routed them before Albuquerque could come to their assistance.

After sacking the town and transporting on board all the provisions and valuables he could collect, Albuquerque gave it to the flames, making a point of destroying the famous Jami Masjid, to the great grief of the inhabitants. Albuquerque's description of this mosque accords with that of Ibn Batuta, who had visited the place about 200 years before, and from these accounts the edifice appears to have been a very fine specimen of Persian architecture. It may be remarked here that no cut or squared stones are to be found at the present day among the ruins of Kilhat; the houses there, and doubtless this mosque also, were built of limestone and coral; the destruction of it, however, has been so complete that no vestige of it now remains to point out the spot where it stood.

Albuquerque here obtained important information from the Persians who had brought off the presents from the Governor, Sherif al-Deen, and who had, until now, been detained on board the flagship, respecting the condition of affairs at Hormuz, and the men were dismissed with gifts. He then gave orders to burn the Arab shipping in the creek, and after consultation with his officers, resolved to proceed at once with the expedition. The fleet accordingly sailed the following day, and having watered at Taiwee, where Albuquerque anchored for two days, and which he represents as a port with a river near, running between lofty hills and forming on the shore a lake surrounded by palm trees, continued his voyage up the gulf towards Hormuz.

The first act in the drama thus terminated in the destruction of Kilhat, and a lull succeeded the stormful visits of the Conquistador, whose track along the Arab coast had been marked by a trail of blood and flame. For five years the Arabs appear to have been left unmolested by their new foes, and in the meantime they had leisure to rebuild their towns and to watch—as they doubtless did with interest—the proceedings of their ruthless invaders at Hormuz and in India.

In 1512 Diego Fernandes de Bega, who had been sent to demolish the fort at Socotra, which had been found useless for the purpose it was intended to serve, came to Hormuz and Muscat to receive the tribute agreed upon with the King.

It was in the year 1514 that the Portuguese first visited and explored the island of Bahrain, on the north-east coast of Arabia. In May, Pedro d'Albuquerque, having finished his cruise in the Arabian Sea, under instruction from his uncle arrived at Hormuz, and from thence proceeded to Menamah, the capital of the Bahrain Islands, which were then subject to the King of Hormuz. The main object of the Portuguese in visiting these islands was probably to gain control over the valuable pearl fishery which then, as now, furnished the bulk of the pearls required for the markets of Europe and Asia. Pedro d'Albuquerque, however, did nothing more than confirm existing arrangements between the Shaikh and the King of Hormuz, and then returned with his squadron to Hormuz. Seven years later, viz., 1521, during the vice-royalty of Diego da Sequeira, a strong force was despatched from Hormuz under the command of Antonio Correa, who successfully stormed and carried the town of Menamah, which was then garrisoned, and with varying fortune, remained in possession of the Portuguese for many years.

It had been the intention of Albuquerque, who had in the meantime become the second Viceroy of India, to return to the Persian Gulf in the year 1512 with de Bega, but circumstances prevented his doing so until two years later, when he sailed from Goa with a fleet of fourteen sail of the line and thirteen smaller vessels. On March 21st, 1515, he sighted land near Ras al-Had, and four days later arrived at Kuriyat. Here he found an armada from Hormuz on the look-out for pirates, and deciding not to molest it he moved on to Muscat, where he anchored for two days to take in provisions and water. The Persian Governor or Agent here at the time was Rais Hamed, a nephew of Rais Noor al-Deen, one of the officers of the King of Hormuz, and Albuquerque was much exercised at observing his tyrannical behaviour over the people. He appears, however, to have behaved civilly enough to the Portuguese, having, doubtless, a lively recollection of what had occurred seven years before.

Having completed the conquest of Hormuz, the Viceroy prepared to turn his face southward, and appointed his relative, Pedro d'Albuquerque, commandant of the fort, with a strong garrison to overawe the city. It was the last important act of his life, for he was very ill when he set sail, and as it turned out on his deathbed. The "terrible Albuquerque," as he was called, died the day of his arrival off the bar of Goa, his end being hastened by the news he had received of his supersession and recall by the King.

De Barros gives a curious and detailed account of the revenue and expenditure of Hormuz at this time. He says that on the coast of Arabia the chief town was Kilhat, the governor and customs master at which overruled those in the other towns in the principality. The revenue collected and remitted by Kilhat to Hormuz was 19,200 sharafins, equal to 5,760 dollars, which was contributed in the following proportion: Kilhat, paid 1,100 ashrafies, Muscat 4,000, Sohar 1,500, Khor Fakan 1,500, Dibba 500, and Lima 700. The Julfar district or pirate coast also paid 7,500, and in addition to the above, the boats engaged in the pearl fishery, which were compelled to go to Hormuz to take out passes, contributed 1,500 ashrafies. The Oman revenue thus came to 28,200 ashrafies. The total revenue of Hormuz is said to have been 198,078 ashrafies, or 59,423 dollars.

The same writer also gives us a glimpse at the political state of Oman at this time, from which we learn that the Imam Mohammed possessed undisputed spiritual and temporal power in all parts, and that the chief cities in Oman Proper, which was the most populous district, were Manh, Nezwa, and Behla, each of which was fortified and had its own quasi-independent king who ruled in a sort of republic. These chieftains had formed a league to protect themselves against the Ben Jaber, a predatory tribe and the most powerful in Arabia, who used to raid Oman every year at the date season, and the Imam had to buy them off from plundering his territories by an annual tribute.

Intermediate between the above towns and the seaboard were other shaikhdoms, who were continually at feud with the Persian governors, a state of distraction which, of course, operated greatly in favour of the Portuguese. Who these Ben Jaber were that appeared so formidable is an enigma that remains unsolved.

After the subjection of Hormuz, three places on the Arab coast, viz., Kilhat, Muscat, and Sohar, became stations for the Portuguese factors and merchants, who were appointed and controlled from Hormuz. They were sufficiently protected by the visits of the King's ships from India which touched at these places on their way to Hormuz and Bahrain; and as no vessel under a native flag was suffered to cross the ocean without a pass, they had practically the control of all seaborne commerce, and thus commanded the markets; but it does not appear that any garrisons were yet stationed on the Oman coast.

In the year 1519 the first check to the prestige gained by the Portuguese in the Persian Gulf was experienced by them, and the effect of this disaster on the native mind found expression two years later in a general revolt at all their Arab and Persian stations. In the original quarrel from which this affair resulted, the Portuguese had been in no wise concerned. The King of Hormuz having found reason to be displeased with the Persian governor of Kilhat, Rais Shahab al-Deen, and being unable to displace or arrest him, besought the aid of the Port Commandant in Hormuz, Dom Garcia de Coutinho, in asserting his authority. In compliance with the request, Dom Garcia directed the Captain-Major or naval chief of the Gulf Squadron, Duarte Mendes da Vasconcello, to arrest Rais Shahab al-Deen and bring him to Hormuz. This order, however, Duarte Mendes found difficult of execution, as the Rais was too wary to be entrapped and too strongly guarded to be taken, and it remained in abeyance until the opportune arrival in the port of Dom Jorge d'Albuquerque, with ten ships, offered him the means of effecting the desired object. Dom Jorge had been despatched from Lisbon this year in command of a fleet, and on reaching Mozambique had received instructions from the Governor-General and Viceroy, Dom Diego Lopes da Sequeira, to rendezvous at Muscat early in 1519, and his appearance at Kilhat at this juncture seemed to put Duarte Mendes in an advantageous position. A plan of operations having been concocted between the Captain-Major and the Admiral, a small force was landed in the town from the ships after dark and marched to the house of the Governor, Shahab al-Deen, with the object of capturing the latter by a night surprise. The attack, however, failed. The Persians were on the alert and in strength, and repulsed the Portuguese at all points. Outnumbered and overpowered, the latter took refuge in a house, but this was set fire to by the Persian soldiers, and after a severe struggle and heavy loss in killed, wounded, and prisoners, the remnant was rescued by a fresh party from the fleet. The fiasco was complete and Rais Shahab al-Deen remained uncaptured and triumphant.

Shortly after this disastrous event and early in the following year, 1520, the Viceroy, Dom Diego Lopes da Sequeira, whose arrival had been long expected, anchored with twenty-three ships in Muscat harbour. He had been cruising in the Red Sea and was now on the way to Hormuz. On hearing of the affair at Kilhat he summoned the Admiral, Dom Jorge d'Albuquerque, and the Captain-Major, Duarte de Vasconcello, and after a full enquiry condemned and censured the whole proceedings. He even went so far as to put Duarte Mendes in irons. Having disposed of this matter the Viceroy continued his voyage to Hormuz with a few galleys, leaving Dom Jorge d'Albuquerque in charge of the major portion of the fleet at Muscat. Fifteen Portuguese, who had been taken prisoners and carried inland from Kilhat, were recovered by Dom Jorge d'Albuquerque during his stay, in wretched plight. No attempt, however, seems to have been made to retrieve the disaster.

In the next year, 1521, only seven years after the fall of Hormuz and the death of the great Conquistador, a concerted insurrection took place at Hormuz, and along the Arabian shore from Bahrain to Kilhat, and the garrisons were taken so completely by surprise that it was only by chance and their own marvellous valour that their entire annihilation was not accomplished. The cause of this revolt, according to the Portuguese officers on the spot, was the dissatisfaction felt by the King at their general supervision of the revenue, and especially at their interference in the arrangements of the Customs House, a measure equally distasteful perhaps to both parties, but lately introduced under orders from Lisbon. Under this system of control a number of court favourites and parasites lost lucrative sinecures and a good deal of wasteful expenditure was thus, no doubt, prevented. But there were counter-balancing disadvantages, and we may without fear ascribe the approximate and predominating cause to the rapacity, insolence and oppression of the Portuguese officials, who made no scruple of taking advantage of their strength in carrying out their duties.

The scheme of revolt appears to have been elaborately planned out and decided upon by the King and his ministers, and when all was ready, letters were despatched to the Persian governors of dependencies on the Arab coast with orders to rise against the Portuguese in their towns on the appointed day and spare none. The scheme was artfully contrived to comprehend all stations for the rising, which would be so simultaneous that the Portuguese would be precluded from finding safety by fleeing from one point to another. The presence of the Port Armada constantly stationed at Hormuz to support the Commandant was an obstacle to success, and a stratagem was therefore devised to get rid of it. The King, pretending that the dependencies on the Oman coast were being ravaged by pirates, requested the Commandant, Dom Garcia de Coutinho, to despatch the armada to protect them. With this request made on the eve of the rising the Commandant unsuspectingly complied, and issued the necessary orders to the Captain-Major, Manoel de Souza Tavares. Judging half his force to be sufficient, Tavares set sail, with two only out of the four ships at his disposal, for Muscat.

The revolt occurred on November 30th, 1521, and commenced with an attack by the Shah Bandar at midnight on the two vessels left in the harbour. The crews, taken by surprise, were easily overpowered, and a fire lighted on board one of the captured vessels gave the signal to those on shore for the massacre of the Portuguese residents in the city, who, unsuspicious of evil, were wrapt in slumber in their houses. About sixty Portuguese were slain or captured by the Persian troops and the populace, but the rest succeeded in escaping to the fort, which was bravely defended against heavy odds by the garrison for some months, until succour arrived from India.

In the outlying dependencies of Hormuz the King's plan was faithfully carried out by his governors. At Bahrain the Christians were attacked and massacred, the factor, Ruy Bale, being tortured and crucified. At Sohar very few, if any, escaped the sudden onslaught that was made. In Muscat alone the Portuguese found friends and protection. The firm attitude and tactics of the Arab Governor, Shaikh Rashid, who was favourably disposed to them and doubtless foresaw their ultimate triumph, kept the Persians in check and prevented a rising, and when the chief factor of Kilhat and of the Oman coast, Vas de Veiga, arrived shortly after, Shaikh Rashid threw off his allegiance to Hormuz and declared for the Portuguese, a step in which he was joined by the principal Arab inhabitants. At Kilhat the Portuguese appear to have received warning in time, from the Commandant at Hormuz, of the revolt, owing to some delay on the part of the Persians, and having collected their valuables made a start for their boats in the harbour, but were interrupted by the Persian Governor and garrison, who killed several of them and captured others. The factor, T. Vas de Veiga, then set out for Muscat, where, as we have said, he made terms with Shaikh Rashid, and where he found at anchor Captain-Major Manoel de Souza Tavares, with whom he sailed at once for the relief of Hormuz. At Hormuz, immediately on the occurrence of the revolt, the Commandant had hired a vessel, which he entrusted to Joao de Meira, directing him to sail at once for India with dispatches for the Viceroy, and ordering him to touch at Muscat and Kilhat on the way.

Setting out with all speed Jaoa de Meira was thus instrumental in warning his countrymen at these two places of the intended massacre. Though this insurrectionary movement had failed in its main object, the number of Portuguese killed at the various stations is said to have been not less than 120. The Viceroy at Goa, at that time, Dom Duarte de Menezes, on hearing the news of the revolt from de Meira, at once despatched Dom Gonçalo in advance to encourage the garrison at Hormuz and to intimate the speedy setting out of a fleet under Dom Luiz de Menezes to their assistance. The arrival of Dom Gonçalo seems to have turned the tables entirely in favour of the Portuguese and to have restored their predominant position in the Persian Gulf, through the dread of their retaliation for the atrocities that had been perpetrated. In the meantime Manoel de Souza, the Captain-Major, had been sent back by the Commandant at Hormuz to try and recover the prisoners in Oman. On anchoring at Muscat he found the place deserted, owing, as he learned, to the fear entertained by the Shaikh that the new Persian Governor of Kilhat, Rais Delamir Shah, was about to attack the town. On hearing of de Souza Tavares' arrival, however, the Shaikh presently returned to the town and solicited Portuguese protection. Having confirmed friendly relations with the Shaikh, Manoel de Souza Tavares proceeded to Kilhat, where his demand for the surrender of the captives met with a decided refusal from the Acting-Governor, Khoja Zein al-Deen, who said he had a letter from the King, Toorun Shah, for delivery to Dom Luiz de Menezes, and that he would wait for the latter's arrival.

It was in February, 1522, when Dom Luiz de Menezes, the brother of the Viceroy, set out from Chaul with a flotilla of three galleys, four fustas and one caravella to punish the authors of the massacres and to re-establish Portuguese supremacy in the Persian Gulf, having already despatched in advance the new Commandant of Hormuz, João Rodrigues da Noronha, to relieve Coutinho, whose three years tenure of office had expired. Dom Luiz anchored first at Kilhat, where he made an immediate demand for the surrender of the captives, the number of whom by this time was reduced to twenty. The Governor replied by sending off the King's letter addressed to the Admiral, and which merely contained a series of complaints against the present and former Commandants of Hormuz, but on a further demand for the delivery of the prisoners, the Governor evaded it by saying that he had no authority to act and must await the new Governor. The Admiral, being in want of water for his ships, proceeded to Taiwee, where a collision occurred with the Arabs, in which the latter suffered a defeat and in their fury vindictively murdered seven unfortunate Portuguese captives that were in their hands. While at this place Dom Luiz received a message from Shaikh Rashid, reporting the approach to Muscat by land of Rais Delamir Shah with a large force and beseeching armed support. The caravella was accordingly detached for this service with orders to support the Shaikh at Muscat from the sea as far as the guns of the vessel would reach, but not to undertake operations on shore. The Shaikh, nevertheless, obtained the aid of five Portuguese volunteers and emboldened by their presence, attacked the Persians in the great wady behind the town with such vigour, that he completely defeated them, their leader, Delamir Shah, being killed in the fight.

Dom Luiz arrived at Muscat two days after this affair, and having congratulated the Shaikh, rewarded him handsomely for his loyalty and for his protection of the Portuguese during the revolt. Having then for the first time apparently established a garrison of twenty men for the defence of the town and stationed a fusta here to guard the port, Dom Luiz de Menezes weighed anchor and stood for Sohar, after a stay of four days, during which time he had been joined by two more vessels from Goa.

Sohar appears at this time to have fallen again under the rule of Hormuz and to have had a large Persian garrison. It was now menaced by two Arab armies, one of which, under Sultan bin Mesood, was in the neighbouring hills and was composed of 250 horse and 3,000 foot. The other and more formidable adversary was Shaikh Hoosain bin Saeed, chief of the great tribe Ben Jaber, who had with him 500 horse and 4,000 foot. These Ben Jaber, we are informed by Barros, were Bedouins and possessed more than 500 leagues of country. Shaikh Hoosain was therefore the lord of all the interior as well as the island of Bahrain and the entire coast as far south as Dhofar.

Dom Luiz, having been informed that these two Arab chiefs were always at war with the Persians of Hormuz, determined to seek their alliance, and accordingly wrote to them, offering to put them in possession of Sohar if they would aid him in ousting the Persians. To this proposal the two Shaikhs readily agreed, but Dom Luiz was detained on his way to Sohar by contrary winds, and in the meantime, by an untoward incident which occurred off the Batineh coast, Sultan bin Mesood became estranged from the Portuguese and withdrew his tribesmen.

The Admiral's plan was that the Arabs should surround Sohar by land while he attacked it from the sea, and on his arrival there on March 11th found Shaikh Hoosain with his force already in position in front of the town. Previous to the fleet casting anchor the Persian Governor, Rais Shahab al-Deen, had with much discretion managed to effect his escape to Hormuz, leaving the garrison of eighty men without a leader to confront their enemies and defend the fort as best they might. Under the circumstances and in view of the warlike preparations of the fleet, it is not surprising that they abandoned the idea of offering a stern resistance. Imitating, therefore, the example of the Rais, the garrison, dreading the resentment of their enemies, did not wait for an assault on the fort, but bribing the Arabs on the watch outside, passed through their lines at night and decamped in the darkness. The Portuguese troops, who had been landed on the beach during the day to make preparations for an attack on the morrow, warned in some way of what had happened, immediately scaled the walls of the fort, massacred or captured the inhabitants and sacked the town, which was set on fire, much to the surprise and indignation of the Admiral, Dom Luiz, who having remained on board his vessel to superintend the preconcerted attack, had not been kept informed of what had occurred on shore.

Shaikh Hoosain bin Saeed also and his following, who had been totally unaware of the flight of the garrison and the escalade of the Portuguese detachment, were furious at what they considered the perfidy and faithlessness of Dom Luiz, and exclaimed loudly at not having been suffered to participate in the plunder of the town, which had been their main objective, but the Admiral made what reparation he could by giving up to them the captives and some of the booty. Furthermore, having declared Sohar independent of Hormuz, he appointed Shaikh Hoosain bin Saeed Governor on behalf of Portugal under a convention. As an agent to support and advise the new Governor, the Admiral nominated a Portuguese scrivener to reside there, and with orders to take note of the revenues and expenses of the place, and then the fleet, after being victualled, weighed and set sail for Hormuz.

In 1526 another revolt occurred on the Oman coast, which appears to have been regarded at this time as being still in subordination to Hormuz. Irritated at the wrongs they considered themselves to be suffering under at the hands of Diego de Mello, the Commandant of Hormuz, the King and his Wazeer, Rais Sherif, threw off allegiance to Portugal and sent orders to the Governors of Muscat and Kilhat to do likewise.

News of these disturbances soon reached Goa, where the provisional Viceroy, Lopo Henrique de Menzes, had died on February 21st, 1526. De Sampayo set out accordingly in May, 1527, with five ships to restore order. In crossing the Gulf of Oman he was delayed by continued calms, in which he lost many men. He anchored first at Kilhat, where he adopted a conciliatory course, and by promising to redress grievances and to punish Captain de Mello, restored confidence without recourse to coercion. Watering at Taiwee, Dom Lopo sailed on to Muscat, where he strove by similar means to pacify the Shaikh, and succeeded.

During his stay here, the Viceroy took advantage of the opportunity to increase the strength of the Portuguese garrison and to order the erection of the new pile of buildings known among the Arabs as the Gareza. This block was intended not only to serve the purpose of a factory, but was also to comprise the residence of the Portuguese commandant, the soldiers' barracks, the warehouse, and the chapel. It appears to have been completed about four years later, 1531, but I never could find a date on it. In modern days it has served as a residence for the Seyyids or Lords of Oman, and though now much dilapidated is still a fine building and one of the chief monuments of Portuguese dominion on this coast. The name it retains—Gareza—is a corruption of the Portuguese "Egreja"—a church.

Before Lopo Vaz left the Gulf of Oman he was joined by Hector da Silveira, who in April or May, 1526, had assaulted and destroyed Dhofar, and after a cruise in the Red Sea had proceeded to Muscat and Hormuz.

In January, 1528, Admiral Dom Antonio da Miranda da Azevedo set sail from Goa with twenty vessels for the Arabian Sea, with orders to make a demonstration against the Turks, who, under Mustapha Pasha, a nephew of Sultan Suliman, had established themselves at the Island of Kamaran to dominate the Red Sea.

Suliman I., Al-Kanooni (the Law Giver), from 1520–1566, made strenuous efforts during his reign to destroy the Portuguese power. The Turks probably occupied Kamaran soon after the conquest of Egypt by Suliman in 1517, as they then sent and conquered the Yemen.

Dom Antonio with his armada visited Kisheen and Aden, but did not venture to attack Shihr, which had been taken and occupied by Mustapha Pasha, nor did he enter the Straits of Bab el-Mandeb, but after destroying Zaili and making a short cruise in the Gulf of Aden, proceeded to Muscat, where he left his great ships under the Captain-Major, Antonio da Silva, and then took his galleys on to Hormuz for the winter. In the following August Antonio da Miranda Silva returned to Muscat, refitted his ships, and sailed again for another cruise in the Arabian Sea to intercept the Mecca ships. In April, 1528, Dom Nuno da Cunha, son of the famous Tristan da Cunha, who had been appointed Viceroy of India by King John, set out from Lisbon with a fleet to take up his post.

After a prolonged stay on the East Coast of Africa, where his disastrous attempt on Mombasa cost him dear, he set sail with the south-west monsoon, and anchored at Kilhat on May 10th, 1529, where he found Chief Captain Aires de S. da Magalhaes, who had been stationed there to guard the coast against the pirates, who infested the sea and robbed the ships trading with India. Da Cunha here received complaints against the factor of Kilhat, Gomez Ferreira, servant to the Duke of Braganza, who had lent money at usurious rate to the native merchants who shipped horses to Goa. Having issued a manifesto on the subject, the Viceroy made enquiry into all cases brought before him, with the result that he suspended several officers, whom he carried with him to Hormuz, much to the surprise of the Arabs, who had never before seen Portuguese officials punished for extortionate conduct.

Nine days later da Cunha was at Muscat, where he arrived on May 19th, and where he was at once visited by the Wazeer of the town, Shaikh Rashid, who had so well befriended the Portuguese in the last revolt. Here da Cunha left most of his ships and all of his men, who were still sick and suffering from the effects of the climate of Mombasa.

Shaikh Rashid had been the object of the Wazeer of Hormuz's (Rais Sherif) vindictive and malevolent hatred ever since the late disturbance, and the Rais had left no means untried to get him into his power. He had been frequently summoned to Hormuz in the King's name by Rais Sherif on the pretext that he had not rendered proper accounts and owed the King more than 20,000 ashrafies, but Shaikh Rashid had been too wary to obey, knowing that his life would not be worth an hour's purchase there.

The Shaikh now represented all this to da Cunha and offered to go to Hormuz under Portuguese protection and meet Rais Sherif's accusations by producing his accounts. The Viceroy, who was aware of Shaikh Rashid's loyalty, approved of this course, and having embarked on board the vessel of his brother, Simon da Cunha, proceeded to Hormuz, where he was received by the King, the Wazeer Rais Sherif, and the Commandant, Christevan Mendoza.

On the Shaikh's accounts being scrutinized and examined by a mixed commission it was found that they were in order and that no revenue was due by him to the King. His accounts were therefore signed in acquittance by the King by the Viceroy's orders. In recognition of the kindness and protection shown by Shaikh Rashid to the Portuguese at Muscat, whom he had been ordered to massacre by the King of Hormuz, but whom he had loyally shielded from injury during the revolt, da Cunha gave him a document in the name of the King of Portugal acknowledging his faithful services and also appointing him Wazeer of Hormuz in place of Rais Sherif, who was shipped off to Lisbon in the vessel of Manoel da Macedo.

Da Cunha's stay at Hormuz was eventful, and was signalized by the disastrous expedition to Bahrain, which proved very injurious to Portuguese prestige and in which his brother Simon lost his life. Leaving Hormuz on September 15th, 1529, da Cunha returned to Muscat, where he picked up the ships and the sick crews he had left there and proceeded on his voyage to India.

The system adopted by the Portuguese in their stations on the Arab coast was to maintain their political and commercial supremacy by retaining the citadel or fort which overawed and commanded the town, and by controlling the custom house and port. This gave them all the protection and trade advantages they required, but they did not interfere with the internal administration or with native habits, religion, and prejudices in so far as they did not affect themselves, and the people were thus left to their own laws and customs in all respects.

In February, 1532, Manoel da Vasconcello set out from Goa with a squadron of two galleys and eight brigantines to cruise after Turkish and Moorish prizes in the Arabian Sea. After sighting Socotra he steered for Shihr, where he expected to find many trading vessels, and where he picked up, among others, a large native craft richly laden, and which, after a struggle, was taken possession of and sent in charge of a prize crew to Muscat.

This expedition was followed shortly after by another of ten ships, under the command of Captain-Major Antonio da Saldanha, who had been delayed at Goa. This fleet, passing by Socotra, also stood for Shihr, where he was visited by the Sultan, who complained to him of the proceedings of Manoel da Vasconcello in seizing ships in his port. Steering for Aden, Saldanha was unable to face the monsoon, and on reaching Ras Fartak changed his course on April 26th and sailed to Muscat, where he arrived on May 6th, 1532. In this port, Antonio da Saldanha found Manoel da Vasconcello with his prize, also several vessels just arrived direct from Goa, commanded by John Rodrigues Pars, Vasco Perez Sampayo, and Antonio Fernandez, who all had the intention of cruising after Moorish craft and enriching themselves by taking prizes, and who, after waiting here till the force of the monsoon had been spent, sailed forth in quest of plunder.

In the following year, 1533, Diego da Silveira left India on his second voyage to Cape Guardafui, where he intended to intercept the craft trading between Sumatra and the Red Sea. On the completion of this cruise he sailed eastward to winter in the Persian Gulf, and on the way captured a large Turkish vessel and several other prizes. On anchoring at Muscat, Silveira found there John Fernandez, the "Taful or Gamester," who had taken a vessel which had produced a false pass, and had brought it in a prize for adjudication. It was condemned by the Captain-Major, and was sold at Muscat for 6,000 cruzados. Silveira left his galleys at Muscat and went on with his rowing vessels to Hormuz to pass the monsoon.

When the season opened the Captain-Major again set out for the Gulf of Aden, where he made many prizes. The smaller ones he burnt and the rest he brought back to Muscat, where they were sold for 80,000 pardaos.

For some forty years the all-powerful Turks, by the despatch of several naval expeditions, by reducing the Yemen and occupying various stations on the Arab littoral, had striven to destroy the growing power and commerce in the East, but they do not appear to have extended their hostile operations to the Persian Gulf until the year 1546, when four Turkish galliots, cruising from the Red Sea, sailed along the South Arabian Coast, and after destroying Kisheen and Dhofar, anchored at Muscat and bombarded the town. The Turkish guns were of very large calibre and threw cast-iron shot of a prodigious size into the place, causing terrible consternation and dismay but not much damage. The Turkish commander, however, did not venture to land his men, and sailed away again as empty-handed as he came. Some days later a vessel arrived from Dhofar bringing the son of the ruler of that province as envoy from his father, to complain of the Turkish proceedings in having battered their town, and built a castle there for their own garrison. The envoy having besought the protection of the Portuguese against the Turks, the Governor of Muscat decided it politic to comply, and issued orders for the Portuguese vessels cruising in the Gulf of Aden against Moorish traders to touch occasionally at Dhofar.

The second appearance of the Turks was in 1552, six years later, when a more formidable fleet, under Piri Pasha, Admiral of Egypt, who had been appointed to the command of this second expedition to the Arabian Sea after his return from his successful attempt to recover Aden. The proximate cause of this hostile demonstration against the Portuguese was the assistance rendered by their fleet, under Dom Antonio da Noronha, to the rebel Arabs at Busra the year before, when anchored in the Port of Muscat. This action had moved the Sublime Porte in retaliation to order Daood Pasha, the Wali of Egypt, to equip a fleet and despatch it with instructions to proceed to Busra direct, and from thence, in conjunction with the force awaiting him there, to sail to Hormuz and reduce it to submission. The Admiral Piri Pasha, to whom this important enterprise had been entrusted, spent many months in collecting ships, men and materials, and having completed his preparations set out from Suez in July, 1552 A.D. [A.H. 960], with a fleet of thirty sail, galleys, bashderdes, galletas and galleons, and 16,000 men. Meanwhile, the Portuguese were not left uninformed respecting the armament that was being prepared against them, and the Commandant at Hormuz, Alvaro da Noronha, having some inkling of the Turkish designs, sent one of his men in disguise to Shihr to collect particulars of the intended expedition. The spy confirmed the report, whereupon Noronha ordered two vessels to watch Ras al-Had, and on sighting the Turkish fleet, to set sail with the news, one for Goa and the other for Hormuz. The Turkish fleet, passing safely down the Red Sea, reached as far as Shihr, where it encountered a violent storm in which several vessels were lost, and then rounding Ras al-Had entered the Gulf of Oman. Here Piri Pasha sent forward five ships under his son to reconnoitre, and this advance guard nearly captured Noronha's two scouts, but by good fortune they eluded the enemy's grasp and succeeded in carrying the news of the Turkish Admiral's arrival to Goa and Hormuz. In the pursuit of one of these vessels Piri's son had been led as far as Ras Mussendom, and on turning back found that his father had already arrived with the rest of the fleet at Muscat.

The Commandant of Muscat at this time was Dom Joao da Lisboa, who had been sent out specially by the King of Portugal to construct a fortress that might command the town and protect the harbour. This fort had only been commenced about three months previously, and was still unfinished. The Commandant, da Lisboa, however, well knowing that the Turks would attack him, hastily provisioned it and threw himself into it with his little garrison of sixty men, after sending off his wife and other ladies in a boat to Hormuz.

The first action of the Turkish Admiral was to sack the town, which was undefended and yielded him a rich booty. He then turned his attention to the fort, which, as it was too strong for assault, he laid siege to and succeeded in battering down part of its unfinished walls by hauling one of his guns up to a height which commanded it. For eighteen days the Portuguese defended the position with vigour and kept the Turks at bay, but provisions and water falling short and the fort becoming untenable, the Commandant, da Lisboa, was induced by a renegade named John da Barrea, in the service of Piri Pasha, to open negotiations for the surrender of the fort. An interview was accordingly arranged between the Admiral and the Commandant, at which the former solemnly guaranteed life and liberty to the whole garrison on condition of immediate capitulation, declaring that the honour of capturing a Portuguese fort was sufficient for him.

The faithless Turk, however, did not abide by his promises, for instead of releasing the garrison he massacred part, probably the wounded and sickly, and chained the remainder, including Joao da Lisboa, to the galleys. Piri Pasha then dismantled the fort, and having shipped his booty and the Portuguese guns, weighed and set sail for Hormuz, where he landed his troops and plundered the town without resistance. The fort, however, held out, and the Pasha, after bombarding it for twenty days and finding he could make no impression, was obliged to raise the siege. An offer made by the Pasha to hold his Muscat prisoners to ransom was unaccountably declined by the Governor, Alvaro da Noronha, and da Lisboa and his comrades were left to their fate as galley slaves. The Turk, nevertheless, released da Lisboa's wife, who had been captured off Khor Fakan, while endeavouring to effect her escape.

The delay caused by the protracted operations at Muscat had afforded an opportunity to the merchants at Hormuz to remove their families and property to the Island of Kishm, of which full advantage had been taken. Thither, accordingly, Piri Pasha, who had been apprised of this manœuvre, and whose grand object in this expedition appears to have been not military glory, but the means of enriching himself, now steered his fleet, and was rewarded by the discovery of immense spoil. He took many captives, including a Spanish Jew named Solomon, who was reported to be the richest merchant in Hormuz.

Meanwhile the Portuguese fleet despatched from Goa had arrived in the Persian Gulf and soon chased the Turkish fleet up to Busra, but Piri Pasha, fearful of losing the treasure he had acquired, abandoned his command, and loading three galleys, which were his private property, with his booty, fled back to Egypt. One of the galleys was lost near Bahrain, but with the other two he arrived at Suez, where he was immediately seized by the Governor and soon after decapitated by orders from Constantinople, all his property being confiscated to the State. The destruction of Muscat was perhaps the most signal success the Turks ever achieved at sea in the Persian Gulf, and might have been attended with more decisive results had Piri Pasha been as eager to injure his enemy as he was to amass wealth for himself. But it had the effect of encouraging Sultan Suliman, the Lord of his Age (Sahib Keran, as the Turks love to call him), to renew his efforts to expel the Portuguese from the Persian Gulf. He ordered Moorad Pasha, formerly Wali of the Sanjak of Kateef, to assume the command of the vessels remaining at Busra (five galleys and one galetta), and to prepare a new fleet, with which he was instructed to proceed to the Red Sea to oppose a Portuguese fleet then cruising off Jedda.

Moorad Pasha sailed in August, 1553, from Busra with a fleet of sixteen galleys, but one sank and was lost, and two barges; but his movements had been closely watched by the Captain-Major, Diego da Noronha, who intercepted him between Mussendom and Henjam, and after a desperate engagement almost exterminated it. Two of the Turkish captains, Suliman Reis and Rajab Reis, with a great number of men, were killed, but the remnant of the fleet escaped in the night and hurried back to Busra.

The Turks could now no longer conceal from themselves the evident superiority of the Portuguese at sea; their efforts against them hitherto, so far from breaking up the Portuguese power in the East, had, on the contrary, only served to extend the prestige of Portugal. Had the Turks been able to foresee more clearly the dire results in the future to their Empire from the change in the course of trade effected by the Portuguese, they would doubtless have put forth the utmost of their strength in the East, and combined with the Asiatics to expel their commercial rivals from India. Being then in the plenitude of their strength, and still invincible at sea in Europe, the Turks might have floated in the Arabian Sea a far more formidable armada than they ever attempted to get together, and by taking advantage of the religious zeal which then undoubtedly burnt throughout Islam, they might have enlisted in their cause, and secured the alliance of, both the Shah Tahmasp Suffar, Ruler of Persia, and Babèr, First Mogul Emperor of India, and thus possibly have kept Europeans out of the Indian Ocean for many years to come. But even the genius of the great Suliman seems to have failed to grasp the vital importance of concentrating his energies in this direction, and instead of cultivating friendly relations with Persia was actually at this time (1553) engaged in preparing for his second war with that Power, and, worse still, in foully murdering the very man who could best have seconded his efforts to crush the Infidel—his brilliant son, Prince Mustafa. This was, indeed, one of the most critical periods of the world—the balance of power had begun to shift from the hands of the Moslem to those of the Christian, and with the death of Suliman in 1566, succeeded as he was by a feeble youth, the opportunity for destroying Portuguese supremacy in the East passed away for ever.

The old Sultan Suliman was not dismayed by Moorad Pasha's discomfiture, but struck one final blow at the Infidels who had dared to undermine his Empire by their energy and enterprise, before relinquishing the contest and leaving them to enjoy the fruits of their discoveries and monopoly. It so happened that this final struggle between the Turks and Portuguese, which took place in the Arabian Sea, was also the most hardly contested and decisive sea fight in which the former had ever been engaged. The Battle of Muscat is described by the Turkish historian, Hajji Khalfa, as being a greater affair than the Battle of Lepanto, which was fought between Kheir-al-Deen (Barbarossa) and the Spanish Admiral, Andria Doria, at Lepanto in 1538.

The remainder of Moorad Pasha's ill-fated squadron formed the nucleus of the new fleet, for the organization and command of which Sultan Suliman took care this time to select a man whom he thought he could trust. This person was a distinguished sailor named Sidi Ali bin Hoosain, who had served under the famous Barbarossa or Kheir al-Deen at Rhodes, and had been governor of the arsenal at Stamboul. He had been appointed Capudan or Admiral of Egypt by the Sultan as a reward for his services and was also well known as an author of scientific works, his " takhallus " (nom de plume) being Katibi. Having received the Sultan's command to attack the Portuguese and bring his fleet round to Suez, he started from Constantinople and travelled by Aleppo, Mosul, and Baghdad to Busra in December, 1553. Having arrived at Busra, Sidi Ali at once set to work with earnest diligence to collect materials to repair and refit the fleet. In view of the recent defeat of Noorah Pasha, it is much to be wondered at that the Admiral did not strain his energies to increase and strengthen his armada, seeing that it was manifestly inadequate to the task of coping with the Portuguese, but this does not appear to have been attempted. The Wali or Governor of Busra, Shereef Mustafa Pasha, who had in the meantime been despatched from that city by the Porte with a frigate to reconnoitre Hormuz, sent to inform the Capudan Sidi Ali that the Infidels had only four ships on the station, and shortly after proceeded to join the Turkish armada, which had set sail from Busra in July, 1554. Expecting an easy conquest over what he supposed the feeble force of his enemy, the Admiral pressed on in eager haste to Bahrain, where he anchored and had an interview with the Governor, Moorad Reis. Thence the fleet sailed on past the Straits of Mussendom and first sighted the Portuguese fleet off the little port of Khor Fakan on the 10th Ramzan, 961 A.H. (10th August, 1553 A.D.). It was much larger than he had been led to anticipate, as it consisted of three galleons, four barges, six guardships and twelve galettas. The Captain-Major at Hormuz at this time, Dom Fernandez de Menezes, had been duly notified of the preparations being made at Busra, and kept himself well informed as to the Turkish Admiral's proceedings. He had, therefore, gathered a considerable force of galleys, fustas, and caravellos to repel the threatened attack, but in order to conceal his real strength he had with much sagacity stationed the superior vessels of his armada at Muscat, and had thus deceived the Turkish scouts, who had not ventured to reconnoitre beyond the Straits of Hormuz. In July, 1554, he sent out three vessels to cruise in the Gulf, and there learned from native boats that the Turks had already started. Spies disguised as fishermen were then sent to sell fish to the enemy and in this way precise intelligence of the Turkish Admiral's whereabouts was obtained. On receiving this warning the Captain-Major, Fernandez de Menezes, embarked the same day with Antonio da Noronha, and proceeded to Muscat with his light vessels to join his armada. Taking command the Captain-Major weighed and began his cruise in search of the Turks and soon learned from a captain in command of a galley, named de Souza, that the Turks had weathered Ras Mussendom and were approaching in single line. He accordingly gave orders to clear for action, and prepared to open the ball with a cannonade.

The Turkish galleys, however, which were off the cove of Lima, made for the land, and as the wind freshened began to drive on shore. De Menezes, not caring to attack under the circumstances, took counsel with his officers, and after some skirmishing decided to retire to Muscat with his fleet, leaving his light vessels to watch the enemy. He accordingly returned to Muscat and watered his ships, sending out more boats to observe the Turkish galleys. The Portuguese were in their first encounter decidedly worsted by the Turks, who compelled their foe to retire to Muscat and followed them up thither. The Turkish account of this action is thus given by Mitchell :—

> "On sighting the Portuguese fleet," he says, "the Moslems immediately hoisted their colours, weighed anchor, and got in readiness all their warlike machines. With flags hoisted and sail spread, and looking in confidence to the Supreme Being, they set up Muhammadan shouts and commenced an attack, the fierceness of which baffles description. By the favour of God their fire struck one of the Portuguese galleons, which was wrecked on the Island of Fakk al-Asad. They fought bravely till nightfall, when the Capudan hoisted the lights. The Infidels, however, fired a gun as the signal of retreat and fled to Hormuz. Thus by the favour of God the victory was left to the Moslems, who, favoured by the winds, departed next day for the city of Khor Fakan, where the troops took in a supply of fresh water, and after seventeen days' sailing arrived in the neighbourhood of Muscat and Aden."

The Captain-Major did not venture out to attack the Turks until they had arrived so menacingly near Muscat that he could no longer refuse battle.

On this day two remarkable events are said to have occurred at Muscat, and were doubtless looked on as omens by the superstitious Portuguese. There came into the cove a marine monster larger than a whale and of a shape so strange that no one had ever seen the like before. It swam several times round the ship of the Captain-Major de Menezes and scared the sailors probably out of their wits.

But this marvellous creature did not frighten the Arabs, who, looking on it as a godsend, soon captured it and towed it on shore at Moculla Chini. The other event was the appearance of a large and fiery comet, which eventually fell over the locality of the coming battle. Whether these were taken by the Portuguese as favourable or unfavourable signs we are not told. While the fleet was at anchor, the fustas sent out on scout returned with the news that the Turks had arrived off the Deymanieh Islands, about twelve leagues from Muscat, and the Captain-Major immediately ordered ensigns to be hoisted, anchors weighed, and sails set to meet the enemy. When the hostile fleets sighted each other, which was at 9 a.m. on August 25th, the Turkish galleys were rowing along the Batineh shore, the wind being contrary, opposite Ghobia or Khaleed and about two leagues from Muscat, while the Portuguese fleet kept to seaward, encircling the coast to prevent the galleys escaping.

The Capudan, Sidi Ali, now tried to obtain an offing and nine of his galleys appear to have cut the Portuguese lines, but the other six were hemmed in as they had remained astern. Jeronymo Castello Branco, who was in advance of all, was the first to engage one of the galleys, and other vessels remaining in shore began to close with the Turks. The fight as regards the six galleys became general, some were burnt and others boarded and carried after severe hand-to-hand combats with the Turks. All the latter, who had thrown themselves into the sea during the fight, were put to death by the Portuguese. All this while Sidi Ali and the nine galleys, being in the offing, took no part in the fight, but watched it from a distance, and on seeing his six galleys surrender waited no longer to try and stem the current of victory, but stood out to sea and steered to the north-east towards the opposite coast, intending to make for Cambay, as he dared not go to Constantinople, where the Sultan would assuredly decapitate him. The carrevellos, seeing the Turks fly, set sail and chased them to the coast of India. The victorious de Menezes then returned to Muscat to look after his wounded. He ordered the six galleys captured from the Turks to be repaired and ransomed from those who had taken them prizes. The spoils included forty-six brass cannon, such as basilisks, esperas (40-pounder guns) and other small pieces known as camels, eagles, etc. It may be interesting to give the story of the fight as told by the vanquished, and I here quote again from Mitchell's translation :—

"On the morning of the 26th Ramzan, 961 A.H. [25th August, 1553 A.D.] the Captain of Goa, the son of the Governor, left the harbour of Muscat and with his barges, guardships, and galleons, with their mainsails spread and colours flying, sailed against the Moslems, who still trusting in God remained near the shore prepared for battle. The enemy's barges first came up and attacked the galleys, when a sharp fire was opened on both sides and a furious engagement ensued. The Infidels then began to shower down their hand-grenades from the main-tops upon the galleys, one of which and a barge, which was near it, they burnt by throwing a bomb into the galley. Five barges and as many galleys were driven ashore and lost. Another barge was driven ashore by the violence with which the wind beat against it and was lost. At length the sailors and the troops on both sides were exhausted, the former being unable to pull at the oars and the latter to work the guns any longer; they were, therefore, obliged to cast anchor; but even in this position they fought for some time with springs to their cables. They were finally obliged to abandon their boats. Elmshah Reis, Kara Mustapha, and Kalfah Mumi, the commanders of the lost galleys, and Duzzi Mustaffa Bey, the commander of the volunteers, with about 200 Egyptian soldiers reached the shore in safety and afterwards returned to the fleet, bringing with them many Arabs to the assistance of the Moslems. The Infidels also recovered the men who were in their barges which had been driven ashore. This battle was even greater than that between Kheir al-Deen and Andeia Doria. Few soldiers are known to have ever been engaged in such a fight. At last when night approached, a strong gale began to blow and each of the barges threw out two stream anchors, but the men on board were so overcome with fatigue that they were obliged to stand out from the shore and sail before the wind. In this way they came to the coast of Bar Jask, where, finding plenty of sea, they succeeded in reaching Bundar Charbar in Mekran. Here they took in water, and by the direction of a pilot reached Bundar Gwadur, the Governor of which, Malik Dinar Oghli Jeladdin, came to examine the state of their fleet and represented to the Sultan the necessity of sending supplies, in consequence of which fifty or sixty vessels with provisions were sent out and joined them before they reached Ormuz. From Bundar Gwadur the Capudan again sailed with nine vessels for the Indian Ocean, and directed his course toward the Yemen. For a few days the weather was favourable and they had arrived in the neighbourhood of Zaffar and Shedjer when the westerly winds began to blow and they were overtaken by the storm called 'The Elephant,' before which they scudded, being unable even to carry the foresail."

The complete defeat of the Turks with the loss of six galleys was thus manifest beyond all dispute, and their disaster was twofold. They not only suffered a severe defeat at the hands of the enemy against whom they had undertaken offensive operations, but being prevented by the monsoon from reaching Suez, were driven back to the Indian coast, where the remainder of the fleet with all their guns, ammunition, stores, and slaves, had to be abandoned or surrendered to the Governor of Surat, with whom also the Turkish soldiers and sailors took service.

The Admiral, Sidi Ali, however, did not remain at Surat but visited other cities in India, not daring to show himself in Turkey, but at last he left Surat in November, 1554, and returned home through Persia overland to Constantinople in May, 1557, with fifty attendants, and his misfortunes having been by that time forgotten and forgiven, he was given a small pension, as were also the fifty men who accompanied him.

This notable sea fight took place between Khaleel on the coast and Fahil, a rocky islet about six miles from Muscat, which was henceforth called by the Portuguese "The Island of Victory." It lasted the whole of the day and must have been a sanguinary and obstinate contest, but we are not told the exact loss of the Portuguese by de Couto, who leads one to believe that Sidi Ali did not take part in it but left the six galleys to their fate. The Turkish account seems to be more candid and trustworthy. The decisive effect of the victory, however, is shown by the fact that they never more confronted the Portuguese navy in the Indian Ocean.

From this time maritime affairs appear to have gone on pretty smoothly in the Persian Gulf; the Portuguese remained undisputed masters of the situation and the utter rout of the fleet of the Grand Turk contributed greatly to enhance their military prestige and had, doubtless, a sobering effect on the logical minds of the Persians and Arabs, for we hear but little of them or of any stirring events on the Arabian coast for nearly thirty years.

In the year 1580 (or 81) news reached the Gulf that an expedition was being prepared at Aden for the purpose of attacking and pillaging Muscat. The rumour was not credited by the Governor of Hormuz, Dom Gonçales de Menzes, who neglected to send any reinforcements, and contented himself with warning the Muscat garrison to be watchful and ready for resistance.

The Governor of Muscat, on the other hand, being better acquainted with the unfriendly feeling of the Oman tribes towards the Portuguese, and having good reason to believe that the scheme had originated in his own neighbourhood among the chiefs who had conveyed intimation to the Governor of Al-Yemen, a renegade Italian named Mirat al-Zeman, that Muscat was in a very defenceless condition and that a rich booty would reward a sudden raid, was fully convinced of the truth of the report, and resolved on making preparations to meet the attack. In order to guard against surprise he despatched a scout named Alvaro Murato in a swift vessel to cruise off Ras al-Had, and bring back instant intelligence of the approach of the corsairs.

As the south-west monsoon then prevailed, fresh rumours of

the expedition were, no doubt, continually being brought to Muscat by vessels arriving from the Gulf of Aden, and every effort should have been made to resist the threatened blow, but as Murato, the scout, did not return with tidings of it, the garrison appears to have been lulled into a false security and to have relaxed their watchfulness.

Mirat al-Zemam, the Pasha, had entrusted the command of the expedition to a Turkish adventurer named Meer Ali Beg, who with four galleys left Aden at the end of August, 1580. In passing along the Arabian coast one of the galleys foundered and was lost, the galley-slaves, who tugged at the oars and were chained to their seats, perishing probably to a man. The filibusters, now reduced to three galleys, continued their voyage, and giving Ras al-Had a wide berth, by which they eluded the vigilance of Alvaro Murato, arrived off Muscat on the evening of September 22nd. Meer Ali Beg, however, suspecting that the garrison would be on their guard and that he might have to encounter superior odds with his little force, had astutely determined not to attack the town boldly in front but to adopt a plan of tactics by which he hoped to confound and surprise the defenders. Instead of entering the harbour, therefore, Ali Beg proceeded to the little bay and village of Sedab, where he quietly landed with 150 men and sent the galleys round to Muscat with instructions to appear before the city at dawn and commence an immediate bombardment, making at the same time a feint of leaving the boats and pretending to land soldiers, in order to concentrate the attention of the garrison in that direction. During the night Ali Beg with his band made his way from the little bay where he had landed to the walls of Muscat, from which it is distant about a mile. Here he divided his men into three parties and posted one at each of the three gates, ordering them to lie concealed until the morning broke and the guns of the galleys opening fire on the town should give the signal for attack.

The Portuguese civil residents in the city at this time, exclusive probably of the garrison, numbered about 500 souls, of whom only about seventy were capable of bearing arms. They had received no warning, as we have seen, from the scout Murato of the approach of the enemy, and having already from the length of time that had elapsed begun to discredit the truth of the rumours, were embowered in a fool's paradise, and were at this moment slumbering in their houses unconscious of danger. They had omitted the precaution of sending their families and valuables to a place of safety, and notwithstanding the corroboration of the impending invasion given by the Arabs to the Governor, they were still unprepared for resistance. An accident first revealed the presence of the Turks, but it was then too late to repair the consequences of negligence. It is related that a merchant named Diego Machád, desiring to bury his treasure outside the town, came to one of the gates with the intention of passing through to the suburbs in the night. He reached one of Ali Beg's posts, and the robbers, fearing discovery, or perceiving the bag of money, stabbed him in the road and relieved him of it. His servant, who was following, fled back to the gate and raised an alarm, while almost simultaneously the three Turkish galleys entered the harbour and began their cannonade.

The sudden appearance of the foe in front and in rear caused the utmost confusion and excitement among both the garrison and the citizens, and led to a feeble and distracted resistance on their part. The gates were soon forced by Ali Beg, who after some fighting appears to have driven the garrison into the citadel or gareza. While most of the citizens took refuge at Muttrah with their women, and some, it is said, even fled terror-stricken as far as Bosher, a village about eighteen miles distant, where they were well received by the Arabs. Ali Beg's main purpose was not, it seems, to expel the Portuguese but to pillage the town, and this he did in the most thorough and effective manner, with the hearty assistance of the rif-raf of the town and negro slaves, who, no doubt, cordially detested their Portuguese masters. He did not remain long in the place, knowing that the Governor would soon obtain reinforcements. One day sufficed to sack the town and collect the booty, which was shipped on board the galleys and on three vessels that had been captured in the harbour, and Ali Beg, triumphant in his enterprise, set sail for Aden.

The Governor of Hormuz, Dom Gonçales de Menzes, immediately on hearing of the arrival of the Turkish galleys at Muscat, despatched Luiz d'Almeida with a squadron, consisting of a galleon, a galley, and six smaller vessels, to intercept and destroy Ali Beg's flotilla. Had this squadron been stationed at Muscat when the rumours of the expedition first arrived it might have annihilated the filibusters and saved the town, but it was a case of shutting the stable door after the horse had been stolen. Luiz d'Almeida, not caring to face the enemy or finding that they had got too long a start, gave up the pursuit, and instead of steering west after the galleys, steered east for Mekran with the object of doing a little plunder on his own account, and looted in succession the seaport towns of Pussnee, Gwader and Teez.

Ali Beg's subsequent career was an eventful one. Elated with his success at Muscat he began to undertake piratical expeditions against the Portuguese settlements on the East Coast of Africa, and nine years later (1589) was taken prisoner during a raid of his on Mombasa, by Thome da Souza Coutinho, who sent him to Lisbon, where, under the gentle persuasions and *supplices* of the Inquisition, he turned Christian and died, probably from the effects of torture.

It was in this same year (1580) that Portugal was brought by Philip II. under the domination of Spain after a bloodless invasion. The Portuguese, however, obtained more privileges and concessions than they could have expected after the passive resistance they had offered, and were allowed, among other things, to retain their monopoly of the trade to India and Persia. The decadence of Lusitanian power in the East is usually dated from this event, and is ascribed by Portuguese historians to the indifference of the Spanish Court during the sixty years that Portugal remained under Spanish subjection. During this period certainly Hormuz and other places were lost, and Portuguese influence declined, but there were other influences at work, such as the Dutch and English rivalry, and other factors combined to produce this result. The Viceroys at Goa were all Portuguese noblemen and displayed no want of vigour, and in the Persian Gulf the loss of Hormuz was partly compensated by the building of forts at Muscat and Sohar.

The exploit of Ali Beg had shown unmistakably enough to the Portuguese authorities that Muscat was unprepared for an attack by sea, and it was obvious that they might again be exposed to a similar blow unless further and more efficient means of defence were afforded. In this way the stroke aimed at it by Ali Beg, though severely felt, was not without good results. It was, moreover, suspected by the Portuguese, that the Turkish Government had an eye on this port, and would at no distant date make an effort to gain possession of it, as in the hands of a naval power it commands the Straits of Mussendom as Aden commands the Red Sea, and it would have been of incalculable service to the Turks in protecting and fostering the Busra trade. It was some years, however, before the dilatory Government at Lisbon could be induced to sanction the erection of the forts, and the year 1586 had arrived before the Viceroy was entrusted to commence them. The first was entrusted to Melchior Calaca, who commanded one of the ships at Muscat, and who erected it on an eminence to the east of the town, which was levelled at the top and scarped for the purpose. This castle, consisting of two towers or bastions connected by a curtain, still stands in its entirety, though somewhat dilapidated and battered by shot, with its guns, embrasures and battlements, mounting guard over the anchorage. It was completed in 1587, and called San Joao—now known to the Arabs as Killa Jalali. The new Viceroy, Dom Manoel de Souza Coutinho, who left Lisbon in 1587 to take up his appointment, appears to have received orders before starting to complete the defences, and under his auspices the plans laid down by his predecessor, Dom Duarte de Menezes, were brought to a conclusion. This latter Viceroy had charged Dom Martin Affonso de Mello Pombeyro, who had distinguished himself by expelling the Turks from East Africa, to undertake the work, but this officer had died at Hormuz before he could take it in hand. His successor in command of the fleet was therefore directed to carry out the scheme, and the fort that had been left unfinished by da Lisboa thirty years before, on the west side of the town, was recommenced and very skilfully and elaborately brought to a termination in the following year, 1588. It contains a chapel with an inscription and holy water cup, and a long inscription still existing almost perfect over the inner gateway records the particulars and date. It was then called Fort Capitan, but it is now named by the Arabs Killa Merani.

Late in the year 1615, or early in 1616, the Chief of Sohar, Mohammed bin Mohenna, instigated by Sultan bin Himyar, raided the district of Seeb belonging to the Ameer Umeyr bin Himyar, who was absent at Bahila at the time. The attack took the inhabitants by surprise and was successful, the Ameer's brother, Ali bin Himyar, being killed in the fray. The Ameer was greatly incensed at the affair, and vowed vengeance against Mohammed bin Mohenna, going so far in his thirst for vengeance as to call in the aid of the Portuguese, whom he seems to have promised to put in possession again of Sohar. The bait was too tempting to be refused, and the Governor of Hormuz, who had been appealed to as the senior authority, delighted at the prospect of recovering Sohar and destroying its trade rivalry with Muscat, at once recommended the Viceroy to accede to the request for aid and send a force for the purpose. The senior officer in command of the squadron of five vessels at Hormuz at this time was Dom Vasco da Gama, whose force was joined in February, 1616, by Dom Francisco Rolim from Goa with six ships, laden with stores and munitions of war. The Ameer made Muscat his headquarters while he collected his troops and got together a number of Arab Bughlas to co-operate with the Portuguese fleet; he then marched to Seeb with 1,200 men, accompanied by a small Portuguese land force. Mohammed bin Mohenna meanwhile had also been seeking allies, and had been joined by Mohammed bin Jafir, who, however, soon quarrelled with the Chief of Sohar and deserted him. This news encouraged the Ameer, who after a halt of seven days at Seeb, moved along the Batineh coast on to Sohar, where he arrived on the 19th of the month of the second Rabi. Here some indecisive skirmishing took place in front of the city between the Arabs, and the suburbs were occupied by the Ameer. In the meantime, the naval expedition having anchored, the Portuguese landed their men and guns and commenced to bombard the fort, using gabions stuffed with cotton, and guns mounted on wooden carriages and fitted with wooden screens for their siege batteries. The first conflict took place at a detached tower which was strongly garrisoned. This was battered, and in a breach entrance was soon effected by the Portuguese, who repulsed a sortie from the fort made by Mohammed bin Mohenna and Ali bin Thebad to relieve it, in which both those leaders were slain. The command of the besieged garrison now devolved on Sultan bin Himyar, who retired into the citadel, which, after a bloody contest in which Sultan bin Himyar was killed, the Arabs surrendered to the Portuguese, who made an indiscriminate massacre of the garrison and inhabitants, and burned the town to ashes in violation of the terms of capitulation. The Portuguese sacked the town before burning it, and carried off a number of Arab girls as slaves. In pursuance of the agreement made with the Ameer the Portuguese remained in occupation of the fort, which they at once set to work to repair, and the expeditionary force returned to Muscat. The Ameer Umeyr bin Himyar, having gratified his revenge and rewarded his adherents, dismissed them and then returned to Nakhl, from whence he proceeded to Semail.

The Portuguese now found themselves confronted by foes of a different calibre to the ill-armed Asiatics they had hitherto had to deal with. The Dutch and English had appeared in the East to dispute the mastery of the sea, to oppose them as commercial rivals, and eventually, as time proved, to cause the disruption of their Eastern Empire. Many and severe were the engagements that ensued between these three nations, but the Portuguese power had already begun to wane and could not long sustain the unequal contest. The Oriental navigations of the English commenced towards the close of the sixteenth century, and it was not very long before they felt strong enough to venture into the Persian Gulf as rivals with the Portuguese for the Persian trade. In 1613 the ship *Expedition*, of 260 tons, with the Ambassador to Persia, Sir Thomas Shirley, on board, arrived at Gwader, from whence Sir Thomas proposed to march up to the capital—Ispahan—overland. A plot of the treacherous Belooches to murder the whole embassy and crew of the *Expedition* was, however, fortunately discovered in time and the vessel proceeded on to India. On the way thither they captured a terada or native trader of fifteen tons, the Nakhoda or Master of which exhibited in defence a pass which he had purchased from the Governor of Muscat to prevent molestation by the Portuguese ships. This pass Sir Thomas Shirley thought fit to transcribe as a proof of the complete subjugation to which the Portuguese had reduced the maritime trade of the Arabian Sea, not allowing any vessel, large or small, to navigate it without their permission.

The first encounter between the English and Portuguese in the Gulf of Oman appears to have taken place in 1620, in which year a fleet consisting of the *London*, 800 tons; *Hart*, 500 tons; *Roebuck*, 300 tons; and the *Eagle*, 280 tons; sailed from Tilbury Hope for Surat, from whence two of the ships, the *Hart* and *Eagle*, set out for Jask. Jask is situated at the extreme south-west corner of Persia in the Gulf of Oman, and about 150 miles from Muscat. Mr. Steel, the original promoter of the English trade with Persia, had recommended this port as a suitable one for the English to occupy and use as their entrepôt seven years before, and the English Company's agent at Ispahan had subsequently obtained a grant from the Shah for this purpose. One vessel with merchandise had been despatched thither in 1614 and had made a favourable beginning in trading with the inhabitants. Jask and Gombroon were now the two points on which the English had cast their eyes for forming depôts. The Portuguese, however, were not blind to this encroachment on their monopoly and had resolved to strain every nerve to counteract and strangle this incipient commerce and to thwart the English in every possible way. With this view General Dom Frere da Andrada had been specially despatched from Lisbon, with Dom Joao Boralho as his vice-admiral, in command of a strong fleet. The *Hart* and *Eagle*, on arrival at Jask, found this force waiting in the Gulf of Oman to intercept and attack them, and judging themselves unable to cope with it, were returning to Surat for reinforcements when they met the *London* and *Roebuck* on their way to join them. The four ships together then steered for Jask, where they arrived on December 15th, 1620, having captured on the way, on November 21st, a Portuguese ship of 200 tons bound from Muscat to Chaul with a cargo of horses. The Portuguese fleet consisted of two galleons, one of which was larger than the *London*, two galliots, and ten frigates, and was accompanied by two Dutch galleons, one commanded by Antonio Mesquitta and the other by Belthazar de Chaves, the Dutch being then as eager as the Portuguese to debar the English from participation in the Persian trade. On December 16th, the English were engaged in fitting up their prize as a fireship, but as it fell calm during the day they were unable to do more than exchange long shots with the enemy. The breeze springing up the following morning, the Portuguese, who had the weather gauge, weighed and closed. The battle began at 9 a.m. and continued without intermission for nine hours, the two fleets manœuvring and exchanging broadsides till, night coming on, the smaller Dutch ship, pressed by the *Roebuck*, turned tail and fled, and was soon followed by the rest of the Dutch and Portuguese fleet, which disappeared in the darkness. The English ships anchored for the night in the road. The prize that had been fitted up as a fireship had been lighted and burnt early in the day, but had failed to injure the enemy's vessels, but the English had shown their superiority and claimed the victory without dispute.

Though none of the Portuguese ships appear to have been captured, their vessels suffered severely and they lost the Vice-Admiral Boralho and thirty men in one ship alone, while the English had but few damages to repair and had lost only one man. The next morning the Portuguese were discovered in the offing to the eastward, from whence they made no attempt to renew the engagement but remained there during the next ten days, watching the English and awaiting supplies and reinforcements from Muscat. Having been worsted in their endeavours to drive away the English by force, they had changed their tactics and now sought to harass and impede them by compelling them to remain together, as if they separated the vessels could be cut off in detail and thus the

Portuguese hoped to frustrate the prosecution of the English trade with Persia. This Fabian policy suited Dom Frere da Andrada well, as he had the fortified strongholds of Hormuz and Muscat as bases of operation and as harbours of refuge to retire to, while the English could get no supplies or seek refuge at any port nearer than Surat. In the meantime the English landed their cargoes at Jask, and on December 28th, having repaired damages as well as they could, and perceiving that their opponents were in greater force and assuming a more menacing attitude, determined to renew the contest, and, with this object in view, anchored within a cable and a half of the Portuguese fleet, on which they immediately opened a heavy broadside fire. The action was fought with great obstinacy on both sides until 3 p.m., when the Portuguese Admiral, finding himself hopelessly vanquished, gave the signal to cut cables and sheer off. The English thenceforward remained in undisturbed possession of Jask, but they had to deplore the loss of Captain Shilling, their commander, who was killed by a cannon shot in the action.

In February the English squadron sailed for Surat, where they refitted and remained until the following May, when they set out to pass the monsoon at the Island of Maseera, where it arrived on June 2nd, 1621. The *London* then seems to have parted company as on July 6th she was found to be lying at Soor, after visiting Taiwee, where she had watered, and where she had lost her surgeon and chaplain's servant, who had been surprised and taken prisoners by the Portuguese and Arabs. A month later the *Hart* and *Roebuck*, having weighed from Maseera, joined the *London* at Soor, from whence they all returned soon after to Surat. On November 14th of the same year another English expedition, consisting of five ships and four pinnaces, was despatched from Surat to the Persian Gulf under the command of Captain Blythe, with orders to co-operate with the Persians in effecting the reduction of Hormuz and thus deprive the Portuguese of their main stronghold in that quarter.

This squadron arrived in sight of Hormuz on December 23rd, but as the Persians were not ready, it occupied the time in harassing the Portuguese and obstructing their trade. The siege of Hormuz was begun by the English on February 9th, in conjunction with the Persian land force, and the result, after a brave defence, was the surrender of that fortress and entrepôt to the English commander on May 23rd, 1622; the Portuguese officers being sent prisoners to India and the European population, said to number 2,000 souls, being allowed to retire to Muscat. This important event was a staggering blow to the Portuguese and commenced the disruption of their Empire in the East. The Arabs, who hated the Portuguese and Persians in an equal degree, contributed to the success of the latter by an attack on, and capture of, Julfar, now Ras al-Khyma, which was the main source of supply the garrison at Hormuz had to rely on. They would, no doubt, have gladly helped to bring about the expulsion of the Infidels from Muscat had they not known full well that the substitution of Persian rule there for Portuguese would have been a case of "out of the frying-pan into the fire." For it was soon spread abroad that the Persians, elated with the recovery of Hormuz, had turned their attention to the conquest of Muscat and Sohar. The occupation of the latter place appears to have been easily accomplished, but for the capture of Muscat the aid of a maritime power was requisite, and negotiations were accordingly set on foot with the English commander. Being reluctant to enter on this service, the latter demanded exorbitant terms. These were that Hormuz should be given over to the English with half the revenues of the Custom House and city, the English on their part maintaining there four ships for the protection of trade in the Gulf. These terms were not acceptable to the Persians, who were as jealous of the English as they had been of the Portuguese, and would rather hold Hormuz a deserted, bare and desolate rock than yield it to the Infidel to be restored to life and prosperity. The negotiations, accordingly, fell through, but the English commander was ready to sell to the Persians, who had determined to carry on the war in Oman alone, a small frigate which was damaged and of no use to himself. The Persian expedition against Muscat appears to have taken place in the early part of 1623, but we have no definite account of what transpired. It certainly failed, however, and it is probable that this was due to the energy of the Portuguese Admiral, Ruy Frere da Andrada. This capable and experienced officer had been taken prisoner by the English at Hormuz and sent to India, but had escaped, and after reaching Muscat had proceeded to Goa, where the Viceroy, Dom Francisco da Gama, gave him the command of six ships, and despatched him in April, 1623, to the relief of Muscat. This he seems to have effected in so decisive a manner that we hear of no more efforts made by the Persians against Muscat. Shortly after Ruy Frere was reinforced by several vessels despatched to him by the Viceroy from Chaul and Diu to continue the war against the Persians, and he now felt strong enough to change the face of affairs and to assume the offensive in the Gulf against the enemy. He determined, first of all, to attempt the recovery of Sohar, and having collected his fleet he accordingly proceeded thither with sixteen ships. This fort had in the meantime been greatly strengthened by the Persians and could now offer a formidable resistance.

Ruy Frere's first assault on the castle was repulsed with a loss of twenty-one men and four officers, but the siege was carried on so energetically that the Persians at length were compelled to capitulate, and it was agreed that they should march out with the honours of war. Having decided to take possession, Ruy Frere ordered the outer fortlet to be razed to the ground, and having garrisoned the citadel he then sailed on to Khor Fakan, which was also held by the Persians, and here he was again successful, storming the little fort and putting the entire garrison to the sword.

Ruy Frere's success had encouraged his men and raised the prestige of his fleet, and feeling secure with Muscat as his base, he determined to delay no longer in undertaking the main object of his expedition, viz., the re-capture of Hormuz. Having anchored in that port, therefore, and satisfied himself that an attack on shore was out of the question with his small force, he established an effective blockade of the island to cut off supplies and communication, and maintained this state of siege, notwithstanding the inadequacy of his means, with great vigour and persistency for about six months.

This blockade and the destruction of much of the coasting craft in the vicinity of Hormuz reduced the Persian garrison to such distress from want of provisions that they were brought to the verge of starvation and almost to the point of surrender. Meanwhile the Viceroy at Goa, Dom Francisco da Gama, was engaged in collecting a powerful armament for the reconquest of Hormuz, designing, as rumour said, and the slowness of his preparations lent colour to the slander, to arrive in time to reap the glory of the capture after Ruy Frere had reduced the defenders to straits. The Viceroy's scheme, however, overreached itself, for he procrastinated so long that Ruy Frere, being unsupported and in want of provisions himself, was compelled to raise the siege and retire to Muscat.

In April, 1624, the first squadron of the great armada against Hormuz, consisting of ten ships, left Goa for Muscat under Sancho da Toar, and shortly after him, five more vessels were despatched. Besides these, three galleons were ordered from Mozambique to join Ruy Frere at Muscat. Before these reinforcements could arrive, however, the Admiral, impatient of delay, had despatched Michael Pereira on April 24th, 1624, with twelve ships to recommence the blockade, but it was not until four months afterwards, August 24th, that having mustered the rest of his fleet, which comprised twenty-five galliots and many boats, and put it in order for the campaign, he was able at length to sail for Hormuz and direct the operations.

Hormuz had in the meanwhile been again strengthened and provisioned, but the siege was now prosecuted by Ruy Frere with such relentless vigour, during the remainder of the year, that it would have unquestionably soon fallen again into the hands of the Portuguese had not a fleet of ten English and Dutch ships arrived to relieve it—both these nations regarding the recovery of Hormuz as highly detrimental to their interests. Ruy Frere immediately detached a squadron to meet it and in January, 1625, an action was fought in which both sides lost heavily and the Portuguese Vice-Admiral, Nuno Alvarez Botello, was wounded.

In the following month another and more severe battle took place between the fleets, in which the Portuguese, who were decidedly superior in force, seem to have had the advantage, but could not claim the victory. Botello now retired to Muscat, from whence he again sailed in September to cruise against the enemy. Off the Indian coast he fell in with three English ships, and a sharp skirmish took place between them, neither being able to claim the advantage. Thus ended the abortive effort of the Portuguese great expedition to recover Hormuz from the Persians, and Ruy Frere, who had shown himself a brave, active, and skilful commander, felt unable to maintain the siege any longer, and was compelled for the second time to withdraw his hand when the fruit was almost within his grasp. He retired first to Larek and from thence to Khasab, intending to wait for the expected main body of the fleet from Goa. He was doomed to disappointment. The ships that had arrived under da Toar were only the first squadron of the armada. The European enemies of the Portuguese were now too powerful in the Gulf to permit them to regain their old supremacy, and all hope of the reconquest of Hormuz had to be abandoned.

But although Hormuz was lost, Muscat still remained and no efforts were spared by the Portuguese to force the trade of the Gulf to this place and to raise it to the same commercial grandeur as Hormuz. The commanding position of Muscat and its natural defensive capabilities combined to make it superior in many respects to Hormuz, but the English, who were now rapidly gaining the ascendency in the Gulf—as also the Dutch—were interested in concentrating the trade at Busra and Gombroon. Moreover, as the Portuguese had never tried to win the confidence and respect of the native merchants, the latter were now eager to remove from the rigour of their sway, and many seized the opportunity of settling at the new and rising town of Gombroon. Nevertheless, owing to the influx from Hormuz, the population of Muscat became at once largely augmented, and the Arab tribes in the vicinity, who had always been kept on good terms by the payment of subsidies, were further conciliated.

By the fall of Hormuz the political connection existing between that island and the Oman coast, which had been established three and a half centuries before, came to an end, though it is related that Mohammed Shah, the nephew of the old King of Hormuz, was brought to Muscat by the Portuguese who endeavoured to compel the coast Arabs to recognize him as their King. Among the improvements undertaken at this time in Muscat were the rebuilding of the town wall, extending from Booma Salih to Bab Methayib, the excavation of the fosse beyond, a new Custom House, the gate of which still bears the date 1625, a landing place, and a boat dock under the western fort. Further protection also was afforded to the town by the erection of the towers at the passes of Kalbuh, Riyam, and Sedab.

In 1623 the Governor of Muscat was Martino Affonso de Mello, who resided for the most part of the year in the factory or " gareza,' but during the hot weather occupied Fort Capitan, which was at this time deemed of more importance than Fort San Joao (now Jalali), the former citadel.

There were two churches, one of which was the See of the Vicar, generally an Augustinian friar, and dedicated to the Virgin del Rozario; the other, known as Della Gratia, being the property of the Augustinians, four of whom resided in it.

As Hormuz had been recovered by the Persians, its rightful owners, during the vigorous reign of a great King—Shah Abbas—so Muscat and the Oman coast were wrested from the grip of Portugal by the force of a national impulse engendered by the rise of a new Arab dynasty. At the beginning of the seventeenth century the Nebhani, the reigning family in Oman, which had lasted about 500 years, was in such a critical condition that power soon fell from their hands altogether, and the country became enveloped from one end to the other in anarchy and civil war. A long and sanguinary struggle took place between rival claimants, which terminated in 1624 in the election of Nasir bin Murshid al-Yaareby as Imam. This Prince proved to be one of the ablest and strongest rulers Oman ever had; he soon made himself master of and tranquillized the interior, and then turned his attention to the task of expelling the foreigners, who held the coast forts and commanded the sea, with whom during his reign he was engaged in incessant warfare.

To face p. 193.

THE FORT AT YABREEN.

[*See p.* 214]

About seven years after the Imam Nasir's accession (1631) the Portuguese, finding that the Persian Gulf trade continued gradually, but surely, to slip from their hands, made an effort to obtain by peaceful means what they had failed to do by force. The Viceroy (Dom Miguel da Noronha) tried to purchase, or to farm, the Island of Hormuz from the Persians, and to this end he despatched an emissary, named Dominic dá Tirale Valdez, to Muscat, where he was to concert measures with the Admiral Ruy Frere da Andrada, who still commanded in those waters, for this purpose; and after conferring together they set out for Hormuz, where, however, the negotiations, though aided apparently by handsome offers to the Persian Governor, came to naught. The indomitable Ruy Frere, determined on doing something, then proceeded to Julfar, where he built a fort adjoining that of the Persians. This new fort does not appear to have been long retained, for in July, 1633, the Imam Nasir succeeded in driving away both the Persians and Portuguese and in taking possession himself. He then ordered Shaikh Hafiz bin Saif to erect a fort at Sohar against that held by the Portuguese, which he vigorously besieged for some time with a force composed of the Beni Khalid, Beni Lahm, and Al-Amoor tribes, but the garrison offered so stout a resistance that the Kadhi Khamis bin Saeed was soon after deputed by the Imam to treat for peace at Muttrah with the Portuguese Governor of Muscat, and it was then agreed that the Arabs should abandon the siege of Sohar. But though foiled in his attempt on that fortress, the Imam in the same or following year attacked Soor and Kuriyat and succeeded in recovering both these places, though both seem to have been soon after retaken; thus within ten years of his accession he expelled the invaders along the whole coast of Oman except at two points.

In 1640 Portugal regained her independence from Spain, and the accession of Dom Joao IV. was signalized at Muscat, as at other places, with much rejoicing. In the same year, too, a decisive success over the Arabs at Muscat contributed to raise their hopes and spirits. The Imam had obtained information that the stores of water and gunpowder were deficient and that the garrison was weak. He therefore had moved down on the plain with celerity in the hope of being able to carry it by assault before it could be succoured from the sea by the arrival of a fleet; but the attack failed. The Portuguese met him with a gallant defence and the Imam was compelled to retire discomfited and with heavy loss.

Three years later the Arab chief of Lawa, Shaikh Saif bin Mohammed, who was in hostility with the Imam, appealed to the Portuguese for assistance, and a small force was accordingly sent from Sohar to co-operate with him. The Imam, however, marched down upon Lawa in force, reduced the rebellious Shaikh to obedience, and, having cut off and captured the Portuguese contingent, followed up his success by laying siege to Sohar, which after a short resistance surrendered on November 7th, 1643, the Portuguese garrison being put to the sword.

The Imam Nasir was now becoming old and inactive, and for five years we hear of no more contests between him and the Christians, but in 1648 a rupture again occurred, and the Imam, who was now perhaps too infirm to take the lead himself, despatched the army under the command of Mesood bin Ramzan and Saeed bin Khalifeh. The siege of Muscat began on August 16th and lasted until September 11th, during which time the Arabs, according to Ross's *Annals of Oman*, captured and demolished the high watch towers of Muscat, and reduced the Portuguese garrison to such straits that they sued for peace. The terms enforced by the Shaikhs were that Kuriyat and the fort of Soor should be surrendered and razed, that the Arabs of the interior should pay no customs duties on goods at Muscat, that the town wall there should be levelled, and that the Portuguese should pay the Imam 200,000 pardaos. These terms were considered too onerous and the siege was resumed with vigour, the Arabs pressing closer until they occupied the heights above Fort Capitan and Moculla. For six weeks longer, however, the Portuguese held out, until, finding that his ammunition was exhausted, the plague raging in the town and carrying off many victims, Dom Juliao da Noronha, the Captain-General or Governor, again opened negotiations and concluded a treaty of peace on October 31st, 1648, on which the

Imam's force retired from before the town. In the treaty the Governor consented to the following humiliating conditions :—That the forts of Soor and Kuriyat should be destroyed, and that both the Arab and Portuguese forts at Muttrah should also be razed, that Muttrah should be evacuated and remain neutral, that Arab vessels homeward bound only should require a pass, that the Arabs should pay no taxes or duties, and that trade should be free, and finally that the Portuguese should erect no fortifications outside Muscat. It would appear that at the commencement of the siege the Governor, Dom Juliao, had sent to Goa for help and that a squadron had been despatched by the Viceroy, Dom Filippe Mascarenhas, which arrived at Muscat in the middle of November, 1648. For not holding out longer Dom Juliao and the Vedor (or Treasurer) were subsequently arrested and confined at Goa. In despatches dated January, 1649, from the Government of Lisbon commenting on these affairs it was directed that every effort should be made to retain Muscat, that more ships should be stationed there, that the Arabs should not be allowed to remain in the town of Muscat, and that the fort at Khasab should be strengthened. It may be presumed that these orders were carried out, but they did not suffice to ensure the retention of Muscat for long. Had the Imam Nasir bin Murshid continued to reign it is possible that the terms of peace would have been observed, and that Muscat would have remained undisturbed for some time, but the death of the sovereign in April, 1649, and the accession of a new ruler, inaugurated a policy of renewed hostility with the Christians, and before the year had closed Muscat was again surrounded and menaced by a besieging army.

According to the Arab writers the Imam Sultan bin Saif, who succeeded, waged war on the Christians at Muscat, and to have personally conducted the operations against them until God gave him the victory. It would seem, indeed, that he disregarded the treaty and undertook the campaign almost immediately after his accession, and that he brought it to a glorious issue within about nine months.

The year 1650 was just dawning when, to the surprise of the Portuguese inhabitants, the small but determined body of besiegers suddenly entered the city by a night attack, and swarming into the streets and bazaars, slew many of the frightened and unresisting citizens. Many crowded on board the vessels in the harbour, two of which with those on board were captured. Seven hundred Portuguese made their escape to Diu. The gareza or factory, in which were stored the ammunition and arms, was at once surrounded by the Imam's troops, and after a short resistance the Governor-General, receiving apparently but little help from the Captain of the Fleet, Braz Caldeira da Mattos, who might have rendered effective aid had he wished, but who seems to have acted with great pusillanimity, retired to Fort Capitan with the garrison, leaving the gareza to be defended by its Arab, or rather, Belooch guard.

Notwithstanding the presence of the fleet, which did nothing, and the weakness of the Arab army, the Governor surrendered Forts Capitan and St. John on January 23rd, though the gareza held out for three days longer, the guard knowing, no doubt, that they could expect no mercy from their assailants. Meanwhile, the fugitives, having reached Diu, sent word immediately to Goa to apprise the Viceroy, Dom Filippe Mascarenhas, who despatched a fleet at once to Muscat to support the garrison, but on arrival it was found already in the hands of the Arabs, and learned that the Portuguese squadron had sailed for Diu. That the garrison were massacred by the Arabs appears to be only too probable, but this is not asserted by the Portuguese writers, and, next to that of Danver's, the most full and circumstantial account of the siege is given by Hamilton in his *New Account of the East Indies*. As this book is scarce I think it worth while to quote the passage :—

> " All the Arab army threatened to mutiny, if they were not forthwith led by their officers to the Scalade of the City Walls. And at last the King, finding that no Perswasions could cool their Fury, tho' the Day was far spent, ordered them to be led on. The Portugueze flank'd them from their Forts on the Mountains, with Plenty of great and small Shot ; but the Arabs never looked back, nor minded the great Numbers of their dead

Companions, but mounted the Walls over the Carcases of their slain. About Sun-set they drove the Portugueze from two of the City Gates, and pursued their Enemy so hard, that not one escaped, tho' they fled in great Haste toward the great Fort, where the Governor staid. That Fort is built on a Rock almost surrounded by the Sea, and has no way to get up to it, but by a Stair-case hewn out of the Rock, above 50 yards high, and not above two or three Persons can ascend a-breast. The Arabs thought it impracticable to attack it, so made a Blockade of it. In the Attack of the Town, the Arabs lost between 4 and 5,000 of the best of their Forces; and the Portugueze in their Forts were reduced to 60 or 70. Those in the small Forts were obliged soon to surrender for want of Ammunition and Provisions, and all were put to the Sword, except those, who, to save their Lives, promised to be circumcised, and abjure the Christian Religion. Those in the great Fort held out about six Months, under great Want and Fatigues; and all Hopes of Relief being cut off, they resolved on a Surrender, on which motion, the imprudent Governor, who was the sole Cause of their Calamity, leapt down a Precipice into the Sea, where the Water being very shallow he was dasht to pieces on the Rocks.

"The little Garison would fain have come to a Capitulation, but the Arabs would grant them no Terms, but that they must yield or be starved; and tho' the Terms were hard, yet they thought best to surrender, and all were put to the Sword, except a few who embraced Mahometism, which in all were eighteen Persons. And this Relation I had from a very old Renegade who was at the Tragedy, being then a Soldier, who reckoned himself about 100 Years old, and by his Aspect, could not be much less."

In an Arab work, known as the *Diary of the Wazeer of Sanaa in the Yemen* the following passage occurs, which is also worth while transcribing:—

"In the year 1052 A.H. [A.D. 1642] a number of merchants

set out on a venture to Hasa, Bahrain, and Basra, and when they had passed the sea of Fars and had reached Bunder Muscat, which was then in the hands of the Franks, they were plundered by the latter. People became afraid therefore to pass that way. The Ocean also became closed to seafarers and remained so until the Omanis possessed themselves of Muscat, as will be recorded presently. When the Moslems occupied Muscat, trade was re-opened to merchants and they obtained security against those wretches, and in the year 1054 A.H. [A.D. 1644] the rulers of Oman, the Kharejites and the Ibadhis, became possessed of Muscat, which is on the coast of their country, and had been up to that time in the hands of the Franks. They had no idea they would be able to take it, but they ordered everyone in it to be slaughtered with knives which they had concealed for the purpose. All that were in the forts were accordingly killed."

This little square fort at Khasab, which still stands untenanted and intact in its solitude, was also captured about the same time. The fall of Muscat closed the eventful career of the successors of the great Albuquerque in the Persian Gulf, and it was still held by the Portuguese in 1648 by which time Soor, Kuriyat and Sohar had been lost. No expedition to recover Muscat seems ever to have been despatched from Goa or Lisbon, but its fall was less surprising and a lesser disaster than that of Hormuz, and was not felt so keenly. But Dom Filippe endeavoured to repair the loss in some way by sending in 1650 a squadron of seven galliots to the Gulf to try and purchase or farm Hormuz, as already stated, and to obtain the aid of the Persians against the Arabs. This squadron sailed to Kong and Kateef, and fell in with an Arab fleet there, which captured one of the vessels and six Portuguese merchantmen without any corresponding success on the part of the Portuguese. The latter obtained the offer of Henjam, but this island was of no value, and on the Viceroy receiving the report he determined to send a stronger fleet to the Gulf to try and recover Khasab or some equally advantageous port. The new fleet arrived in the Gulf of Oman in March, 1650, and encountered off Muscat an Arab fleet, which entered the cove and anchored under cover of the forts. The Portuguese here had an opportunity of striking a blow at the Arabs and recovering their prestige, but no battle took place and the Portuguese Commander sailed on up the Gulf where, however, he did nothing.

In 1718 the Portuguese thought they had a chance of recovering their position in the Gulf. The Persians having recently lost Hormuz to the Turks and Bahrain to the Arabs, sent an embassy to Goa to get the help of the Portuguese. Accordingly a fleet was sent in February, 1719, to Kong, and on August 4th, an Arab fleet appeared off that port. On the 5th the fight lasted from 9 a.m. to 7 p.m. The Portuguese attacked with guns and the Arabs retired in good order. The next day the contest was resumed, the Arabs making a running fight, which continued until night, the fleets passing the Straits. The day following the Portuguese again went for the Arabs, who fled and took refuge apparently in Malcolm Inlet or thereabouts. The Portuguese retired to Kong, and the Arabs then went to Julfar, to obtain supplies from Muscat and from the English and Dutch. The Arabs are said to have lost 500 killed and wounded and the Portuguese lost 10 killed and 35 wounded. On the 27th the Portuguese Admiral sailed for Julfar with four ships, and the Arabs retreated, while three days later a fight took place and the Arabs were completely routed; again next day the fleets came in sight, but the Arabs retired, and on September 1st the Portuguese chased them all day, while on September 2nd the Arabs fled to their own ports. This signal defeat of the Arabs was followed by riots at Muscat, and the death of the Imam, who was succeeded by his nephew, led to attempts to negotiate a peace with the Portuguese, which the latter would not agree to. The Shah refused to besiege Muscat as he had promised to do, and the Portuguese, after wintering in Persian ports, retired to Goa at the end of the year.

For many years vessels continued to be sent occasionally to war with the Arabs and destroy their trade, and met with varying success. Towns and villages on the Oman coast were burnt and sacked. The Arabs on their side had been taught by experience to increase the size of their ships, and they profited by this to make successful expeditions to the coast of India and harry the Portuguese trade.

The long protracted, needless, and vindictive maritime war between the Arabs and Portuguese may be said to have come to an end about the year 1739, when the Portuguese were driven from the Northern Concan by the Mahrattas, who dispossessed them of Bassain and all the adjoining territory.

CHAPTER IV.

THE YAAREBA DYNASTY.

FROM the beginning of the seventeenth century our materials become somewhat more copious and precise, and we have now more than one Arab work to refer to for this period.

At this time the Nebhani Dynasty, which had ruled Oman for over four and a-half centuries, had fallen into a declining state and could extend its authority over little more than one-half of the kingdom, owing in some measure to the rapacity, misrule and oppression of the Maliks, or rulers, but in a greater degree, perhaps, to political causes. The dynasty at this time was represented by a Malik named Makhzoom bin Fellah bin Mohsin, who resided at Yenkal, and who was being vigorously opposed by his brother, Nebhan bin Fellah.

On the death of Makhzoom, about 1615, further disorder and strife arose in the Nebhani family, and Nebhan bin Fellah, who claimed the sovereignty, was confronted by his cousin, Omair bin Himyar, and was attacked and defeated at Yenkal in 1617 by the latter, in conjunction with Saif bin Mohammed al-Hinay.

In the anarchy and confusion resulting from this contest, direction of affairs was assumed by the two victorious generals, Omair and Saif bin Mohammed, for about seven years, when, apparently on the death of Omair bin Himyar, the countries fell again into disorder and the Nebhani Dynasty became extinct. Competitors for the leadership arose now in various tribes, and notably among the Yaareba, one of the oldest and most influential clans in Oman.

The Shaikh in possession of Rostak in 1624 was Malik bin Abul Arar al-Yaarebi, one of the foremost in attempting to seize power, but was opposed and thwarted by the learned and energetic Kadhi

Khamis bin Saeed al-Shakasi, under whose guidance an assembly of several notables was convened, at which the Shaikh Nasir bin Murshid al-Yaarebi was elected Imam unanimously. This election not only inaugurated a new dynasty, but opened a new era in the history of Oman, in which the country advanced to a previously unknown pitch of prosperity and glory, while in Nasir bin Murshid it brought to the front a man of unusual sagacity and power, who was to rank as one of Oman's most famous princes. But the decision of the Rostak assembly was by no means a national one, nor did it find universal acceptance, and when the news spread abroad the dissentient towns and tribes stood aloof and awaited events. Assisted by the Yadmad tribe, the Imam Nasir had little difficulty in taking the fort of Rostak from his cousins, who had held it since the death of his grandfather, Malik bin Abul Arar, which had occurred in 1620. On looking round, however, the Imam soon saw that his position was precarious, and that he would have to encounter much hostility and opposition in maintaining his office, particularly in view of the threatening attitude of the Nizar tribes. It may here be remarked as worthy of note that the Sunni or Nizar tribes had greatly increased at this epoch and had become equal in strength to the Yemenites.

In the time of the Khalifs, the Nizar were decidedly in the minority, but from that period, owing to immigration and other causes, they had gradually augmented and were now able to hold their ground.

In 1625 the Imam, having collected a force, marched against the fort of Nakhl, which was held by his great uncle, Sultan bin Abul Arar. This fort he had no sooner captured than he was surrounded and besieged by a party of those disloyal to him, and it was not until he was succoured by reinforcements that he was able to return to Rostak. Shortly afterwards, having gathered an army of Yahmad, Beni Ruwaihah and other tribes, the Imam, attended by the Kadhi Khamis bin Saeed, moved to Zikki, which surrendered to him, and thence proceeded to Nezwa, which he also entered and where he resided for some months in the walled quarter of Al-Akr, from which he had expelled the Beni Saeed.

Turning eastward, the Imam then captured the towns of Semed al-Shan and Ibra, on which the whole of Al-Sharkiyeh submitted. For some time after this the Imam was engaged in further small operations in various places, where he found himself strong enough to undertake a campaign against the hostile Nizar tribes, who held all the principal forts in Al-Dhahireh. The chief leader of the Nizar was Nasir bin Katan of the Beni Hilal, who possessed the forts of Ghabbi and Dhank. The Imam's troops first attacked Ghabbi, which was eventually taken after heavy fighting, in which the Imam's brother was slain.

At Dhank the Beni Hilal were again worsted, and Nasir bin Katan, who throughout the Imam's reign remained his most powerful and relentless foe, surrendered the fort, of which, however, his brother was made Wali.

Obre was also taken by the Imam, but Makiniyat held out and the Yemenite tribes allied with the Imam were repulsed. The campaign appears to have been protracted for some years with varying fortune in Al-Dhahireh, and though Bahila, Makiniyat, and other forts were captured by the Imam, the disaffection in that province was never entirely suppressed, as the Nizar continued to observe an attitude of enmity and independence towards the Imam Nasir during his life. The greater part of Oman, however, had by this time been reduced to obedience, and the Imam then retired to Rostak.

A force was now sent against Beraimi and Lawa, and both these forts were captured, notwithstanding the assistance given to the garrison of Lawa by the Portuguese.

Emboldened by his success with the tribes, and confident in his military skill, the Imam next raised a numerous army, placed it under Mesood bin Ramdhan, and sent it to attack Muscat, but it had barely reached the outskirts of the town, when it was defeated and dispersed by the Portuguese. The Imam, soon after this, contrived to compass the death of Mani bin Sinan by inviting him to Lawa on promise of safety, which was perfidiously broken.

Julfar was the next point to which Nasir turned his attention, where there were two forts, one held by the Portuguese, who had two ships stationed there, while the other was held by the Persians under Nasir al-Din. The Imam's army was commanded by Ali bin Ahmed, who succeeded in capturing both forts and expelling the Persians. The army then returned in triumph to Nezwa.

This success encouraged the Imam to try his strength against Sohar, and Hafiz bin Saif, the Wali of Lawa, was ordered to assemble a force for this purpose. He reached Sohar in Moharram, 1043 A.H. [A.D. 1633], and attacked the town, but was soon defeated and driven off by the Portuguese.

The latter then stopped all communications with Muscat from the interior, and the Imam was compelled to sue for peace, which was negotiated by the old Kadhi Khamis bin Saeed. Shortly after, however, the Imam undertook operations against Soor and Kuriyat, which he recovered from the Portuguese, who were now in a very decayed and despondent condition.

At this time, the Beni Hilal, under Shaikh Nasir bin Katan, in conjunction with other Nizar tribes, invaded Al-Jow and the Batineh. The Imam sent forces against them with but little success, for the raids continued, and the Beni Hilal carried off slaves and other booty. In a subsequent invasion Shaikh Nasir advanced to Lawa, where a battle took place betweem him and the Imam's troops, commanded by Ali bin Ahmed. The latter was victorious, and Shaikh Nasir fled to Al-Shemal pursued by the Omanis. He then suddenly turned upon his enemies and slew the foremost pursuers.

Shaikh Nasir bin Katan al-Helali contirued his raids on Oman, and became a terror to the whole country, which he ravaged as he pleased. The Imam's counter-attacks against him were failures, and on one occasion, in the south, the Imam's army was almost cut to pieces. Shaikh Nasir continued unsubdued, and was at length only pacified by the payment to him of a large subsidy by the Imam, and after this we hear little of him.

In 1648 war was resumed between the Imam and the Portuguese, which resulted, in October of that year, in a treaty of peace which was very disadvantageous to the latter, the particulars of which have been already given.

The Imam, Nasir bin Murshid, died on the 11th Rabi al-Akhir, 1059 A.H. [April 14th, A.D. 1649], at a good old age, after a reign of twenty-six years, and was buried at Nezwa.

It was late in the sixteenth century before the English attempted to follow in the footsteps of the Portuguese and make an effort to ascertain the real prospects of the Indian trade, and it would be as well, therefore, to take a glance at their initiatory steps in this enterprise. The first action was due to two intelligent and enterprising directors of the Turkish Company, which had been established in 1581. These two gentlemen, Messrs. Smith and Staper, selected four persons to form a party to proceed to the East to gather information on all subjects with a view to the participation in the Venetian overland commerce. The party consisted of Messrs. Newbery and Fitch (merchants), Mr. Storie (painter), and Mr. Leeds (jeweller). In 1583 they sailed for Tripoli in Syria, from whence they travelled to Baghdad and Busra, and embarking at this place, they sailed to Hormuz and Goa. Newbery and Leeds remained in India and died there, but Fitch, having collected a mass of information on all the places and countries through which he passed, returned to England by the same route in 1590.

The immediate consequences of this mission was the despatch in 1591 of three vessels under Admiral Raymond round the Cape to the East Indies, and the acquisition in 1592 by the Turkish Company of an exclusive right from the Queen to trade between India and England.

In the meantime war had broken out between Spain and England, and Philip II. had passed a decree prohibiting the English, as he had already done in the case of the Dutch, from coming to Lisbon to trade. Philip thought by this to strike a deadly blow at Holland and England, but he was egregiously mistaken. The result of his policy was contrary to what he expected. It only turned their trade into another channel and incited them to venture by the Cape route to India, which they followed with such success that in a few years they supplanted the Portuguese in their Oriental commerce.

In 1610 the East India Company, which had been chartered in December, 1600, despatched its sixth venture, consisting of the *Trade's Increase, Peppercorn,* and *Darling,* under Sir Henry Middleton. The *Trade's Increase* was of 1,000 tons burthen, the largest merchant ship ever built in England up to that period.

Sir Henry sailed first for Mocha, where he was treacherously treated and where he subsequently retaliated by pirating the Arab vessels. The next year he was joined by Captain Saris with three ships, the *Clove, Hector,* and *Thomas,* and together they forcibly bartered their goods with Arab traders and sailed for Bantam.

In 1613 Captain Newport in the *Expedition,* as already stated, took out Sir Thomas Shirley, the Ambassador to the Shah, who narrowly escaped being murdered at Gwader on the Mekran coast, whither he had proceeded in order to travel overland to Ispahan.

In 1613 Mr. Steel, who had left England in search of a runaway debtor, and had proceeded overland to India, making good use of his opportunities to ascertain the condition of trade, proposed to the Company that they should endeavour to open up trade with Persia, where he thought a lucrative business would result. He was accordingly sent thither in 1614 with Mr. Crowther from Surat to report, and after examining Muscat, Kong, Bushire, etc., they fixed upon Jask as the most convenient station at which to locate a factory and commence trade. The attempt succeeded at first beyond expectation. Mr. Berker and Mr. Cormack were sent from Jask to Moghistan, where the Governor received them favourably and gave them a firman to trade.

Sir Thomas Roe, for certain reasons, strongly opposed the trade with Persia and solemnly warned the Company to abandon it, but he afterwards gave the project his assistance. Sir Thomas Shirley, who was for years Resident at Ispahan, was an enemy to the English trade and supported the Spano-Portuguese interests, but on the other hand, Mr. Cormack was in favour of it and pointed out to the Company the danger of allowing the Spano-Portuguese to monopolize the Persian trade, as it would render them a most formidable nation. In June, 1617, a Spano-Portuguese Ambassador arrived at Ispahan, and at this time, the English Agent in Persia advised the Agent at Surat to despatch all the Company's ships to Jask and to defend it, as the Portuguese fleet had assembled at Muscat to obstruct the passage of the English into the Persian Gulf.

The letter written by Sir Thomas Roe to the Shah had a good effect, and it produced three favourable firmans, which were followed by an important treaty which was concluded in 1618. A second letter in 1619 was followed by a further confirmation of the Treaty, and in March, 1620, King James addressed a friendly letter to the Shah thanking him for his favour and requesting a continuation of his protection to the English.

When the Portuguese took the Oriental trade out of the hands of the Venetians and made Lisbon the new commercial mart of Europe, the old lines of trade in that continent became deranged, the old depôts fell from their high position, and the merchants had in all European countries to make new arrangements for the sale of their wares. Previously, Bruges and Augsburg had been the markets of Venice, now these towns were left to decay.

In 1515 the English chose Antwerp as the most suitable site for the northern mart in place of Bruges, and it soon grew into a great city. In 1585, Antwerp was destroyed by Parma and Alva, and its place as a commercial depôt was taken by Amsterdam.

About this time the Dutch determined to seek the products of the East in the East itself and to submit no longer to receive them at second hand but to reap the full profits of the trade. Stimulated to this new enterprise by the vindictive and unstatesmanlike policy of Philip, who had interdicted them from coming to Lisbon, encouraged by the suggestions and information imparted by a countryman, Linschoten, who had opportunely returned from India after long service with the Portuguese, and who at this time had published a useful compendium, the States-General chartered a company, which prepared a fleet under the command of Molesar. This fleet of four ships sailed from Amsterdam in 1595 under the auspices of the "Company for Remote Countries," and these ventures became from the very first a surprising success. They waged war against the Portuguese and enriched their own country while adding to its maritime importance; and they succeeded in greatly crippling that power and in annexing some of its factories. Their chief object soon became the entire monopoly of the Spice Islands, and towards the attainment of this end they scrupled at nothing and committed the most atrocious barbarities.

The English everywhere in the East found the Dutch as hostile to them as the Portuguese were, for though the Dutch owed their existence as an independent nation to the English, they did not hesitate to sacrifice the latter to their own avarice and to wrest the spice trade out of their hands by the vilest means. They went even further and omitted no measures of violence, fraud, and intrigue to ruin the trade of the English.

As the countries were at peace the disputes were referred home and Commissioners were appointed to inquire into them. The Dutch were anxious to amalgamate the Dutch and English Companies, by which they would soon have destroyed the English trade and taken all into their own hands; this was understood in England and the plan failed. The Dutch, therefore, sent orders to their agents to injure, harass, and annoy the English in India to the utmost, and especially to monopolize the spice trade altogether.

In July, 1619, however, a hollow treaty was concluded between the two Companies, by which they agreed to assist each other, and enjoining that each should maintain ten ships of war in the East for protection of trade.

In the following year the conduct of the Dutch had become so intolerable that the English Company had been obliged to equip six men of war for the purpose of protecting their trade against the Dutch. This fleet was under Sir Thomas Dale, with Captain Parker as second in command.

The Treaty of 1619 was no sooner made than broken by the Dutch, and it did not interrupt their outrages for a day. In 1620 they expelled the English from the Iantore, and in 1622 committed the famous massacre of the English at Amboyna.

The first encounter between the English and Portuguese in the Persian Gulf took place in 1620, as we have seen above.

In 1621 the attention of the English agents in India was wholly engaged in promoting the trade with Persia, which appeared to them of great importance. The *London* after the battle appears to have sailed to the Oman coast and remained at anchor at Soor, where she was joined by the other two ships and returned afterwards to Surat.

On November 14th, 1621, a trading fleet, convoyed by Sir Thomas Dale with some men-of-war, and consisting altogether of five ships and four pinnaces, left Surat for the Persian Gulf. The English subsequently removed their factory from Jask to the town of Gombroon or Bundar Abbas and erected a strong building. About 1626 they endeavoured to erect a fortress at Hormuz, but the jealousy of the Shah prevented them. The Persians, meantime, did not desist in their efforts to possess themselves of Muscat. The Khan or Governor of Shiraz began to prepare an expedition against Muscat in 1632, and the English, partly to avoid incurring the displeasure of the Khan and partly to prevent the Dutch having the chance of aiding the Khan themselves, which they would readily have embraced, offered the assistance of their ships in the attack. The scheme lingered on till 1635 and the enterprise appears then, from various reasons, to have dropped altogether.

At this time in England the Members of the Third Joint Stock Company took over the concerns of the special voyages to Persia, and in 1639 they sent Messrs. Thurston and Pearce on a mission to re-open trade in the Persian Gulf at Busra, a town which was not only outside the territories of the Shah but in which European influence was more strongly felt. They reached Kong in April and Busra on May 31st, 1640, and obtained a firman from the Pasha more favourable than that granted to any other nation. The samples of cargo they took with them, however, were disposed of at a low rate, owing to a Portuguese fleet from Muscat having just previously glutted the market with similar goods. Mr. Thurston proposed to erect a permanent factory at Busra and probably did so.

By the capture of Malacca from the Portuguese by the Dutch in 1641 the latter obtained the undisputed supremacy of the Indian Archipelago. Having a coast trade in the East besides their great commerce with Europe, they profited greatly by carrying commodities, especially spices, from port to port, spices being their monopoly and being greatly in request from Arabia to China. This coasting trade was almost as lucrative as that with Europe.

The Treaty of Munster, signed by Spain in 1648, acknowledged the independence of the Netherlands and agreed to the humiliating condition that the Spaniards would refrain from rounding the Cape of Good Hope, but sail to the East by Cape Horn only. From this time for about a hundred years the commercial career of the Dutch was one of almost uninterrupted activity, prosperity and success.

Returning now to Muscat affairs, we find the vigorous sway of the Imam Nasir had been so beneficial to the country in restoring order and extending its power, that the continuance of the Yaareba Dynasty was fully assured, and universally accepted without hesitation, opposition or dispute. As the Imam had died without issue, the judges and elders who assembled at Rostak on the very day of his death, elected and proclaimed his cousin, Sultan bin Saif bin Malik, successor and Imam. The choice appears to have been generally approved, as we hear of no hostilities taking place, the larger tribes and governors of forts acknowledging the new ruler without demur.

The Treaty of 1648, between the Imam Nasir and the Portuguese Commandant, had shown clearly enough that the Portuguese tenure of Muscat was coming to an end, and that it was only necessary to make one more strong and united effort to ensure final expulsion. The Imam Sultan bin Saif, however, had at once perceived how essential it was for his country to possess maritime equality with the enemy, and to this end, before attacking the Portuguese, increased the number and size of his warships to protect his coast from insult and his commerce from destruction. The year 1649 was drawing to a close when the Imam undertook the final campaign, which he had deliberately planned against the domineering Christians, who had held the chief port and castle of Oman in defiance of the Arabs for a hundred and forty years. The tribes had responded with alacrity to the Imam's call to arms, and had collected in the Sih al-Harmel, outside Muttrah, ready to strike. The assault, however, was delivered on the town of Muscat by only a small band, which took the garrison by surprise at night and soon gained possession. The Captain-General retired into Fort Capitan, where, on January 28th, he laid down his arms and capitulated. The Imam then appointed the son of Belarab Governor of Muscat, and ordered the wall of the town, which had been partially destroyed, to be rebuilt.

This triumph inspirited the Imam and his people not only to embark on a policy of foreign adventure and aggression, but to carry the war into the enemy's country and to harass the Portuguese in the Indian Ocean by land and sea. The Portuguese never attempted to equip an adequate expedition to retake Muscat, but for many years kept up a desultory warfare with the Arabs, and in their turn sent ships to ravage the Oman coast. One of the squadrons despatched from Goa to the Persian Gulf arrived at Muscat in 1652, and found there a number of Arab vessels, which, fearing an attack, took shelter under the guns of the fort. The Portuguese, having the superiority, might have made short work of the Arab ships, and might possibly have recovered possession of Muscat itself, but the Commander did not even venture to make an attack, and thus the opportunity of striking a severe blow at the enemy was lost.

During the same year in which Muscat fell the Dutch factory at Gombroon received large stocks from Europe, two of their ships having arrived there from Holland, which gave them temporarily the preponderance in the Gulf trade. The fall of Muscat was an event in their favour, and the arrival of eleven more ships in 1651 with valuable cargoes from the Hague still further augmented their trade.

The prestige of the Dutch was now so high that in this year, 1651, the Imam Sultan bin Saif proceeded to Gombroon and offered the Dutch, who in 1641 had quarrelled with the Shah of Persia about the trade in silk, and who were anxious to evade the Persian customs, a land route to Busra for their goods from Abu Thubi, the Shaikh of which town would furnish camels from thence to Kateef and Busra. This offer, however, was declined by the chief of the Dutch factory with thanks.

Neglecting nothing by which he could retaliate on his enemies and pillage or extend his dominions, the Imam Sultan, as soon as the pressure of home affairs had lessened, sent out several maritime expeditions against the Portuguese. One of these, in 1655, raided and plundered Bombay, then known to the Arabs as Colabah, another fleet proceeded to East Africa to succour the inhabitants of Mombasa, who, being unable to tolerate the oppressive yoke of their masters, the Portuguese, had some time previously sent a deputation to Muscat to solicit the intervention of the Imam, whose rule they were willing to accept. After being blockaded for five years the fort of Mombasa surrendered, and the Portuguese retired from the place, an Arab Governor, Mohammed bin Mombarek, being located there with a strong garrison. The Imam's hold on the fort, however, was of short duration. The Portuguese returned in force and expelled the Arabs, treating the inhabitants with great severity and cruelty. The members of the deputation were put to death, and the people were treated with increased rigour and tyranny until the return of the Arabs to Mombasa thirty-seven years later.

Meantime, the affairs of the English East India Company were steadily declining, while those of the Dutch were rapidly increasing, and though Cromwell did his best to dissipate the clouds that overhung the English Company by confirming their charter, so much confusion and disorganization prevailed in India that in 1657 the company offered its privileges and property for sale. This brought matters to a crisis, and Cromwell at once assisted them to re-establish their factory and continue their operations. Before Cromwell's death (1658) the East India Company had, in virtue of this aid, somewhat recovered its position. The trade in the Persian Gulf, however, had dwindled so much in 1659, partly owing to the superiority of the Dutch and partly to the current belief among the natives that the company had been dissolved, that the President at Surat, Mr. Whish, in this situation projected the plan for obtaining possession of Muscat as a port of safety for their shipping and as a means of overawing the Persian Government in recovering their proportion of trade. Accordingly, Colonel Rainsford, who had come to India as an interloper and commercial traveller, was instructed to proceed to Muscat to negotiate with the Imam Sultan-bin Saif, for the acquisition of the place. There can be no doubt that if the project had been successful the possession of this port would have greatly benefited the company and given it the complete command of the Persian Gulf trade, but as the object of the President was not merely the erection of a factory, but a lease of the town and fortress, which it was estimated would require a garrison of one hundred men, the negotiations did not progress, as the Imam, having expelled the Portuguese, was naturally averse from handing it over to any other Christian Power, and by the following year the President found that his plan had failed.

In May, 1660, occurred the Restoration in England, and Charles II., eager to outshine as far as possible the prestige of Cromwell, seized the opportunity of granting to the company a new Royal Charter with new privileges and advantages. This gave the company a fresh impetus and enabled it to carry on its operations on a greatly extended scale. At this juncture an island and harbour of the first importance opportunely came into their hands and gave them an independent and sure depôt, for which they had long been sighing. Bombay formed part of the dowry which Catharine of Braganza had brought to Charles II. in 1662, and two years later the King sent to take possession of it. Being useless to the King, however, it was handed over to the East India Company in 1669, and it at once became the chief emporium in the Arabian Sea in supersession of Surat, which now occupied a subordinate position.

The reign of the Imam Sultan bin Saif appears to have been one of comparative tranquillity, as we hear little of dissensions and internal troubles in his time. He had thus been able to devote his leisure to organizing naval expeditions, and he set the example to succeeding Imams of engaging in commerce, for which latter occupation he incurred the odium of the religious party, who considered trading as unlawful in one holding the spiritual office of Imam. It is recorded that he constructed the Banana tank or aqueduct near Zikki, and that he spent twelve years in building the great circular fort or tower at Nezwa, which is described in another chapter, at a cost of eighty thousand dollars, as well as other public works.

There is much discrepancy concerning the date of the death of the Imam Sultan bin Saif. Sir Edward Ross in his *Annals* gives it as the 16th Dhu'l-Kaada, 1090 A.H. [October 4th, 1679 A.D.], Guillain suggests vaguely 1668 or 1669, while Badger reckons it as occurring on November 11th, 1668. Imam Sultan bin Saif was buried at Nezwa.

Belarab bin Sultan was elected Imam without opposition on his father's death and began to reside at Nezwa, and is said to have been of generous character and studious disposition and was styled "Abor al-Arabi" by the people. Soon after his election he erected a new fort at Yabreen in the Wady Bahila on the site of an ancient tower, and also built a famous madrasseh or college, which existed for many years but of which there now remains no trace. Two years after his accession he despatched an expedition against the Portuguese town of Diu, which was surprised at night, stormed, and sacked. The best account of this affair is given by Alexander Hamilton and is here transcribed :—

> "About the year 1670 the Muscat Arabs came with a fleet of trankies and took an opportunity to land in the night, on the west of the island, without being discovered, and marched silently close up to the town, and at break of day, when the gates were opened, they entered without resistance. The alarm was soon spread over the town, and happy was he who got first to the castle gates, but those who had heavy heels were sacrificed to the enemies' fury, who spared none; so in a moment that fair city and churches were left to the mercy of the Arabs, who for three days loaded their vessels with rich plunder, and mounted some cannon in a beautiful church and fired at the fort, but to little purpose. The Governor, who was in the castle, could soon have obliged them to move farther off the castle by the force of his heavy cannon, yet the priesthood forbid him firing at the church on pain of excommunication, lest some un-

lucky shot should sacrilegiously have defaced some holy image. But the Arabs, like a parcel of unsanctified rogues, made sad havoc on the church's trumpery, for besides robbing them of all the sanctified plate and cash, they did not leave one gold or silver image behind them, but carried all into dismal captivity, from whence they never returned that I could hear of. And as for the poor images of wood and stone, they were so rudely treated by those barbarous infidels that they came well off if they lost but a limb, and I saw some who lost their heads; but by the indefatigable industry of the clergy their churches are again as well or better furnished with well carved images of wood and stone than they were before, but I saw none of gold or silver to supply the places of the poor captives. However, before the Arabs had done plundering they became secure and negligent, which the Governor having notice of, proclaimed freedom to all slaves who would venture to sally out on the enemy. Accordingly about 4,000 soldiers and slaves made a sally with success, killing above 1,000 Arabs and made the rest flee from the town, the assailants losing but very few; and by that one sally the town was regained."

This enterprise was probably under the command of the Imam's warlike and ambitious brother, Saif bin Sultan. It was perhaps at this time the Muscat Arabs besieged the Persian garrison at Hormuz in the castle for three months, but failing in their efforts to take it, they retired.

According to annual custom, the Viceroy of Goa sent out a strong squadron to sweep the Indian Ocean and assert their maritime superiority. The fleet that sailed in accordance with this rule in September, 1673, visited Muscat, but the Admiral commanding, not liking the look of the powerful batteries in the forts and fearing to engage in a duel with them, went round to the little bay of Sedab and ravaged to the walls of Muscat before he retired. On their departure the Imam equipped ten merchant vessels as men-of-war and in the following December attacked a Portuguese grain fleet near Diu, escorted by several grabs and galleots, of which the Arabs took and destroyed the greater part.

In February of the next year (1674) the Imam's fleet sailed to the Portuguese colony at Bassain and landed 600 men, who raided the country, plundered the town and churches, and committed many outrages; the garrison is said to have been stronger than the Arab force but did not dare to sally out against them.

The well-known traveller Dr. Fryer, who was at Muscat in March, 1676, quaintly describes the city as follows:—

> "Those vast and torrid mountains no shade but heaven does hide. Within their fiery bosom the pilots find secure harbour for their weather-beaten ships. The prince of this country is called Imam, who is guardian of Mohammed's tomb. It is much frequented by merchants, who pay gold for Indian commodities. They are a fierce and treacherous people, gaining as much by fraud as by merchandise."

At this time there seems to have been a lull in the piratical expeditions of the Imam, owing probably to the distraction caused by the civil war that had arisen between the brothers Belarab and Saif, who had never been on good terms; the main cause of the quarrel was jealousy, but the sources of it are differently related in Oman. The country became divided into two camps and the war was conducted with so much virulence and bitter animosity that the Imam and his brother received opprobrious epithets, the former being called the "Calamity" and the "Butcher," while Saif was known as the "Scourge." Saif being the more active and energetic was generally regarded as the better fitted to rule and consequently obtained the more hearty support of the tribes. His adherents soon possessed themselves of the chief fortresses of the land, Sohar, Nakhl, Zikki, Semail and others, and the Imam was at last reduced to his stronghold of Yabreen and compelled to stand on the defensive. Besieged by his implacable brother and becoming weary of the struggle, the Imam Belarab ended his life with his own hands. This event, there is reason to believe, took place about the year 1679, but the date is uncertain.

The election of Saif bin Sultan to the Imamate followed immediately on Belarab's death, and he was acknowledged by the tribes without hesitation. The popularity of Saif was, at this time, unbounded as he had won the respect and admiration of the Arabs by his warlike and adventurous character, and his qualities as a leader were quite in harmony with the spirit of enterprise and love of foreign aggression that had been fostered among the Omanis by the preceding Yaareba Princes.

The new Imam began his reign by devoting his attention to the building of ships, the size and force of which he increased, in order that they might better cope with those of the Portuguese, thus he was soon able to put to sea a more numerous and formidable fleet than Oman had ever before possessed.

Much of the interesting information to be found in the pages of Hamilton and Ovington concerning the operations of the Muscat Arabs at this period was obtained by those writers from a journal kept by Captain Edward Say, an interloper, who in September, 1682, not venturing to settle in India, came to Muscat, where he resided at intervals for many years and traded direct to Europe. His journal, however, which no doubt contained many useful particulars, has unfortunately perished. Captain Say was wrecked in 1684 off Maseera Island in his ship *The Merchant's Delight*, from London, and was rescued by the Jenebeh tribe, who faithfully performed the engagement they had made with him about salvage.

About this time an event occurred which caused much resentment among the English merchants in India against the Imam Saif, though the latter does not appear to have been directly responsible. This event was the attack in the beginning of 1683 on the Company's ship *President*, commanded by Captain Hyde, bound from Masulipatam to Bombay, off Rajapore, by a flotilla of two Arab ships and four grabs, which were in the employ of Sumbaja Angria. Three of the grabs grappled while the fourth attempted to board. A sharp fight ensued in which the *President* lost eleven killed and thirty-five wounded, but at last the pirates were beaten off with the loss of some of the grabs. The *President* was obliged to put into Goa to repair damages before proceeding on her voyage.

About three years later, in 1686, Aurangzeeb's son, Sultan Akbar, who had made friends with Sivajee, the founder of the Mahratta Empire, by warning him of a plot against his life, fled from his father's wrath and took passage in Captain Bendall's ship at Rajapore in October with a few attendants for Muscat, where he was kindly received by the governor and by Mr. Stephens, an English gentleman, who sent him on to Persia in another ship. A royal welcome awaited him on his arrival at Bushire, and he is said to have subsequently obtained the Shah's sister in marriage.

The accounts of the Arab writers at this period are very meagre and we are mainly indebted to Alexander Hamilton for notice of the more salient events that took place. But it seems clear that the long and desultory naval warfare which had begun on the recovery of Muscat by the Arabs in 1650 was still being vigorously carried on with the Portuguese, and many engagements are said to have taken place between the squadrons and cruisers in the Arabian Sea.

We are told that the Arabs had the superiority on the whole, though in one of the most decisive actions, which occurred in 1693 off the bar of Surat, the Arab fleet was completely routed and dispersed. The Portuguese, finding their commerce seriously harassed in this war, endeavoured to retaliate on the Arabs by inducing the Zamorin of Calicut and other native chiefs on the coast of India, Sumatra, etc., to prevent their subjects from trading with Muscat, and the Viceroy of Goa is said to have quarrelled with the English of Bombay for supplying the Imam's ships with powder and shot. In 1694 the King of Persia, Shah Suliman, was succeeded by Shah Hoossain, a weak and incompetent prince, whose loose grasp of the reins was soon felt throughout the Empire.

At this time, probably, the Imam Saif was busily engaged in home affairs and carrying on commercial ventures and speculations; but he by no means neglected his shipbuilding operations, and in 1694 his naval resources were so strong that with renewed activity he sent out several expeditions against the Portuguese settlements in India, Persia, and Africa. One of these fleets sailed to Damaun, which was raided and sacked, thence proceeded to Salsette, where, according to Hamilton, great depredations were committed by the Arabs, who burned villages and churches, killed the priests, and carried off 1,400 captives into slavery and returned to Muscat with immense booty. Another of the Imam's squadrons, consisting of five ships manned by 1,500 men, was sent to the Persian Gulf and plundered Kong to the extent of 60,000 tomans, and soon after took a rich Armenian merchant ship. The squadron then threatened Gombroon, which the Persians prepared to defend, but no attack was made. The Persian Governor, however, asked the English factory to detain their ship, the *Nassau*, for twenty days, in order to keep off twelve Arab cruisers, whose arrival was shortly expected. The Governor further desired the co-operation of the English in his intended expedition against Muscat, for which preparations were being made, but to this the English agent was not inclined to accede, although it was well known that the Dutch were very eager to help the Persians in the affair, hoping thereby to secure the monopoly of the Gombroon trade for themselves, but as the expedition was eventually abandoned the naval aid asked for was never required. Nevertheless, much disquiet was caused among the native merchants in the Gulf by the rumours of war, while at the same time the piratical operations of the Imam Saif tended still further to paralyze trade and greatly terrified the traders, who gradually deserted Kong and other towns on the coast open to Arab attack; so much was this the case that Captain Brangion, the chief of the English factory at Gombroon, declared that the Muscat Arabs would prove as great a plague in India as the Algerines were in Europe.

The Imam Saif was well aware of the projected Persian campaign against him, and had taken measures for the defence of his country. He had given warning also that he would attack any European nation venturing to lend the Persians naval assistance, but so far he had refrained from interrupting the English trade, as they had hitherto acted with strict neutrality.

In 1695, war having broken out with that "potent prince," the Rajah of the Carnatic, a powerful armament was fitted out at Muscat for the purpose of ravaging the coast of that country. The expedition was entirely successful and the towns of Barsalore and Mangalore and other places were burnt and sacked, the fleet returning laden with valuable loot of all kinds as a contribution to the Imam's already immense wealth.

In the following year the Imam having learnt, apparently from Captain da Silva, who commanded the squadron cruising in the Persian Gulf, that the Portuguese Government had decided to co-operate with the Persians in a new expedition against Muscat, lost no time in equipping a fleet and despatching it to destroy the Portuguese factory at Mangalore.

In April, 1697, the Muscat Arabs seized an English ship called the *London,* belonging to Mr. Affleck of Bombay, and compelled her crew to join with them in their operations against the Portuguese. Many of them were wounded, as those who refused to fight were bound with cords in exposed positions on deck. The Imam was assured that the *London* was a peaceful trader and had not molested the Arab ships, but the Imam replied that as the English had lately taken one of his ships, he had confiscated the *London* in retaliation; he was ready to fight the English but would not give her up. The ship referred to by the Imam was probably one of those captured by the pirate Avory in the Red Sea.

About the same time, the Imam, having been appealed to by the inhabitants of Mombasa to free them from the tyranny of their Portuguese rulers, despatched a squadron to East Africa and laid siege to that town, which was stubbornly defended for two years by the garrison, who did not capitulate until about the end of the year 1698, when the Arabs succeeded in gaining possession of the fort. The fall of Mombasa happened soon after the arrival at Goa of the new Viceroy, Dom Gonsalvo da Coutinho, who had succeeded Dom Pedro da Noronha, and caused the failure of the new trading company that had been established at Goa and which had made Mombasa its chief business centre.

The Admiral of the Muscat squadron now sailed southward along the African coast, reducing successively Pemba, Zanzibar, Patta, and Kilwa. At Mozambique, however, his triumphal progress was checked; his attack was repulsed and he returned to Mombasa.

The operations of the Arab fleet were followed with the keenest interest by the natives, who saw in them the prospect of a speedy release from their oppressors. A general revolt took place, resulting in an indiscriminate massacre of the Portuguese at many places. For the time the power of the Portuguese was completely broken from Cape Delgado to Ras Guardafui, but except at Mombasa, where he left a strong garrison, the Imam Saif's Admiral refrained from establishing his authority on the Zanzibar coast, and on his departure to Muscat the land fell at once into a condition of anarchy and confusion, in which it remained for thirty years. During this period, though many Omani Arabs took the opportunity to migrate thither, the Yaareba Princes evinced no inclination to do more than claim a nominal ascendancy in that region.

The governor appointed by the Imam Saif to rule over Mombasa was Shaikh Nasir bin Abdulla al-Mezrui, but he was shortly after supplanted by one Saasah bin Rumbah.

The occurrences on the East African coast during the next half century are narrated in the *Tarikh Mombasa*, an Arabian work, an abridged translation of which has been given in English by Captain Owen and in French by Captain Guillain.

In May, 1698, two Portuguese frigates were met off Ras al-Had by eight Arab dhows, commanded by the Wali of Muttrah, and an engagement ensued in which the frigates, probably by superiority of seamanship, were able to beat off their assailants, though not without the loss of five killed and eleven wounded.

At the opening of the eighteenth century the maritime power of Oman was paramount to that of all the native rulers along the entire shores of the Indian Ocean, even to that of the pirate Angria.

This extensive area was swept by the Muscat Arabs with their marauding fleets to such a degree that they were dreaded not only by the Oriental traders but also by European merchantmen, except the larger vessels of the English and Dutch East India Companies.

Since the expulsion of the Portuguese from Muscat the Arabian Sea had ceased to be policed and guarded by their warships and no other power had stepped in to afford protection to sea-borne traffic, and the Indians, Persians, and Portuguese had in consequence suffered severely at the ravages done to their commerce by the Arabs, who fearlessly scoured the ocean in all directions with impunity.

The Imam Saif, to whose indomitable energy was mainly due the rapidly rising strength of the Muscat navy, and whose success might have been greater had not his spirit of enterprise been curbed by his miserly disposition, was at this time revolving in his head many schemes of foreign aggression in the Persian Gulf and India.

The fleet, which had torn Mombasa from the grasp of the Portuguese, had hardly returned from East Africa in 1699 when the Imam began to prepare another expedition against Salsette. The Arab commander of this new expedition arrived at a critical juncture when the Portuguese were threatening to attack and invade Bombay.

A short time previously a rupture had occurred between Bombay and the Portuguese Government of Salsette, owing to the seizure of a Portuguese vessel in Bombay Harbour. The Portuguese Governor had refused to accept apologies, and cut off all food supplies, on which Bombay was largely dependent, had collected troops and was preparing to cross over to the island and attack the town of Bombay when the Arab fleet hove in sight off Salsette. In their usual way, the Arabs lost not a moment in landing at Bersona, attacking the castle and massacring the people and soldiers. While the Arabs were engaged in plunder, the frightened Portuguese fled in numbers for refuge to Bombay and besought the aid of the English, who gave them protection and stood between them and the Arabs. The latter being on good terms with the English did not venture to molest the fugitives.

After sacking Salsette and scattering the inhabitants, the Imam's troops were re-embarked with the exception of about 300, who were left on shore on guard. Meanwhile, the Portuguese Governor, who had taken shelter at Bandora, had been reinforced by a strong contingent from the mainland and attacked the Arabs who had been left on shore with such vigour that they would unquestionably have been cut to pieces if they had not received timely succour from the fleet.

By their help, however, the tide was turned against the Portuguese, who were completely routed and dispersed with heavy slaughter. Content with their victory and enriched by great booty, the Arabs returned to Muscat. The fear inspired by this and other disasters now compelled the Portuguese to increase their naval armaments and strengthen their garrisons along the Indian coast.

The next point to which the Imam Saif now turned his attention was the Island of Bahrain in the Persian Gulf. This island possesses the finest pearl-fishery in the world, and was at this period held by Persia. The enterprise was fully accomplished by the Arab commander, but the length of time of the Imam's retention of the island is uncertain, as owing probably to the exaction and oppression of the new rulers the pearl-fishers deserted the island in a body.

About this time the Directors of the East India Company had received reports that the Arabs had become extremely insolent on account of their great successes, and were only deterred from attacking the English from fear of their being too strong for them. They had also been advised that the old Portuguese fort at Bombay required strengthening, and apprehensions were rife, which were not altogether without foundation, that the Muscat Arabs meditated a raid upon the island. This led to the receipt of orders from London to improve the fortifications and to place Bombay in a proper position as a well-defended commercial emporium. The Imam Saif, however, though too prudent to undertake actual hostilities against Bombay, continued, nevertheless, in an aggressive attitude towards the English for some time.

In 1704 the Agent of Gombroon reported that the Arabs were obstructing English trade in the Gulf to such an extent that the Persians were able to use this as a pretext for not paying up the arrears of customs due to the Company. A few months later, the Governor of Madras reported that Arab ships were still scouring the Coromandel coast and intercepting native craft, while in the following year the Muscat Arabs went so far as to capture a small English vessel belonging to Captain Maurice, who was detained with all his crew in perpetual slavery.

Lockyer, who was at Muscat in 1705, tells us that the Arabs had greatly improved the town and forts after their recovery of it from the Portuguese, and that they were a terror to the traders of India, and did not scruple to take English vessels of small size. Their shipping was daily increasing; some of their vessels were built at Surat and some in the River Indus, in dockyards of which the English had very little knowledge.

He saw fourteen men-of-war in the harbour, and learnt that many more were cruising about, the largest of which had seventy guns and none had less than twenty.

A short time previous to Lockyer's arrival the Arabs had taken a rich Calcutta ship, belonging to Captain Murvill, and Lockyer laments that some notice of this outrage had not been taken and restitution demanded by the East India Company, but apparently nothing had been done.

In February, 1707, another English trader, the *Diamond*, bound from Bombay to Gombroon, fell into the hands of the Arabs as a prize, and this event, together with numerous other recent captures of Persian vessels, so perturbed the Government that the Shah determined to solicit the co-operation of the English and Dutch in hostilities against the Imam Saif, who was now predominant in the Persian Gulf, in which sea he now possessed most of the islands. In pursuance of this plan the Shah nominated one, Meerza Nasir, as envoy to Bombay, and a nobleman as envoy to Batavia, but the President at Bombay, being apprised of the project, promptly resolved to forestall it, knowing well that if the Dutch complied with the Shah's request they would undoubtedly obtain a preference in the Persian markets. He accordingly instructed the Agent at Gombroon to promise that as soon as the war in Europe should cease, a naval force would be sent to operate against the Muscat Arabs. This promise had the desired effect, and the Shah's intended deputation to Batavia was never despatched.

It was about this time that the two English East India Companies, which, after four years of destructive rivalry and competition, had been nominally united in 1702, but had continued to quarrel with and thwart each other, were now finally amalgamated under the famous award of Lord Godolphin in 1708, which arranged for the control of the English trade being divided into three Presidencies, and placed the Company's trade on a more sound and prosperous footing than before.

The Imam Saif bin Sultan al-Yaareba died at Rostak, after a reign of thirty-two years, on October 4th, 1711, though it must be noted that the author of the Kashf al-Ghummeh gives the date as 1708. He was buried at Rostak, where a handsome tomb was erected to his memory, but it was destroyed in the early part of the nineteenth century by the iconoclastic zeal of a Wahabee general.

The Imam Saif bin Sultan was the greatest of the Yaareba Princes, and at no time before or since has Oman been so renowned, powerful or prosperous as under his sway. Ambition and love of glory, combined with a lust for wealth, were his ruling passions, and in pursuit of these objects he was as unscrupulous and unswerving as he was capable and energetic. His eventful career is chiefly remarkable for his policy of waging an incessant and vindictive war against the Portuguese, plundering their settlements and destroying their ships and commerce, as well as for his systematic piratical excursions against the merchantmen of India, Persia, and even of European powers. Whether the Imam personally commanded any of the military expeditions undertaken by him we are not informed, but it seems probable from his character that he accompanied many of them, and that their success was due in great part to his presence.

We hear but little in the local historians of internal troubles and wars during his reign; we may therefore infer that the Imam had the skill and tact to divert the more restless and ambitious spirits from tribal broils, jealousies and dissensions by employing them in piratical and other expeditions, and in encouraging them to venture their trading operations in distant regions, for it is beyond question that under his auspices the commerce of Oman greatly extended and developed.

He appears to have invested part of the great wealth he had accumulated in the purchase of land, and thus acquired about a third of the date trees in his dominions. He carried out many public works for the improvement of the country, such as felejes or underground rivers—used for irrigating the land. We have no means of ascertaining the number of vessels of which his navy was composed, but it must have been very considerable. Many were square-rigged ships after the European model, but the rest were Arab war dhows. They were all well armed, and were used indifferently for war and trading purposes, and he often employed Englishmen to command his trading vessels, while he did not scruple to send them under English colours for better security.

It may be as well here, perhaps, to glance at the insecure state of trade at this period in the Indian Ocean, it being infested with swarms of European pirates, mostly English, scouring the coasts in search of prey, and doing incalculable mischief to the merchants of all nations.

Far less numerous than the Mahrattas, Muscat Arabs, and other marauding ruffians, but infinitely more formidable, enterprising, and skilful were these freebooters, of whom Anderson in his *Western India* observes: "Such reckless captains created a terrible sensation. Native piracy, with its hole-and-corner business, was completely eclipsed. Instead of small boats from Malabar and Sind, which took by surprise boats smaller than themselves, there were now in the Indian Seas vessels with tiers of guns and manned by the first seamen of Europe." Most, if not all, of these pirates hailed from the West Indies, where they had followed the same trade, and on arriving in the Eastern seas were at no loss to find ports at which to refit and watch the trade routes. At Muscat, they commanded the entrance to the Persian Gulf. At Aden they could intercept the rich stream of vessels passing between India and the Red Sea, while on the coasts of Madagascar they made settlements in which they lived in freedom and luxury. In comparison with the various naval powers in the East, the rovers felt themselves strong enough to defy any attempts at capture, while the game they played was so easy and lucrative that they had no difficulty in obtaining sufficient volunteers and recruits. Many of them secured considerable wealth during their adventurous career, though it rarely proved of any use to them. The destruction of vessels was so great and the booty they acquired was so enormous that the fame and notoriety of their actions were only equalled by the universal dread and alarm inspired among merchants along the shores of Southern Asia. Fortunately the campaign of these robbers in the Indian Ocean was, comparatively, short lived, for it only lasted from about 1690 to 1720. Very little is known about them, and most of their exploits and atrocities have passed into oblivion. Our information about the whole of this period is as meagre as it is unreliable. Nor were these "Reckless Captains" many in number, and it may be doubted whether there were more than fifty of them altogether.

One of the first cases of European piracy we find mentioned as having occurred in the Arabian Sea was that of 1686, when two corsairs, acting in concert, plundered vessels in the Red Sea to the extent of six lakhs of rupees.

Among other similar events about this time, we hear that an English pirate attacked and plundered the long-suffering Portuguese settlement at Kong in the Persian Gulf, which led to the despatch from India of the Company's cruiser *Cæsar*, commanded by Captain Wright, to intercept her, but the pirate escaped unhurt. Off the Malabar coast the *Charming Mary*, commanded by Captain Babington, was about this time (1689) on the look-out for prizes. Six other rovers from the West Indies were in the same year cruising off the northern coast of India and making rich harvests.

The pirates, indeed, had already begun to give serious trouble and the heavy losses sustained by merchants caused much anxiety. So far hardly any of the names of the rovers have come down to us, but in 1691 we hear of Captain James Gilliam, an English pirate, being beguiled on shore by the Nawab of Mungrole, a tributary of Joonagur, and made prisoner with some of his men. Gilliam could obtain no help from the President of Surat and was afterwards sent to Delhi, where he remained in captivity.

One of the ablest and most successful of these "Monarchs of the Main" was a Frenchman, who took the name of Misson and went to sea in the *Victoire*, a merchant vessel. While this ship was at Naples he visited Rome and made the acquaintance of an Italian priest named Caraccioli, whom he persuaded to exchange the cowl for the pigtail and who remained his companion for life. In the West Indies the *Victoire* turned pirate and steered for the East. On the way, Misson captured an English ship, which he re-named the *Bijoux*, and gave the command to Caraccioli. After a stay at Johanna, which he made his headquarters for the time and where he took several prizes, Misson resolved to found a settlement, and selected British Sound on the north of Madagascar as the locality. Here he erected an octagon fort, which he mounted with guns taken from a Portuguese prize, built houses, and made docks. Besides French and English pirates, many of whom possessed several wives apiece, a large number of freed negroes were collected, who proved of great use in manning the squadron. This colony was founded in 1694 and was named by Misson "Libertatia." In one of his piratical voyages, in which he took a Portuguese ship of fifty guns with £200,000 on board, Misson met with Captain Tew, who fraternized with him and agreed to join forces.

Another pirate, who acted in concert with Misson, was Avory, as will be seen presently.

Eventually Libertatia was overwhelmed by a large body of the natives, Caraccioli was killed and the other Europeans massacred or dispersed. Almost simultaneously the *Victoire* was wrecked in a violent storm and Misson with all on board perished.

Tew returned with his booty to America, but after a time revisited his old haunts and was killed in an engagement with an English ship in the Red Sea. In the same year, there came to the Indian Ocean the famous John or Henry Avory, who, when mate of a Bristol ship off Corunna, turned pirate and put the captain on shore. Re-naming his ship the *Fanny*, Avory sailed for the East and cruised in the Arabian Sea, to intercept the Red Sea and Indian trade. In 1695, while cruising between Aden and Muscat, he took a Surat ship laden with pilgrims returning from Jedda, and after relieving her of what little booty she had, set her at liberty.

With the object of levying toll upon all ships passing in and out of the Red Sea, a measure he was able to perform as his vessel carried 46 guns and 130 men, he chose the Island of Perim in the Straits of Bab al-Mandeb, as a safe and convenient spot to form a station, and began to dig a well, as the island had no spring of water. Though the rock was pierced to the depth of nearly 100 feet nothing but brackish water was found and Avory was compelled to abandon his project. Seeking for another locality to form a station, Avory's choice fell upon the little island of St. Mary's in the north-east of Madagascar, which he fortified as a storehouse, while a colony sprang up on the mainland, where the pirates intermarried with the natives and bought the negroes to cultivate the ground.

In the following year (1696) in company with Misson in the *Victoire*, Avory cruised between India and the Gulf of Oman, where he fell in with, and took without resistance a large ship of 110 guns, commanded by Nakhod Ibrahim Khan and belonging to the Malik al-Tajar of Surat, Abdul Ghafoor. This vessel, the *Gunjsowaee*, was bound for Jedda with pilgrims and is said to have had 1,500 souls on board, from whom he obtained loot in money and jewels to the value of more than a quarter of a million sterling, part of which, viz., £30,000, formed the annual subsidy paid by the great Mogul to the Shereef of Mecca. Avory took from the ship a young lady of rank with her attendants and carried her to St. Mary's and had by her a son known as "Mulatto Tom," who afterwards became factotum to Plantain, King of Ranger Bay. The lady was generally spoken of at the time as Aurangzeeb's granddaughter, but her identity does not appear to have been established. From the *Gunjsowaee* were removed also about a hundred girls of from twelve to eighteen years of age and put on board Misson's sloop to be carried to Libertatia. The ship was then released and sailed back to Surat, where, on the news of the outrage becoming known, a storm of fanatical fury and indignation against the English broke over the town and the Governor, Itimad Khan, was forced to act with vigour. President Annesley and the whole of the factors at Surat and Broach, about eighty in number, were imprisoned, and the English trade was, much to the satisfaction of the Dutch and French, stopped for many months, and the East India Company suffered severely for Avory's conduct, though the Governor behaved, on the whole, with praiseworthy moderation and justice.

Avory returned to St. Mary's surfeited with loot and remained for some time organizing the settlement, after which he reached England in safety and died in obscurity. Five only of his men appear to have been taken, tried, and hanged.

Among other piracies in this year was the *Rampoora*, a very rich Surat vessel and Bombay ship, which had embarked a cargo of horses at Muscat for Surat and was taken to the Gulf of Oman. The pirates, having taken off the master, Captain Sawbridge, and his crew, set fire to the vessel and burnt the Arab horses. As Captain Sawbridge persisted in rebuking his captors his lips were sewn up with twine to keep him silent; but was subsequently landed at Aden, where he died in consequence of the ill-treatment he had received.

Perhaps the most notorious pirate that ever lived was William Kidd, whose reputation has survived to this day, though there were probably but few rovers who did less mischief. He was a native of Greenock, and had served in the West Indies. In 1696 he was given a King's Commission as a privateer in the *Adventure*, a galley of 30 guns, to suppress piracy in Eastern seas, and arrived in the Gulf of Aden about the middle of 1697. Having traitorously and with the consent of some of his crew turned pirate, he did not hesitate to attack an Indian ship, but was prevented from capturing her by the *Sceptre*, a cruiser, which Sir John Gayer had sent from Surat as convoy to the Delhi ships; he cruised chiefly between Madagascar, Malabar and the Red Sea. In August he took a small brigantine, the *Mary*, commanded by Captain Parker, and later on (1698) an Armenian ship, the *Quedah Merchant*, the master of which was Captain Wright. The prize was worth about a lakh of rupees, and as it was a better ship than his own, Kidd shifted into it. After this he sailed for Madagascar, where he met Culliford, and remained some time. Though of a cruel and savage nature, he seems to have had no stomach for fighting and is not known to have attacked a single strong ship. During his short piratical career of about two years Kidd had made but few prizes and could have amassed but little wealth; not venturing, however, to tarry longer in the Indian Ocean, he sailed for Boston in New England, in the *Quedah Merchant*, where he arrived in June, 1699. He was soon after arrested and sent to London, where he was convicted and hanged in chains in 1701.

The European pirates at this time in the Indian Seas were very numerous, and were robbing all nations indiscriminately. Some of the crews had run away with the ships on which they served, and among these were the men of the Dutch ship *Hare*, bound from Java to Gombroon. Having set aside the officers they ran up the black flag and sailed to the Red Sea, where they took and plundered many Arab vessels, and then, being short of food, returned to Gombroon. Here the officers succeeded in recovering authority and restoring the vessel to the Dutch factory.

We learn that about 1701-2 three of these rovers agreed to cruise in the Red Sea, and keeping company as arranged, they seized an Arab ship with a heavy cargo of slaves off Aden, the sale of which gave a handsome share to each man. After committing further depredations on native shipping they shaped their course to the Malabar coast, where they arrived in November, 1698. The pirates of this squadron were Culliford in the *Resolution* (late *Mocha*), 40 guns, the former master of which, Captain Edgecombe, had been murdered. Shivers, the grand old Dutch pirate, as he was called, in the *Soldada*, alias the *Algerine*, 28 guns, had previously captured the *Sedgwick*, commanded by Captain Skinner, off Comorin, but had released her after taking only some stores; and, thirdly, Captain North in the *Pelican*, which was afterwards exchanged for the *Dolphin*. North subsequently went to Madagascar, where he held command of the pirate settlement at St. Mary's for some time, till he was killed by the natives. Culliford and Shivers also proceeded to Madagascar, where they surrendered to Commodore Lyttleton, who gave them the King's pardon, on which they sailed for Europe in the *Vine*.

At the solicitation of the East India Company, Commodore Warren was commissioned in 1699 in the *Anglesey*, to proceed to the Indian Ocean with three other ships to suppress piracy, and was empowered to offer pardon to any pirate who would surrender themselves, except Kidd and Avory. Warren died on reaching Tellicheri in November of that year, and was succeeded by Captain Lyttleton of the *Harwich*, who six months later sailed for St. Mary's, Madagascar, where he remained for some months but made no attempt to capture pirates. About 1702 Captain Bowen in the *Speedy Return*, in company with Captain Howard in the *Prosperous*, captured two Arab ships off the Muscat coast, and then entering the Persian Gulf took several small craft. These rovers afterwards attacked a Surat ship and carried it by boarding, the pirates losing thirty men in the encounter. The prize is said to have been worth £42,000.

Another corsair, Captain Halsey, in the brigantine *Charles*, first took an Arab grab with 2,000 dollars, and then two English ships, the *Rising Eagle* and the *Essex*, the former having £10,000 and the latter £40,000. These vessels were taken to Madagascar, and the cruiser *Greyhound* was soon after despatched from Madras to obtain restitution, but was herself captured by the pirates.

A year or two later, Captain Read, in a brigantine, cruising in the Persian Gulf, took an Arab grab laden with woollen goods, which the pirates deemed useless and jettisoned, and thus lost their booty, for in one of the bales the merchant had concealed a quantity of gold, which went overboard with the rest.

Sometime afterwards Captain Booth, in the *Speaker*, with Captain White also on board, sailed for Zanzibar, where Booth with twenty of his men were entrapped by the Arab Governor and made prisoners. Deserting his comrade, White slipped off to Aden, and there captured an Arab ship, which proved a rich prize, as the loot, when distributed, gave £500 per man. After taking two more Arab vessels near Perim, White stood over to the Somali Coast, where he seized the *Malabar*, a large slaver with 600 negroes on board. White then transferred his crew to the *Malabar*, and sent the slaves away in the *Speaker* to be sold. The proceeds of the sale, together with the gold concealed in a jar under the ship's cow, was a goodly harvest to the captors. Two other prizes were a Portuguese and an English ship, the latter, the *Dorothy*, commanded by Captain Penruddock, being strong and newly built, was retained as a consort, Captain Penruddock and his crew being sent off in the Portuguese prize. The *Malabar* then sailed for Dhofar on the Arabian coast, where she took a ketch, and some time after steered for Hoppel Point in Madagascar, where White divided the plunder, which came to £12,000 per man, and formed a settlement, but fell ill and died soon after.

In the Persian Gulf great havoc was wrought by Captain Cornelius in the *Morning Star*, with a mixed crew of French, Dutch, English and negroes. Cornelius lay off the Island of Karrack and was refitting his ship there, when he was chased by two Portuguese men-of-war. The *Morning Star*, having escaped this danger, then ran for East Africa, where the men mutinied and replaced Cornelius by Williamson.

One of the more notable freebooters before piracy was extinguished was Captain England, who had been mate of the *Onslow*, a small pirate which had been captured by the *Terrible*, probably in the Atlantic. In command of the *Fanny*, and having the *Victor* as consort, he sailed to the Indian Ocean in 1719 and visited the pirate settlements in Madagascar.

In the Red Sea he took an Indian pilgrim ship, which was taken to St. Mary's, where the plunder was landed and the Indian ladies distributed among the crew, England only reserving two for himself.

In the following year he steered for the Malabar coast, and fell in with an Arab dhow from China, which proved a good prize. The *Fanny* and *Victor* next went to East Africa and on arriving at Johanna found Captain de la Bouche building a new ship, his own vessel, the *Indian Queen*, in which he had come to pirate the Arabian Sea, having been wrecked. England also found here two English merchant ships at anchor, the *Cassandra*, commanded by Captain Macray, and the *Greenwich*, commanded by Captain Kirby, which he immediately attacked. The brunt of the action fell on Macray, as Kirby, besides deserting him at the outset, sheered off.

After a long and gallant fight, in which the *Cassandra* had thirteen killed, Macray took to his boats, and landing at Johanna, escaped inland. Subsequently he surrendered to England, who had in the meantime changed to the *Cassandra*, and who, admiring Macray's courage and skill in defending his vessel, took advantage of his mate, Taylor, being drunk and insensible. He allowed Macray and his crew to take the *Fanny* and sail away to Bombay. The mate, Taylor, a cruel and ferocious brute, enraged at Macray's escape, instigated the pirates to dispose and maroon England, but this was not agreed to, and the latter found his way to Madagascar, where he died a few days later, reformed and repentant. On the departure of England, Taylor assumed command of the *Cassandra*, and cruised off India and in the Arabian Sea, capturing one European and several Arab ships. Among the latter were two vessels from Muscat laden with horses and bound for India. The Arab merchants were put to the torture to make them disclose treasure, but they had none to reveal. Whilst thus engaged, Taylor sighted the squadron of Commodore Upton, which had been sent from Bombay to operate against the pirate Angria, and releasing the dhows, fled to the northward. One of Taylor's prizes was the *Sedgwick*, the captain of which, Skinner, was savagely treated by that ruffian, who bound him to the windlass and pelted him with broken bottles and whipped him up and down the deck till he fell, and then shot him.

This sketch may be concluded with a notice of John Plantain, who was a native of Jamaica and first joined the pirates in the *Terrible*. He sailed to the Indian Seas with Captain England and was present in many piratical cruises under Avory and other captains. Having amassed considerable wealth, he settled in "Ranger Bay," or Antongil, to the north of St. Mary's, where he built a fort, collected many slaves, and established a large harem. He also repaired Avory's fortifications at St. Mary's and became known as the King of Ranger Bay.

There were many English pirates in that part of Madagascar, some of whom joined him, while others, among whom was King Kelly of Manningory, treated him as an enemy. One of the chief native rulers in the island was King Dick of Massalage, whose grand-daughter, Eleanor Brown, was demanded in marriage by Plantain. King Dick not only refused to give her up but defied Plantain, who thereupon made war on him and killed him and carried off the girl. Among Plantain's principal adherents was Mulatto Tom, said to have been a son of Avory by the Indian lady he had taken from the *Gunjsowaee* in 1696. Mulatto Tom, though a very young man, was in the confidence of Plantain, who employed him in collecting recruits and slaves, and obtained through him about 1,000 men from St. Mary's. Mulatto Tom was also instrumental in serving Plantain in other ways.

In 1721 Commodore Matthews, who had been commissioned to act against the pirates, arrived with his squadron off St. Mary's and had an interview with Plantain, but beyond looting the wreck of an Arab ship which had been captured by the pirate Condent in the *Flying Dragon* in the Red Sea, Matthews did nothing and sailed away to Bengal.

Plantain's successes made him aim at the complete sovereignty over Madagascar, but his ambition overreached itself, and the hostility of the natives convinced him at length that his stay in the island was impossible. He accordingly sailed for India about May, 1722, and after being nearly wrecked on Bombay Island reached Gheriah, where he was joyfully received by Angria, who made Plantain Admiral of his piratical fleet.

Saif was succeeded in the Imamate by his eldest son, Sultan, who was elected without opposition in the same year. Sultan continued the policy of his father with a firm and unbending hand, carrying on the war with the Persians and Portuguese by land and sea, and ruling the tribes of Oman with justice and sagacity.

One of the most notable actions of his administration was the transference of the seat of government from Rostak to Al-Hazm in the Batineh, where he constructed a substantial fort, generally considered by the Arabs as next to Nezwa, the strongest fortress in Oman. On this fortress the expenditure incurred was enormous, and the Imam is said to have expended not only the bulk of his father's accumulated wealth but also large sums borrowed on the "wakf"—or religious endowments—of mosques throughout the land. Al-Hazm lies close under the range of hills known as Jebel Hajar and does not occupy a very advantageous position and has, therefore, notwithstanding its strength, never been much used as a residence by later rulers.

It is to be regretted that though the native annalists inform us that the Imam Sultan continued warlike operations by land and sea against his enemies, they are absolutely silent as to the details of the campaigns and even as to the objective of the various military expeditions sent out by him from Muscat, and we have to rely on other sources for particulars of these events.

So far as we can learn, the first enterprise undertaken by the Imam Sultan was when he set out in the early part of 1714 to make a descent on the Indian Coast which resulted in disaster. The squadron succeeded in capturing a Portuguese vessel that had arrived from China and committed other depredations on Portuguese territory, but was intercepted by a Portuguese fleet sent after it by the Viceroy of Goa. The battle took place off Surat on February 19th, 1714, and it is said to have ended after a long day's fight in the complete defeat and dispersal of the Arabs, whose flagship was sunk during the engagement. Incensed at the unexpected reverse he had sustained in this affair at the hands of the Portuguese, Sultan lost no time in equipping another fleet to operate against the enemy and to recover his lost prestige.

The Armada sailed direct to Kong in the Persian Gulf, where the Portuguese factory was attacked, pillaged, and burnt without resistance. The Shahbunder of the place, however, having obtained the aid of some Persian troops in the vicinity, fell upon the Arabs and drove them back to their ships. To cruise against the Arabs, the gallant Dom Francesco da Silva, who had commanded the Portuguese squadron in the Persian Gulf for many years, was despatched thither by the Viceroy of Goa, but apparently without result.

We are told by Hamilton that the Imam's naval power in 1715

comprised one ship of 74 guns, two of 60, one of 50, eighteen smaller vessels of from 32 to 12 guns each, and some trankies, or rowing vessels, of from 4 to 8 guns. He adds, that the Imam keeps all the coasts in awe from Cape Comorin to the Red Sea. It may be here observed that the Imam's military expeditions were largely composed of armed merchant ships, which joined the fleet in the hope of sharing in the booty. We learn from Ross's *nnals of Oman* that Sultan attacked and took Bahrain and engaged in hostilities with the Persians. This island had been taken from Persia by the Imam Saif in 1700 and it seems probable that Sultan in 1717 re-occupied and garrisoned it.

The general disaffection in, and disruption of Persia at this period, under the timid rule of Shah Hoossain, undoubtedly emboldened the Arabs to continue their insults and depredations, and in this way the whole of the islands in the Persian Gulf gradually fell into the hands of the Muscat Arabs. In the same year (1717) a Muscat piratical fleet of thirteen sail made a descent on the towns of Diu and Damaun, and cruised along the coast to intercept the Portuguese traders. The Viceroy, Dom Luiz de Menezes, promptly despatched a squadron of five ships under Dom Lopo da Almeida to protect his territory, but no decisive results appear to have followed.

Early in the year 1719 a fleet sailed from Goa to Kong, in compliance with a request made by the Shah of Persia for Portuguese naval co-operation against the Muscat Arabs. The Imam Sultan bin Saif, on hearing of this fleet being stationed at Kong ready to act in conjunction with the Persians, prepared an armament to oppose it. This force arrived off Kong on August 4th, and the Portuguese, accepting the offered battle, at once weighed anchor and sailed out to meet it. The particulars of the engagement that ensued have been given in the preceding chapter.

The Imam Sultan bin Saif appears to have died shortly afterwards in 1719, though it must be noted that according to the *Annals of Oman* his death occurred in the previous year (1718). He was buried in the fortress he had himself completed, and which he had chosen for his residence—Al-Hazm.

During the eight years of the Imam's sway, Oman seems to have enjoyed to an unusual degree the advantage of internal tranquillity, prosperity, and freedom from tribal feuds. Less ambitious, less avaricious, and less adventurous than his father Saif, Sultan preferred to engage in legitimate commerce rather than in piracy, and we consequently hear of no complaints from the English and Dutch factors of Arab outrages. With the death of the Imam Sultan the peace which had so long and happily prevailed in Oman came abruptly to an end. The event was the signal for a series of dynastic troubles, disputed successions, and misfortunes, that not only caused internecine strife that deluged the country with blood for thirty years, but also brought on the land the calamities of a foreign invasion, and resulted eventually in the collapse of the Yaareba power and the establishment of a new dynasty.

Sultan had left several children, the eldest of whom, Saif, was about twelve years old. The general voice was in favour of this boy succeeding his father, but the more enlightened portion of the community saw serious objections, legal and political, to a minor being raised to the Imamate and supported the claims of the boy's great uncle, Muhenna, a younger brother of the great Imam Saif bin Sultan, to act as Regent.

At an assembly of Shaikhs and notables convoked at Rostak for the purpose of electing a successor to Sultan, the Kadhi Adey bin Suliman, after a long discussion, reluctantly proclaimed the youth, Saif bin Sultan, as Imam. In defiance of this decision the adherents of Muhenna, among whom was included the sister of the late Imam Sultan, about the close of the year 1719 smuggled him into the castle and recognized him not as Regent but as Imam, expelling therefrom the young Saif, who probably fled to Al-Hazm.

For some reason not recorded by the Arab writers, Muhenna was not popular with the people of Oman generally, and it may be naturally supposed that his unauthorized assumption of the Imamate was regarded with resentment and indignation by those who had opposed his election. Feeling the insecurity of his position he endeavoured by all the means in his power to disarm opposition and conciliate all classes. With this view he abolished the customs at Muscat and allowed merchandise from foreign countries to be imported free. But it was all in vain; even his victory over the Portuguese did not avail to ward off the fate that awaited him.

While Muhenna was seeking to win popularity and consolidate his position in Oman, the doomed dynasty of the Sefawis in Persia was struggling to extricate itself from the dangers by which it was surrounded and repel its enemies, not the least among whom were the Muscat Arabs, who had ravaged the Persian coast, and were in possession of all the islands in the Gulf. To recover these islands, protect the coast, and punish the Arabs, General Lootf Ali Khan was despatched with an army in 1720 to Gombroon, and a Portuguese fleet of warships and transports, which at the request of Shah Hoossain had been sent by the Viceroy in India to the Gulf, was on its way to embark the Persian troops at Gombroon, when it was met and attacked by a Muscat squadron, by which it was worsted and driven back to India.

Not long after this event the disaffection and enmity towards Muhenna and his chief supporter, the Kadhi Adey bin Suliman, rose to a head at Rostak, where Yaarab bin Belarab, a nephew of Muhenna, was persuaded to rise against him. Yaarab with a small following first marched to Muscat, where the gates were opened to him without resistance, the governor at this time being Masood bin Mohammed al-Ryamee. Mohammed happened at the moment to be at Felej al-Bagly in the district of Jow, but on hearing of Yaarab's seizure of Muscat, immediately returned to Rostak and prepared for defence. Yaarab with his force, which had meantime gathered strength, now besieged Rostak Castle in which Muhenna, almost entirely deserted by his friends, had shut himself up.

Despairing of aid from any quarter, Muhenna soon perceived the uselessness of further opposition, and relying on Yaarab's guarantee of personal safety for himself and adherents, abandoned the castle and surrendered. The promise of life had been given only to be broken; Muhenna had no sooner fallen into the hands of his nephew than he was seized, bound, and thrown into prison, where he was a few days later perfidiously murdered, which occurred about the end of the year 1720.

No disturbances followed this crime and Yaarab bin Belarab was quietly allowed to assume the government. He was astute enough, however, at first to forego the title of Imam and declared himself as Regent, on behalf of his young cousin, Saif bin Sultan. Under this guise he was able to rule for about a year, working cautiously but indefatigably to gain the allegiance of the tribes and to get possession of all the chief fortresses in the country.

In the month of May, 1722, Yaarab felt himself sufficiently strong to throw off the mask of Regent and allowed himself to be proclaimed Imam at Rostak by the influential Kadhi Adey bin Suliman, who had now warmly espoused his cause, and forgetting his scruples had given him plenary absolution for the murder of Muhenna and other crimes and misdemeanours. The conduct of Yaarab, in thus exalting himself to the Imamate, instead of raising his fortunes, served on the contrary to hasten his downfall, and caused the deepest offence to the people, who remained steadfast in their loyalty to the young Prince, Saif bin Sultan. At Rostak, in particular, the excitement was so great that Yaarab, within a few days, was obliged to fly to Nezwa, where he arrived about June.

The disaffected party at Rostak now conspired with Belarab bin Nasir, the brother-in-law of the late Imam Sultan bin Saif, to oppose and overthrow the Imam Yaarab; and Belarab, who had been residing at Nezwa, lost no time in gaining the adhesion of the Beni Hina tribe, which is very powerful in that district. Leaving Nezwa in August, Belarab marched to Rostak, escorted by a body of the Beni Hina, who set fire to the castle and expelled Nebhan, the Wali or Governor of the town, who was an adherent of the Imam Yaarab.

On hearing that Belarab had commenced hostilities against him, Yaarab despatched from Nezwa a party of about 400 men to recover Rostak, but this force was unable to proceed further than Awabi in the Wady Beni Kharoosi, and was obliged to retreat.

The Wali of Muscat, Himyar bin Munir al-Ryamee, on being written to by Belarab to give up that place, obeyed the order, and his example was followed by the Wali of Nakhl. A few weeks later, a force was detached from Rostak under Malik bin Saif al-Yaarabi, who took Semail and then, in conjunction with the Beni Ruwaihah, captured Zikki without opposition. The townspeople of Zikki, however, being in favour of the Imam Yaarab, encouraged him to try and recover that fort, and he accordingly moved against it with two guns and besieged Malik bin Saif. While the Imam Yaarab was thus engaged, he was suddenly attacked by a strong body of the Beni Hina, which had arrived from Rostak under Ali bin Mohammed, the Sahib al-Anbar, by whom he was completely routed and driven back to Nezwa.

The Kadhi Adey bin Suliman meanwhile, who had accompanied the Imam to Zikki, proceeded to Rostak, where together with his colleague the Kadhi Suliman bin Khalfan, he was immediately seized and put to death by the order of Belarab, the bodies of both being afterwards dragged through the streets by the people. Elated with his success, the Sahib al-Anbar pushed on to Nezwa in pursuit of Yaarab and his supporters, the Beni Ryam, and after a short blockade, compelled Yaarab, who had taken refuge in the great tower, to capitulate and resign the Imamate, which he did on the stipulation that he should be permitted to reside in peace and safety at Yabreen in the Wady Bahila.

To the general satisfaction of the people, the young Prince Saif bin Sultan was then for the third time elected Imam at Nezwa and Rostak, Belarab being at the same time proclaimed as Regent.

To all appearance the tranquillity of the land was now restored, and under a Regency the prospects of future harmony, security, and prosperity were fully assured. But it is the unexpected that always happens, and as we shall see, Oman was on the brink of an abyss and on the eve of the most tempestuous period of its history, for the civil war that now ensued has left its mark to the present day.

Among the Shaikhs of tribes and other personages who flocked to Rostak to offer their allegiance and congratulations to the newly restored Imam Saif bin Sultan was Mohammed bin Nasir, the "Temeemeh" of the Beni Ghafir, a Nizar tribe occupying the valley of that name on the borders of Dhahireh.

For some unaccountable reason, the Regent, Belarab, quarrelled with and grossly insulted Mohammed bin Nasir, who, vowing vengeance, wrote to Yaarab bin Belarab exhorting him to raise the standard of rebellion, and to take the field against Belarab. Having taken this decisive step, Mohammed, in furtherance of his designs, proceeded at once to Dhahireh to concert measures with the Naeem, Beni Kattab and other northern tribes, which were in Suff (or alliance) with the Beni Ghafir.

The Regent, Belarab, apprehending that war was inevitable, sent to the Beni Hina at Nezwa for support, and despatched an army under his brother, Suliman bin Nasir, by the Wady Semail, to operate against Yaarab bin Belarab. On reaching Nezwa, however, he found the great tower already in possession of Yaarab, and retired to Zikki, where he occupied the castle. Another force was sent by Belarab against Behla, but this failed also, and many of the troops were made prisoners. Belarab's third expedition was equally unfortunate. It was sent to the Wady Beni Ghafir, where it encountered the Nizar forces collected by Mohammed bin Nasir, and was ignominiously defeated.

Meantime, Yaarab bin Belarab had made three separate and ineffectual attempts to capture the castle at Zikki, which had been reinforced by Malik bin Nasir from Rostak. Yaarab was soon after obliged to fall back upon Nezwa, and was followed up by Malik, who encamped at Fark. Further fighting now ensued, and in one of the attacks upon Yaarab's position, Malik bin Nasir was slain.

Shaikh Mohammed bin Nasir al-Ghafiri, whose superior ability and military skill had become daily more conspicuous, and who in the interval had been operating in Dhahireh, at Dhank, at Ghabbi, and elsewhere, now moved upon Nezwa and delivered an assault upon the enemy's camp at Fark, which, after heavy fighting, was evacuated during the night.

Mohammed bin Nasir, after a short stay at Nezwa, now retraced his steps to the Wady Beni Ghafir, and marched down it to Rostak. Here he encamped at Felej al-Shamal and a day or two after was attacked by Ali bin Mohammed Sahib al-Anbar, who was killed in the contest that took place under the walls of Rostak. On this defeat of his troops Belarab bin Nasir sued for peace, which was granted on his agreeing to surrender Rostak and all the other forts in Oman. As they proceeded together to the castle, Belarab laid a trap for Mohammed, but the latter was too wary and evaded the stratagem. In revenge for the murder of Muhenna and the two Kadhis, Mohammed then gave over the town to be sacked by the soldiers, who are said to have committed shocking barbarities.

While these events were passing at Rostak, the ex-Imam Yaarab bin Belarab died at Nezwa on March 16th, 1723.

About this time, Mohammed bin Nasir's army was strengthened by the arrival of some of the Shemal tribes, to whom he had applied for assistance. Four thousand of these men appear to have been composed of the Kowasim and Shihiyyeen tribes from Julfar under Khamees bin Munir al-Hawaly, while 1,500 more belonged to the Al-Kaab, Beni Kattab and other tribes. Mohammed bin Nasir having now ascertained that the forts of Muscat and Burka had not been surrendered as promised, ordered Belarab bin Nasir to be fettered and confined. Both these forts were garrisoned by the Beni Hina, and the Wali of Muscat was Jaid bin Murshid al-Yaarebi, who soon afterwards withdrew to Nakhl. His place was taken by Khalf bin Mubarak al-Hinawi, a native of Ghasb, and known as the Dwarf, who was now to assume the leadership of the Yemenite faction, and to prove a most formidable antagonist to Mohammed bin Nasir al-Ghafiri.

Khalf, leaving Muscat, then rode to Burka and awaited the arrival of the Wali sent by Mohammed to take possession of the fort. This Wali was Ali bin Mohammed al-Kharoosi, who had no sooner set foot at Burka than he was slain by Khalf.

Knowing well the man with whom he had to deal Mohammed now set in motion from Rostak nearly the whole of his force in six divisions and camped at Mesnaah, about fifteen miles from Burka.

Khalf appears to have had command of the sea, but as his land forces were far inferior to those of Mohammed, he left Burka with a strong garrison to oppose the enemy, and hastened along to Muscat, where he at once became actively engaged in corresponding with and summoning the tribes in alliance with the Beni Hina to come to his assistance.

Mohammed, after beleaguering Burka for four months, was compelled by want of food to raise the siege and break up his army. On returning to Rostak, he was prostrated with a severe attack of small-pox, which nearly cost him his life. Two months later he started for Makiniyat in Dhahireh, taking with him the young Imam Saif bin Sultan as a hostage, as well as Belarab bin Nasir, whom he still detained as a prisoner. His object in this campaign was to subdue the Yemenite tribes in that province, and for this purpose he collected a fresh army composed of the Beni Yas and other Nizar tribes to the number of about 12,000 men. He captured Yenkal in the Wady Howasina by destroying the aqueduct and cutting off the water supply, and then turned upon Sedab, which offered a vigorous resistance.

While Mohammed was thus engaged, Khalf bin Mubarak marched direct on Rostak, where he was opposed by the Wali Sinan bin Mohammed, who was killed in the encounter. Mohammed al-Harrase then surrendered the place to Khalf, and the people at Rostak also submitted. Khalf then moved against the fort of Nakhl, which was soon captured.

Meantime, Sohar, the chief town on the Batineh coast, was taken possession of for Khalf bin Mubarak al-Amuri. Khalf, pursuing his advantage, now invested Al-Hazm and summoned the Wali Omair bin Masud bin Saleh al-Uhaferi to submit. Refusing to do so, Omair wrote to Mohammed bin Nasir al-Ghafiri for aid, and Mohammed, with a large force, moved down on Al-Hazm and attacked Khalf with such fury that the latter's troops were utterly routed and dispersed.

Satisfied with this result, Mohammed bin Nasir returned to Dhahireh and spent some time at Ghabbi and Saifam, after which, with a view to harass and ravage the districts of the Beni Hina, he moved down with a strong force to Belad Sait and Nezwa, where he met with tolerable success and remained six months. He next raided the fertile little district of Manh, where he destroyed the date-trees and greatly humbled the Beni Hina, after which he retired again to Dhahireh.

After his flight from Al-Hazm, Khalf took refuge at Rostak for a time, and then, gathering a force composed of the Beni Maawal and other tribes, carried on operations against the enemy in the Semail Valley and at Nakhl, but apparently without any decisive result.

The scene now shifts to Al-Sharkiya in the Eastern province, where the Beni Hina, led in all likelihood by Khalf, had allied with two powerful tribes, the Awamir and Al-Waheebeh. To combat this combination the energetic Mohammed bin Nasir marched across Oman and confronted it near Akil, where a great battle was fought. At first the Hinawa had the best of it, but eventually the northern tribes rallied, checked the Hinawas and put them to flight. Taking with him Saif bin Sultan, Mohammed bin Nasir returned to Yabreen, from whence he moved back to Dhahireh.

During the absence of Mohammed in Sharkiya, a fresh coalition of the Yemenite tribes had been formed in the Nezwa district under the leadership of Shaikh Said bin Juwaud al-Hinawi. Mohammed now laid siege to Saifam and Ghafat, where they had assembled. The Hinawa strenuously confronted Mohammed, and while the siege was in progress Said bin Juwaud visited Yenkal, Sohar, and other places to collect levies. Returning to Ghafat, after an absence of seven months, Said bin Juwaud prepared to enter the field against Mohammed bin Nasir, and a decisive battle was fought, in which Mohammed again proved completely victorious. Said bin Juwaud and Ghassan al-Alowi, the chief of Yenkal, were slain in the fight, and the body of Said was ignominiously dragged along the ground before the walls of Ghafat to terrorize the inhabitants, when the garrison not long afterwards surrendered to the victors.

After reducing Ghafat and Al-Akr, the quarter of Nezwa belonging to the Beni Hina, Mohammed undertook a second expedition to Sharkiyeh, where Khalf bin Mubarak, supported by the Al-Haboos, had taken up a position between Al-Roudha and Madhaiby. In the contest that ensued, Khalf was defeated and fled to Ibra, where he was joined by the Harth, one of the most important tribes in Sharkiya. The Harth being unable to resist Mohammed's army, accepted terms, one of which was that Khalf bin Mubarak should quit Sharkiya, and the latter accordingly proceeded to Muscat.

After resting some time at Yabreen, his favourite residence, whither he had retired after his campaign in Sharkiya, Mohammed bin Nasir made his way to Dhahireh ; here he gathered a numerous following and moved down the Wady Jezzi to the Batineh, where he devastated the property of the Yemen tribes.

Khalf bin Mubarak, who was still at Muscat, hearing of Mohammed's new movement, also gathered a force and marched northward to oppose him. A collision took place at Al-Felej al-Arar, where Khalf was routed and his army scattered.

Mohammed now led his troops to Rostak, which promptly submitted to him. Leaving Rostak, Mohammed then proceeded to Makiniyat, where he confirmed Mubarak bin Saeed bin Bedr as Wali of the town, after which he returned to Yabreen. His almost uninterrupted success in the field had by this time turned his head, and he now resolved to throw off the mask as Regent, to set aside Saif bin Sultan, and seize the dignity of Imam, the desire for which he had long and secretly cherished.

Having stayed a considerable time at Yabreen maturing his plans for his elevation to the Imamate, Mohammed set out for Nezwa, whence he despatched couriers to all parts of Oman to summon the Shaikhs and notables to that capital. Before this assembly, which was presided over by the Kadhi Nasir bin Suliman bin Mohammed and the Wali Abdulla bin Mohammed bin Rashid, Mohammed bin Nasir al-Ghafiri, dissembling his real wishes, announced his desire to give up control of affairs and offered to resign his post as Regent for Saif bin Sultan. The plot, which had been carefully laid, fully succeeded, and Mohammed was earnestly besought by the Kadhi Nasir to reconsider his decision and to accept the Imamate, which, after a great show of hypocritical reluctance, he ultimately did, and the proclamation of his accession to that office took place accordingly on October 2nd, 1724.

The civil war, which practically terminated with the election of Mohammed bin Nasir as Imam, is a landmark in the history of Oman and divided the country more widely than ever into two rival factions—the Hinawi and Ghafiri—so called from the tribes which supported the leaders, and by which names they are known at the present day.

On this subject it may be convenient to quote the judicious remarks of Colonel Sir Edward Ross in the notes to his translation :—

> " This civil war was one of the fiercest recorded in the annals of Oman, a great number of the clans ranging themselves under their respective leaders, declaring either for the 'Hinai' or 'Ghafiri.' Those faction terms have survived to the present day, and almost entirely supersede the older classifications, the rival factions being now termed Al-Hinawiyeh and Al-Ghafiriyeh. This is the explanation of the undue pre-eminence assigned by European writers on Oman to these two tribes, whose importance was accidental and temporary. For a time the Ghafiris gained the day, and their chief became Imam, but the Hinawis soon regained the ascendancy. At present the power of the two sections is tolerably evenly balanced, the Ghafiris preponderating in the West and their rivals in the East."

After his election, Mohammed bin Nasir continued to look upon Yabreen as his chief residence and always returned thither from his various expeditions. Owing to his military talents and his prudent and magnanimous administration, he was now completely master of the situation. But his career as Imam was by no means uneventful, as his presence was constantly required in the provinces to put down petty revolts and disturbances, and to frustrate the designs of his arch enemy, Khalf bin Mubarak, who was ever on the alert for an opportunity to oppose and annoy him. At different times he was drawn away to the eastward to suppress trouble at Birket al-Mouz, Tanoof, Zikki, Semail, and other places ; towards the north, in Dhahireh, he had to recover Ghabbi, Dhank, and Yenkal ; in the Batineh he had to vindicate his authority, and occupied Hail, for some time, to intercept Khalf, who was on his way from Muscat to Rostak to collect troops, and whose scheme he was able to frustrate. Khalf bin Mubarak, being unable to oppose Mohammed, remained at Muscat, and the latter eventually returned to Semail and thence to Yabreen.

It was moreover probably due to Khalf's machinations that the Bedouin tribes of the Yemenite faction kept the country to some degree in a state of insecurity and confusion by their predatory raids and highway robberies, which Mohammed was never able to entirely suppress. From the time he had assumed control of affairs to the day of his death, a period of about seven years, Mohammed bin Nasir was most careful to keep the young Prince Saif bin Sultan constantly near his own person, taking the boy with him wherever he went, and never allowing him to remain behind at Yabreen, even in close custody. Being naturally universally regarded as a usurper, Mohammed was fearful lest Saif should be carried off and made the focus of an insurrection so widespread and irresistible as to render hopeless any attempt to withstand it.

After three years of rule as Imam, Mohammed bin Nasir contemplated the reduction of the three important coast towns of Muscat, Burka, and Sohar, which together with Rostak were still independent of him, and under the control of Khalf bin Mubarak. With this view, towards the end of 1727, the Imam gathered a powerful force from the northern tribes, on whom he had always reckoned for his chief support, and marched to Sohar, to which he laid siege in March, 1728.

On hearing of his movement, Khalf hastily started from Muscat to aid in the defence of Sohar, established a camp at Saham, east of Sohar, and resolved to engage the enemy, though the force he was able to muster was far inferior to that of the Imam, which appears to have numbered some 15,000 men. Mohammed's army had hardly reached Sohar, when the inhabitants of the town, terrified at the formidable array of troops, tendered their submission and allowed Mohammed to enter the city.

The citadel, however, which was gained by the Al-Amoor, held out bravely, and Mohammed, conscious of his strength, sent Rabiah bin Ahmed al-Wahshi as envoy to demand its surrender. Instead of doing this, Rabiah with great duplicity, advised the garrison to reject the Imam's terms and returned to the camp. Mohammed, having taken up his quarters in the town, now detached a force of 12,000 men to mask Khalf's camp at Saham, and prevent his approaching Sohar, and the plan succeeded so well that Khalf at once understood that the fall of the citadel was inevitable unless he could devise some stratagem to save it. Khalf's plot is said to have caused an estrangement between the Imam and the Shemal tribes, the Naeem, Jowasim and Beni Kattab, who withdrew to their own homes. Their departure so weakened the besiegers, that Khalf was emboldened to advance against the enemy, but in the engagement that ensued, he was slain, and his troops put to the sword. Elated at the sight of his flying foe, the Imam immediately proceeded to the citadel, expecting an easy triumph, but had scarcely begun the attack when he was struck down by a musket ball in the breast. Mortally wounded he was carried to the house of Mahmood al-Ajamee, where he shortly after expired. His body was secretly buried at night, and his death was not made known to the army for three days.

In the same month and year, March, 1728, which witnessed the death of the valiant Imam Mohammed bin Nasir, Oman lost also its valued possession Mombasa in East Africa, which was recaptured by the Portuguese and retained for about three years. The way this was brought about was as follows:—Near the close of 1717, a native of the town of Patta, having quarrelled with the negro Sultan, found his way to Mozambique, and besought the Captain-General, Dom Luis de Sampayo, to come to Patta and expel the Sultan. The Captain-General was nothing loth to seize the opportunity, and sailed to Patta with four ships, where he easily obtained possession of the town. While here, he seems to have received an invitation from the people of Mombasa, who had rebelled against the governor of the fort, and accordingly proceeded to that place, which surrendered to him, it is said, without resistance. In this way the whole coast submitted to the domination of the Portuguese, whose tyranny and violence again compelled the people (about 1731–2) to send a deputation to Oman, to represent their grievances. The Imam Saif bin Sultan, in compliance with their petition, sent an expedition of three ships—*Kabras*, *Malek*, and another—under the command of Mohammed bin Saeed al-Maamiri, who, after some opposition, regained the fort for the Imam, whose successors have retained it to the present day. Mohammed was shortly after succeeded by Saleh bin Mohammed al-Hadhrami.

Reverting now to Oman we find that on the demise of Mohammed bin Nasir being known, Saif bin Sultan with his Yaareba adherents proceeded to the citadel, the gate of which was thrown open to him, and where he remained for a few days, while the combatants on both sides, in the vicinity of Sohar, broke camp and dispersed to their homes. From Sohar, Saif went first to Rostak, where he was loyally received by the people as their rightful sovereign and from thence made his way by the Wady Beni Ghafir to Nezwa. In this capital, at a vast assembly convened by the Kadhi Nasir bin Suliman al-Narbyah, he was proclaimed Imam for the fourth time on April 2nd, 1728, a dignity to which he was now fully entitled, having obtained his majority.

Meanwhile a cousin of Saif's, Belarab bin Himyar al-Yaarebi, rose as competitor, and having obtained his election as Imam by a small and uninfluential party at Bazily in Al-Jow, where he had been staying, hastened to Nezwa and made energetic efforts to secure adherents to his cause.

About this time, Saif bin Sultan, quitting Nezwa, proceeded to Nakhl, where he demanded the surrender of the fort from Jasses bin Omair bin Rashid al-Hairaney, who, however, refused to give it up. Saif, not being in a position to compel obedience, went to the Wady Maawal and received the allegiance of that tribe. Subsequently Saif bin Sultan sent his uncle, Saif bin Nasir, to negotiate with the Beni Hina, who formed the garrison left by Khalf at Muscat, concerning the Imam's desire to adopt that place as his capital, and the latter arrived there to take up his residence shortly afterwards.

Belarab bin Himyar's first campaign was undertaken against the Beni Ruwaihah, who, though of Nizar stock, were allied with the Hinawis. The Imam Saif sent his brother, Belarab bin Sultan, with a force to assist the tribe against the enemy, and a battle was fought in which the Beni Ruwaihah were defeated, and transferred their fealty to Belarab bin Himyar. On returning to Nezwa after this triumph, Belarab began operations in the surrounding district with a view to humble the Hinawis, and having attacked Belad Sait, soon reduced it to submission. He then appeared before Bahila, which he captured after a short siege and expelled the Beni Hina garrison. For some years after this the rivalry between Belarab bin Himyar, who had fixed his residence at Nezwa, and the Imam Saif continued unabated, but without actual hostilities. Belarab bin Himyar was supported by the Nizar or Ghafiri faction, which had previously formed the mainstay of Mohammed bin Nasir's power, and having possession of most of the interior, was gradually gaining the superiority. Saif, on the other hand, held the navy, the Sharkiya and Batineh seaboard, with Muscat, Burka and Sohar, and could only rely on the Beni Hina and a few of the confederated tribes. Under this divided authority the administration of the state was deplorable and chaotic, trade languished, and prosperity and enterprise were almost at a standstill.

It was the same abroad; the prestige of the Arabs had everywhere greatly waned. The ubiquitous fleets of Muscat Arabs, once so dreaded and respected along the Indian and Persian coasts, even by Europeans, were now but rarely, if ever, seen.

The one achievement of which the Imam Saif had reason to be proud was the final re-conquest of Mombasa from the Portuguese in 1731–2, which was the foundation of the Arab Empire in East Africa. So far each party had refrained from drawing sword upon the other, but about the year 1736 the Imam Saif thought he had found an opportunity to take the initiative against his rival, and put his cause to the issue on the field of battle. At this period, the tribes of Oman appear to have been but scantily provided with fire-arms, their usual weapons being the bow, spear, curved dagger and double-edged sword.

The matchlocks in use were heavy, clumsy and expensive, and were manufactured in and imported from Persia, the Arabs themselves being deficient in mechanical ingenuity and incapable of making guns of any kind.

Learning that the Belooches of Mekran in Southern Persia were considered brave and well-armed with matchlocks, the Imam determined to send agents across the Gulf of Oman and request the Chiefs of that country to allow their men to be enlisted in his service. The men selected by the agent belonged to the Hôt tribe, of whom a large body were brought to Muscat and placed by the Imam, in conjunction with a force of coast Arabs, under the command of his brother, Belarab bin Sultan. With this army Belarab bin Sultan moved to Al-Jow, whither Belarab bin Himyar, on being apprised of the Imam Saif's action, had marched with his forces, and a great battle was fought, in which Belarab bin Himyar proved victorious and held the field. The Commander of the Belooch was among those who perished on the field. The survivors apparently did not return to Mekran, but remained in Oman and formed the nucleus of the settlement known as Mazoon, a walled town in Al-Dhahireh, inhabited to this day exclusively by Belooch.

When the news of this disaster reached the Imam Saif at Muscat, he was filled with consternation and despondency and realized the truly critical nature of his position. The promise of his early youth had not been fulfilled in manhood, and since his election his unpopularity had increased to such a degree that all his best friends and advisers had become estranged from him. There can be no doubt that he would have been deposed in favour of another had it not been for the people's recollection of, and pride in, the glory and prosperity given to Oman by the deeds of his ancestors. The cause of his decline in popular favour must be looked for in Saif's character and conduct. He was certainly a weak and effeminate prince, and is said to have been given to favouritism and injustice, and to have ignored the precepts of the Koran. But there is also reason to believe that he had acquired intemperate and vicious habits.

Early in the next year (1737), within a year of his being crowned

King of Persia, Nadir Shah directed his attention to the Persian Gulf and despatched a small expedition to recover Bahrain and the other islands which had been wrested from the Sefawi rulers by the Imam Saif's father and grandfather. This enterprise was doubtless dictated by the desire not only of again possessing the rich pearl-fishery but also of retaliating on the Arabs for their predacious attacks on the coast. The objects of the expedition were successfully accomplished, and the Commander, after replacing the Arab by a Persian garrison, set sail for the coast of Julfar.

Whether the Persians invaded Oman at the invitation of the Imam Saif bin Sultan or of their own accord is very dubious, but it seems indisputable that Saif met them on their arrival and arranged for the junction and co-operation of his own troops with the Persians.

Belarab bin Himyar did not remain on the defensive at Nezwa, but hastily collecting the tribes advanced at once to meet the enemy. The contest took place at Fèlej al-Semeny and was fatal to Belarab, whose troops were utterly routed. Belarab fled back to Nezwa, where he strengthened the garrison and awaited events. After the battle, the combined forces pushed on through Towwam to Obre, pillaging the inhabitants of Dhahireh and committing great atrocities and cruelties. Indignant at their behaviour, the Imam Saif quarrelled with the Commander and removed his troops. A reconciliation was effected soon after, but the invaders now decided to retire, and having gathered their plunder, returned to the coast and re-embarked for Persia. After their departure the Imam marched first to Bahila, which he captured and garrisoned, appointing Shaikh Salim bin Khamis al-Ofri as Wali. He then moved to Timsa, from whence, cautiously avoiding Nezwa, where Belarab bin Himyar was waiting to intercept him, he made his way to Zikki and down the Semail Valley to Muscat. In this city Saif bin Sultan continued to reside for some years, during which time no event of importance occurred in Oman.

In 1739 the Wali of Mombasa, Saleh bin Saeed al-Hadhrami, who had been appointed four years previously, was replaced by Mohammed bin Osman al-Mezrui, whose descendants ruled at Mombasa for nearly a century.

The remarkable events occurring in India at this time could not but affect Oman more or less directly in their results, as will be seen later on. Perhaps the most important of them was the famous conquest of India by Nadir Shah, who entered Delhi early in March, 1739.

Another event was the Mahratta campaign against the Portuguese in Northern Concan, from which country the latter were ultimately expelled by the Mahratta General, Chimnajee Appa, in 1739, after the successive loss of Mahin, Tanna, Bassain, and other places. One of the results of this curtailment of Portuguese power was the termination of the long protracted naval war between them and the Muscat Arabs, which had lasted for nearly 100 years. The successes of the Mahrattas, which were partly due to the jealous neutrality of the English, to whom the Portuguese had vainly applied for assistance, were a cause of much disquietude to the English settlements, as it was now in close propinquity to, and overawed by, the Mahratta garrisons on the mainland, who were far worse neighbours than the Portuguese, and it was in view of possible contingencies under their menacing attitude that the Bombay fort was strengthened by a ditch and other works.

Owing to Belarab bin Himyar having renounced, by the advice of his friends the Beni Ghafir after his defeat by the Persians in 1737, any claim he might have had to the Imamate, there was at this period no dynastic discord, and Saif bin Sultan continued to be undisputed ruler in Oman, though most of the tribes held aloof, and only four of the larger castles, *i.e.*, Muscat, Rostak, Burka, and Sohar, remained steadfast in their devotion to him. But the tranquillity was not destined to last; it was the lull before the storm, and it was not long before the unhappy land felt the full force of the blast; the change came towards the close of the year 1741.

Disgusted with the conduct and inertness of the feeble voluptuary, the Shaikhs and Kadhis of Nezwa, Semail, etc., assembled at Nakhl and, in the early part of February, 1742, elected Sultan bin Murshid bin Jadi, a grandson of the great Saif bin Sultan, as

Imam in place of Saif, who was accordingly for the fourth and last time deposed. After receiving the submission and homage of Zikki, Semail, Nezwa, Bahila, and other places, the new Imam took the field and marched upon Rostak.

Greatly disconcerted at the course events had taken, and alarmed at the success of the revolution, Saif bin Sultan at once set out from Muscat with what force he could muster to oppose his rival. Saif's endeavours to save Rostak, however, were foiled by the superior strength and activity of his adversary, who had already taken possession of it and appointed Saif bin Muhenna as Wali, and he fell back on Muscat, where, relying on his forts and ships, he stood on the defensive.

Sultan bin Murshid now turned his face towards Muscat, which he besieged for some time, but being unable to force an entrance, occupied the adjacent town of Muttrah, where Saif bin Himyar was made governor. Here he did his utmost to attract trade and divert it from Muscat by reducing customs and offering facilities to merchants, and not only did the inhabitants feel the rigour of the situation, but more important still, Saif bin Sultan, by being deprived of his revenue, was left without resources. Seeing that his rival, Sultan, had received universal recognition and that his own deposition was now a reality, Saif became convinced, in his despair, that his only hope lay in obtaining help from Persia and he accordingly sent messengers with a petition to implore the intervention on his behalf of Nadir Shah, who received them at Ispahan in the spring of 1742.

Nadir Shah had returned from his brilliant expedition to India in 1740, and the easy triumph he had obtained there had turned his head, which became full of ambitious designs for the aggrandisement and prosperity of Persia. He perceived clearly that its wealth and power would be most effectively increased by the encouragement of external trade and that towards this end the possession of a strong navy was indispensable. But the measures he at first adopted were futile. He ordered ships to be built at Howaza and directed that timber should be brought from the forests of Mazenderan, 600 miles distant, but this absurd scheme proved abortive.

According to the Journal of M. Otter, the French Consul at Busra, Nadir Shah then purchased two ships from the Dutch and took forcibly two ships from the English, one at Bundar Abbas, and one at Busra, but these were afterwards paid for and the English agreed to build two more ships for him at Surat. Saif bin Sultan's appeal for intervention for reinstatement on the throne fell in with that monarch's plans so admirably that his decision was not for an instant doubtful, and he immediately ordered the Governor-General of Fars, Mirza Mohammed Taki Khan, to prepare an expedition for the invasion of Oman. Nadir Shah's motives were very far from being disinterested, as the ready compliance with the Arab chief's request was merely a pretext for carrying out his own ambitious aims, and for revenging himself on the deposed Imam, who had some time previously assisted the powerful Hawala tribe with six ships in their rebellion against the Persians. The most important object Nadir Shah had in view, however, it may be surmised, was to gain possession of Muscat, then next to Busra the best trading centre in the Persian Gulf. There were, of course, other considerations which must have influenced Nadir Shah in undertaking this enterprise, such as the fact that Oman produced a hardy race of sailors useful for his new fleet, while Persia could boast of few, if any, men suitable for this service.

It was in the month of September, 1742, that Mirza Mohammed Taki Khan's expeditionary force, which consisted of 6,000 men, with Mirza Kelb Ali Khan as second in command, embarked at Bushire and landed at Julfar about a month later. While here, Mirza Mohammed Taki Khan was engaged for some time in erecting a small fort at Khor Fakan and establishing a base of operations, and also, it is said, in expelling a number of the Hawala or Joasmee tribe, who held the fort at Khasab. Meanwhile, Saif bin Sultan, being informed of the Persian military preparations, remained at Muscat impatiently awaiting the arrival of their ships off the coast, and on hearing of the disembarkation at Julfar, immediately set out with four ships for Khor Fakan. On reaching Khor Fakan, Saif bin Sultan proceeded overland to Julfar to express his gratitude for the

Shah's response to his appeal and to concert measures for the future with the Persian general. The exact nature of the convention between Saif bin Sultan and Mirza Mohammed Taki Khan is not known, but it was to the effect that Saif was to be restored to the Imamate under the suzerainty of Nadir Shah, and that he was in return to transfer to the latter in full possession the town and fort of Sohar. The Arab officers of the ships left by Saif bin Sultan at Khor Fakan, we are informed, entirely disapproved of the deposed Imam's conduct, in inviting the Persians to invade their country, and resolved to support him no longer. Weighing anchor, therefore, they set sail for Muttrah, where they put themselves at the disposal of Sultan bin Murshid.

Mirza Mohammed Taki Khan then commenced offensive operations without delay, and having collected all his ships and transports embarked the greater portion of his troops with siege-guns, stores, etc., and despatched them under Mirza Kelb Ali Khan to Sohar, giving him instructions to invest and attack that fort on the land side. The Persian assault took place shortly after, but was met by such a determined and effective resistance that the assailants were driven back with heavy loss.

Mirza Mohammed Taki Khan, meanwhile, with his larger ships, of which the Admiral in charge appears to have been Mootta Ali Shah, directed his course to Muscat, where he anchored in the cove. The Arab and Hindoo traders, on his approach, were thrown into consternation, and began hastily to remove their goods and desert the town. The fleet at once opened fire, but the defence was so vigorous that the Persians could not sustain the bombardment and were forced to retire to Sohar.

In January, 1743, the Persians, chagrined at the ill-success of their first efforts, made preparations to renew hostilities, having received reinforcements of men and stores from Shiraz. To increase his navy, Nadir Shah at this time arranged with the English president at Surat for the acquisition of eight more ships.

Four of these had to be laid down and built, but four were obtained at once by purchase, and these, as soon as they could be got ready, set out for Bundar Abbas. They never arrived, however, at their destination, and appear to have been captured on the way by pirates.

A second attempt on the part of the besiegers to carry the fort of Sohar met with no better success than the first had done, their repulse by the Governor, Ahmed bin Saeed, being of so decided a character that it was some time before fighting was renewed.

This man, Ahmed bin Saeed, who not only liberated his country from Persian oppression but was afterwards found worthy to assume and control the government during his lifetime, was the son of a camel driver belonging to an uninfluential tribe, the Al-Bu Saeedi. He was born at the remote town of Adam on the border of the great desert about the year 1700 A.D. As Ahmed grew up, he took service with successive Imams, and is said to have brought himself into notice in the reign of Mohammed bin Nasir al-Ghafiri, who was killed at Sohar in 1728. After this Ahmed's promotion was rapid, and in 1737 he was appointed by the Imam Saif bin Sultan Governor of Sohar.

Mirza Mohammed Taki Khan now concentrated his efforts on the main object of his expedition, viz., the acquisition of Muscat, and having returned thither with his fleet recommenced hostilities, and we learn from Otter that Sultan bin Murshid, who continued to reside at Muttrah, devised a stratagem which proved successful.

He ordered the garrison of Muscat to quit the town ostentatiously, leaving the gates wide open. The Persian Sirdar, hearing that the Arabs had fled and left the town defenceless, landed a strong force to take possession of it, and the soldiers not finding any resistance seized the gates and dispersed in search of plunder. The Imam, informed by his spies that the Persians were off their guard, fell upon them with the combined garrisons of Muscat and Muttrah, and put them to the sword. Some of the Persian ships were also captured on this occasion.

Smarting under this disaster, Mirza Mohammed Taki Khan's next operation was to detach Mirza Kelb Ali Khan with a large portion of the army besieging Sohar to attack Muttrah by land. In his march along the Batineh coast Kelb Ali took the towns of Sowaik, Khaboora, Burka, and Mesnaah. He also took and occupied the town of Nakhl, but in penetrating the neighbouring passes and defiles, parties of his troops suffered heavy loss. Crossing the Wady Semail, Kelb Ali then fell upon Muttrah, which was defended by the Imam Sultan and the Commander of the fort, Saif bin Himyar. In spite of a strenuous resistance, Muttrah was eventually taken, the Commander, Saif bin Himyar, being slain during the assault. The Imam Sultan escaped to Sohar, where he was soon after killed in a contest with the Persians, or, as some accounts relate, committed suicide.

Emboldened by this success and being able to invest Muscat by land as well as by sea, Mirza Taki soon appeared there with his fleet, but this time he took the precaution to bring the deposed Imam Saif bin Sultan with him. By the joint operations of the two commanders the town was stormed and occupied, but the two forts, Jelali and Merani, still held out. The deposed Imam firmly resisted Taki Khan's demand that the Commanders should be directed to surrender the forts, and the wily Persian, finding threats and persuasion equally fruitless, invited him to dinner on board his ship and supplied him so liberally with wine that his seal was easily affixed to letters authorizing the Commanders to deliver up the forts without delay, and by this device Taki Khan was soon in possession.

An exulting Kharita apprising Nadir Shah that the city of Muscat, which he so much coveted, was now his own, was speedily despatched to that monarch.

Saif bin Sultan, ashamed and humiliated at the part he had played in the loss of the city, and indignant at the treachery of Taki Khan, broke with the Persians and retired to the fort of Al-Hazm in the Batineh, where he lived in seclusion until his death.

During the war the Arab ships which were in allegiance to the Imam Sultan bin Murshid rendered important service to their country by harassing and attacking the enemy, and especially by supplying Sohar with provisions, stores, and reinforcements.

Ahmed bin Saeed, indeed, could never have kept the Persians at bay, owing to the absence of naval organization, had it not been for these blockade runners, who were able occasionally to pour supplies into the town, which was often in dire distress for want of food and ammunition. The only general engagement that appears to have taken place between the fleets was fought about this time at Al-Sowadi. In this affair Shaikh Salim, the Arab commander, who was on board a large ship (captured some time before from the enemy), attacked a Persian squadron with great bravery, made prizes of three of them, and put the rest to flight.

In the month of May, 1743, Mirza Mohammed Taki Khan and Kelb Ali Khan, leaving strong garrisons at Muscat and Muttrah, returned to Sohar, where they made preparations for a vigorous assault on the fort. A great battle ensued outside the walls, in which, though both sides suffered severely, the result was indecisive, as the fort was not taken and the siege was not raised. Gaining fresh courage by his successful defence, Ahmed bin Saeed repaired his fortifications, collected new reinforcements and supplies and resolved on a more stubborn and formidable resistance than ever.

During the rest of the year 1743 the struggle for the possession of Sohar continued, the Persians actively maintaining the siege and bombarding the fort, while the defenders successfully kept them at bay. The military skill and resourcefulness of Ahmed were shown in the way in which he made frequent sorties from the town, keeping them in constant alarm and preventing them from making incursions. The knowledge of the topography of the country gave the Arabs great advantage in making night surprises and attacks. The town of Sohar, where this memorable siege took place, is situated on that part of the coast of Oman known as the Batineh, and lies about 150 miles north of Muscat. It stands close to the sea and is surrounded by a high wall and rampart about a mile in circuit and is protected by a moat on the land side. The citadel or castle, which is also the residence of the governor, is a plain, square building near the centre, with a strong entrance. There are several shallow wells within the enclosure, from which the water is drawn by swipes, but the town was chiefly supplied by an aqueduct drawn from a spring in the Wady Jezzi, fifteen miles off, but this was, of course, destroyed at the commencement of the siege by the Persians.

At the end of 1743, or the beginning of 1744, Taki Khan, becoming hopeless of reducing Sohar and wearied by the discontent of his troops, solicited and obtained permission from Nadir Shah to conclude peace and to return to Persia. He accordingly opened negotiations with Ahmed bin Saeed, and at an interview a convention was signed at which the terms agreed upon were, that the siege of Sohar should be raised and the besieging army quit Oman, that Nadir Shah should retain Muscat and receive tribute from the Imam, and further that Burka and Sohar should remain with Ahmed bin Saeed. On the conclusion of this treaty hostilities ceased and Mirza Mohammed Taki Khan, having re-embarked his troops, proceeded with his ships to Bundar Abbas, from whence he returned to Shiraz.

Mirza Mohammed Taki Khan is said to have been rapacious and covetous as he was remorseless and cruel, and the barbarities perpetrated by his troops were terrible. Mirza Mohammed Taki Khan had come to Oman in the hope of enriching himself and had to some extent succeeded, but in spite of ruthless ravages had found the land poorer, and had extorted from it less than he had expected. By his incompetence as a general he had allowed the campaign to drift into a protracted, costly, and disastrous war, and had thus justly incurred the severe displeasure of his royal master, Nadir Shah, who expecting an easy and glorious conquest had found himself confronted with defeat and loss of prestige. Soon after his return to Persia, Mirza Mohammed Taki Khan raised a revolt against his sovereign and endeavoured to make himself independent in Fars, but the insurrection was easily quelled and its author disgraced and punished.

In his negotiations with Taki Khan, Ahmed knew well that he was acting entirely without authority, as the Imam Belarab at Rostak, who alone had the right to treat with a foreign power, had been contemptuously ignored in the matter till after the treaty was signed. With the full knowledge that the convention was null and void, therefore, Ahmed apparently considered himself justified in making the retention of Muscat by the Persians impossible, and thus put an end to their occupation of Oman altogether.

As soon as the last Persian soldier had quitted the Batineh

coast Ahmed bin Saeed marched to Burka with a large following, and having appointed his friend, Khalfan bin Mohammed bin Abdulla, governor of that fort, took measures to isolate Muscat by land and sea, by stopping all trade and intercourse with the Persians there as far as possible; and with this object he invited all Arab craft to come to Burka, where he offered every facility to merchants. The plan succeeded admirably. No vessels touched at Muscat and no traders resorted thither from the interior, and the garrison were soon reduced to extremities. The earnest appeals of the Persian governor for succour had remained entirely unheeded, owing, no doubt, to the disorders in that empire occasioned by Nadir Shah's mental aberration, which continued to increase during the last three or four years of his life.

All hopes of aid having at length vanished, the governor resolved to come to terms with Ahmed bin Saeed, who lost no time in despatching Khamees bin Salim from Burka to invite the governor and chief Persian officers to meet him on promise of safe conduct; Having no alternative but to trust in Arab pledges, the governor and officers accepted the invitation and arrived at Burka only to find a Barmecide feast awaiting them. The assurances of safety given by Ahmed bin Saeed were treacherously broken, and most of the Persian officers were barbarously murdered. After this tragedy the Muscat garrison perforce surrendered at discretion, but it is difficult to reconcile the conflicting accounts respecting their fate. Probably they were all allowed to embark in safety and return to Persia.

We must now revert to the time when the Imam Sultan bin Murshid was mortally wounded under the walls of Sohar and was carried into the fort, where he died about the middle of 1743. As soon as the news reached Rostak, two members of the Yaareba family rose at once to claim the succession. One of these was Belarab bin Himyar and his rival was Majid bin Sultan, a brother of the deposed Imam Saif. The choice fell upon the first, Belarab bin Himyar, who was duly elected Imam in the capital and then became the virtual ruler of Oman. Notwithstanding that he was now in undisputed authority and holding most of the resources of the State at his disposal.

Belarab did not attempt to join in the war and operate against the enemy. His jealousy, indeed, of Ahmed bin Saeed was so great, that Sohar, which was in sore straits at this period, was left without any pretence of help or encouragement from the central government. Belarab's selfish policy, however, could not but act prejudicially to the interests of himself and his dynasty. The land, consequently, had no sooner been swept of its foes than the people began to show their appreciation of Ahmed bin Saeed's patriotism, and many of the Kadhis, Shaikhs, and Electors, having assembled at Muscat, declared him to be worthy of being their ruler and proclaimed him as Imam.

Ahmed bin Saeed's first care was to re-occupy Muscat and restore it to its previous condition. The forts were garrisoned, Khalfan bin Mohammed bin Abdulla was appointed Wali or governor, and all the traders and others who had been scared away by the insolence and exactions of the Persians were brought back to their homes again.

Having passed through the horrors of a foreign invasion, the Omanis were in turn to experience the vicissitudes of a civil war between the rival Imams. In this contest the Imam Belarab bin Himyar was supported chiefly by the Ghafiri tribes of Dhahireh and the Semail, while the Imam Ahmed bin Saeed's adherents belonged to the Hinawa tribes of the Batineh. The news of the important conclave at Muscat, at which the popular hero was elected, threw the Yaareba family into a ferment, and roused Belarab to immediate activity. In collecting his followers he showed so much skill and energy that he soon had a formidable levy of 4,000 or 5,000 men, including the Joasmees, Naeem, and other tribes of Al-Sirr, with which to assume the offensive. His plan was to wrest the two fortresses on the coast from Ahmed's grasp, and with this object in view he first marched on Muscat, but threatened that stronghold in vain, and had to retire. His next operations were undertaken against Sohar, and Ahmed having hastened back to that town began to gather forces for the coming struggle. The result of the Battle of Bitnah, which happened probably in the early part of 1745, was unfortunate for Ahmed. Almost at the last moment, as is so often the case in Arab warfare, he was deserted by many of those on whom he most depended, and his troops, being greatly outnumbered, took to flight.

Ahmed himself escaped with difficulty, but being unable to reach Sohar as his pursuers were close upon him, he made his way to Yenkal in the Wady Howasina, where he remained a long time in concealment. Belarab's attempt to capture Sohar, however, was frustrated by the gallant attitude of the governor of that fort, and Belarab returned to Rostak.

For some years the war between the rivals continued, but the hostilities were chiefly local and of a minor character. During this interval, Belarab was undoubtedly recognized as the true ruler, and exercised supreme power throughout the interior, but it is equally certain that the Yaareba influence and power were rapidly waning. The year 1747 saw the end of the extraordinary career of Nadir Shah; and his son, Kareem Khan, who succeeded, demanded the annual tribute, which had been regularly paid under the treaty with Mohammed Taki, from the Oman government, but the demand was not complied with.

Two years now passed before the rival Imams resumed operations, and Ahmed having collected an army moved up against Belarab bin Himyar, who was encamped in the vicinity of Jebel Akhdar. In this campaign Belarab stood on the defensive, as the forces he had been able to muster were hardly sufficient to cope with those of his rival in the field. The final conflict which took place in the latter part of the year 1749 was decisive. Ahmed's attack was completely successful, the Ghafiris were routed and dispersed and Belarab bin Himyar was pursued by Hilal bin Ahmed and slain. According to Guillain this battle was fought in the Wady Maawal, but Salil bin Rizak more correctly perhaps places the event at Fark in the Wady Kalbuh.

The death of Belarab was a blow from which the Yaareba never recovered. The deposed Imam Saif bin Sultan's two sons and his surviving brother Majid remained in seclusion, and the only member of the Yaareba family who endeavoured to oppose him and subvert the authority of Ahmed bin Saeed was Mohammed bin Suliman, a cousin of the late Imam Sultan bin Murshid, who, being unsupported, soon collapsed and was glad to accept the appanage of Nakhl, which he henceforth enjoyed.